America
in a Changing
World Political Economy

America
in a Changing
World Political Economy

William P. Avery
David P. Rapkin

Longman

New York & London

America in a Changing World Political Economy

Longman Inc., 19 West 44th Street, New York, N.Y. 10036
Associated companies, branches, and representatives
throughout the world.

Developmental Editor: Irving E. Rockwood
Editorial and Design Supervisor: Diane Perlmuth
Manufacturing and Production Supervisor: Anne Musso

Library of Congress Cataloging in Publication Data
Main entry under title:

America in a changing world political economy.

    Papers originally delivered at the Fifth
Annual Hendricks Symposium on "US International
Economic Policy in an Age of Scarcity," presented
by the Dept. of Political Science, University of
Nebraska—Lincoln, April 10–11, 1980.
    Bibliography: p.
    Includes index.
    Contents: United States international economic
policy in a period of hegemonic decline/David P.
Rapkin and William P. Avery—American policy and
global economic stability/Stephen D. Krasner—

Hegemonic leadership and U.S. foreign economic
policy in the "long decade"/Robert O. Keohane—
[etc.]
    1. United States—Foreign economic relations—
Addresses, essays, lectures.   I. Rapkin, David P.
II. Avery, William P.   III Hendricks Symposium on
"US International Economic Policy in an Age of
Scarcity" (5th: 1980: University of Nebraska—
Lincoln)
HF1455.A65   337.73   81-12377
ISBN 0-582-28269-1   AACR2
ISBN 0-582-28270-5 (pbk.)

Manufactured in the United States of America
9 8 7 6 5 4 3 2 1

Contents

CONCLUSION 225

Contributors

William P. Avery is Associate Professor of Political Science at the University of Nebraska, Lincoln. His articles have appeared in the *American Journal of Political Science*, *International Organization*, *International Studies Quarterly*, *Journal of Common Market Studies*, *Journal of Political and Military Sociology*, and *Mondes en Development*. In addition, he is co-editor of two volumes on the international and comparative aspects of rural development. He is currently working on a book with David Rapkin entitled *The Comparative Analysis of Dependency: Theories and Evidence*.

Christopher Chase-Dunn is Assistant Professor of Social Relations at Johns Hopkins University. He is engaged in an NSF-sponsored research project on the development of city systems in the context of the world division of labor and is writing a book with Volker Bornschier entitled *Core Corporations and Underdevelopment*.

Stephen D. Cohen is Associate Professor in the School of International Service, American University, Washington, D.C. Among his books, essays, and journal articles on international relations is *The Making of United States International Economic Policy: Principles, Problems, and Proposals for Reform* (1977), a revised edition of which is forthcoming in 1982.

Robert O. Keohane is Professor of Political Science at Brandeis University. He is the author, with Joseph S. Nye, of *Power and Interdependence: World Politics in Transition* (1977). His current work constitutes an attempt to understand the international politics of modern capitalism through an analysis of how and why international regimes change and the effects that regimes, and changes in regimes, have on the world political economy.

Stephen D. Krasner is Associate Professor of Political Science at UCLA. He is the author of *Defending the National Interest: Raw Materials Investment and U.S. Foreign Policy* (1978) and numerous articles in scholarly journals. He is currently working on a study concerning economic and political aspects of Third World demands for a New International Economic Order.

Pat McGowan is a Professor and Chair of the Political Science Department at Arizona State University, Tempe, Arizona. His research has focused on African international relations, the comparative study of foreign policy, and most recently on international political economy. His articles on these topics have appeared in such journals as *World Politics*, *International Organization*, *International Studies Quarterly*, *American Political Science Review*, and *Journal of Modern African Studies*. He is currently writing a textbook on international political economy.

Karen Mingst is Associate Professor of Political Science at the University of Kentucky. Her research interests include the politics of international organizations, regional economic integration, and international commodity policy. Her published articles have appeared in a number of journals, including *International Organization*, *Journal of Developing Areas*, *Journal of Common Market Studies*, and *International Interactions*.

George Modelski is Professor of Political Science at the University of Washington, Seattle. He is the author of *A Theory of Foreign Policy* (1962) and *Principles of World Politics* (1972) and editor of *TNCs and World Order: A Reader in International Political Economy* (1979). His area of research is the long cycle of world leadership.

Robert Paarlberg is Assistant Professor of Political Science at Wellesley College and Research Associate at the Harvard University Center for International Affairs. His principal research interests are in the areas of international political economy and the politics of world food markets. His articles have appeared in a number of journals, including *International Security* and *Foreign Affairs*.

Roger B. Porter is Associate Professor of Public Policy at the John F. Kennedy School of Government at Harvard University and is currently serving as Special Assistant to the President for Policy Development and as Executive Secretary for the Cabinet Council on Economic Affairs. He has previously served as Executive Secretary of President Ford's Economic Policy Board. He is the author of *Presidential Decision Making* (1980).

David P. Rapkin is Assistant Professor of Political Science at the University of Nebraska, Lincoln. His research interests include systemic approaches to international politics and to the political economy of North-South relations. His articles have appeared in the *Journal of Conflict Resolution*, *Comparative Political Studies*, and *International Interactions*. He is currently working on a book with William Avery entitled *The Comparative Analysis of Dependency: Theories and Evidence*.

Stephen G. Walker is an Associate Professor in the Political Science Department at Arizona State University, Tempe, Arizona. His research has focused on the reunification problems of divided nations, the management of international crises, and the impact of psychological variables upon foreign policy decisions. His articles on these topics appear in the *Journal of Peace Research, International Interactions, Journal of Conflict Resolution, British Journal of International Studies, Journal of Politics, Behavioral Science,* and *Political Psychology*. He is currently writing a monograph on signaling during international crises.

Preface

As the title of a previous Longman volume, *Eagle Entangled*,* suggests, American foreign policy has become increasingly encumbered by a variety of external and internal constraints and contradictions. That book explored these constraints and contradictions and their specific functional and areal manifestations. The purpose of this book is to examine more intensively those constraints that arise out of the position of the United States in a rapidly changing world political economy. Toward this end, the volume employs two principal foci, or levels of analysis: systemic and national. The systemic level is concerned broadly with the relative decline of American capabilities over recent decades and the effects of this decline on the ability and willingness of the United States to exercise world economic leadership. The systemic-oriented chapters in part 1 are complemented by the national-level analyses of part 2, which focus on the organization and process by which U.S. international economic policy is formulated and the effects of organization and process on policy content.

Most of the papers in the book were originally delivered at the Fifth Annual Hendricks Symposium on "U.S. International Economic Policy in an Age of Scarcity," presented by the Department of Political Science, University of Nebraska-Lincoln, April 10–11, 1980. The Nebraska Lectures in American Government and Politics have been made possible through the generosity of G. E. Hendricks, an alumnus of the University of Nebraska and later a Colorado attorney. Mr. Hendricks had a lively interest in American politics and was especially concerned about the limitation of public discussion during the early 1950s. Therefore, from 1949 to 1957 he gave to the University of Nebraska Foundation a substantial sum of money to be used to deal with "current controversial political questions . . . in a nonpartisan, unbiased manner." Mr. Hendricks believed that a more intelligent examination and consideration of political questions would lead to better government. We believe that the fifth symposium sponsored with his gift, as well as this volume, is consonant with these aims.

---

* Kenneth A. Oye, Donald Rothchild, and Robert J. Lieber, eds., *Eagle Entangled: U.S. Foreign Policy in a Complex World* (New York: Longman, 1979).

In addition to the Hendricks Fund, several others at the University of Nebraska contributed generously to the funding of this symposium: International Studies Center supported by a Title VI grant from the U.S. Office of Education; College of Arts and Sciences; Scholars-in-Residence Program of the International Studies Center; University Convocation Committee; and University Research Council. The support of Max Larsen, Dean of the College of Arts and Sciences; Susan Welch, Chair of the Department of Political Science; Les Duly, Director of the International Studies Center; and Lloyd Ambrosius, Director of the Scholars-in-Residence Program is also gratefully acknowledged. Mrs. Velma Schroeder and Mrs. Lori Davison provided invaluable staff assistance.

Lincoln, Nebraska   David P. Rapkin
                                                        William P. Avery

Introduction

1

U.S. International Economic Policy in a Period of Hegemonic Decline

David P. Rapkin and William P. Avery

CHANGE IN THE WORLD POLITICAL ECONOMY

It is now commonplace to note that the world political economy has undergone significant structural change during recent decades. While change is of course ubiquitous and can be readily observed in almost all spheres of global affairs, several related developments in the evolution of the postwar international system suggest that major transformations are in train. One such development—and from the perspective of this volume the most fundamental—is the relative decline of American power. In the military-security realm, it is clear that the era of decisive American strategic superiority has passed. Moreover, the range of issues and problems to which America's still formidable military capabilities can be usefully and legitimately applied has sharply diminished. In the economic realm, it is apparent that the vast productive, commercial, and financial superiorities enjoyed by the United States earlier in the post–World War II period have deteriorated markedly. The hegemonic leadership based on these superiorities also has deteriorated, with the result that, for better or worse, the United States is no longer able (or in many cases willing) to impose or project its liberal version of international order upon the rest of the capitalist world.

A second major development has been the growth of economic interdependence, especially among the United States and its advanced capitalist counterparts.[1] The growth of interdependence refers to the increasing economic interconnectedness among countries and to the tendency for this interconnectedness to transmit macroeconomic events and trends more rapidly and certainly from one country to another. Interconnectedness is reflected in the dramatic increase in the density of international

3

economic transactions, including, *inter alia*, flows of capital, goods, services, people, technology, and information. One consequence of these phenomena is that national economies are less insulated from trends, dislocations, and shocks emanating from elsewhere in the system (e.g., inflation, unemployment, recession, rapid price increases, or supply interruptions of key commodities). If we regard national political boundaries as filters or gradients that function so as to dilute, ameliorate, select among, or shut out altogether unwanted, externally determined effects, the main implication of interdependence is that political boundaries decreasingly serve these functions. A corollary implication is that the traditional macroeconomic policy instruments employed by national governments to manage domestic economies have diminished in effectiveness. The notion of a national economy as a discrete entity has therefore become less salient for either understanding or coping with problems of contemporary political economy. Compounding problems arising from interdependence is the fact that these changes have unfolded over a period during which the citizenries of the advanced capitalist countries have escalated demands on their respective governments for increased services and macroeconomic management. The dilemma of interdependence, which seems conspicuously apparent in the current American context, thus lies in the acceleration of popular expectations for governmental provision of macroeconomic management and performance while, concomitantly, the ability of governments to fulfill these expectations has been reduced.

The erosion of American power and the growth of international interdependence have been accompanied by a third major development: The less developed countries have been increasing their cohesion, assertiveness and collective bargaining strength in an effort to radically restructure the existing international economic order. The demands of the world's poorer states for a redistribution of global wealth and power through the instrumentality of a New International Economic Order further complicate the ends and means of American economic policy, both domestic and international.[2] The challenge posed by the demands for a New International Economic Order has become less rhetorical and more concrete with the growing awareness that a variety of natural resources—principally fossil fuels—that are crucial to industrial civilization as it is at present conceived are finite and thus exhaustible. The prospect of raw material scarcities, whether real or imagined, has served to weaken the competitive position of consuming countries (including the United States) while augmenting the bargaining power of Third World raw material producers.

While we do not claim that the erosion of American power, the growth of interdependence, and the nascent Third World challenge exhaust all significant possibilities for transformation, these three areas do seem the most likely sources of fundamental systemic change. From the standpoint of American interests and policy, the lessening of American dominance of the international economic system is the most basic and far-reaching development. In fact, if we look back over the whole of the post–World War II period, the policy problems and dilemmas posed by interdependence and the Third World challenge can be viewed in large part as consequences of the decline of American hegemony. The two paramount goals of American international economic policy in the late 1940s and early 50s were the economic reconstruction of Western Europe and Japan and the formation of an open international economic order premised on liberal economic principles. The accomplishment of these goals, however, served to establish the systemic matrix of interdependence within which the United States now finds itself enmeshed. The successful reconstruction of Japan and the nations of Western Europe provided the other elements of the matrix, that is, viable industrial capitalist competitors. The creation and maintenance of an open international economic order promotive of free movements of goods and capital enabled the interactional density among these elements that is the defining feature of interdependence. As long as the United States enjoyed the dominance derived from its various initial economic advantages, interdependence raised few serious problems for American policy. But as the structural position of the United States has slipped to one of *primus inter pares*, it faces many of the same problems and dilemmas encountered by the other national elements of the interdependent matrix. Thus, while we do not mean to reduce the complex subject of interdependence to an epiphenomenon of the erosion of American hegemony, it is clear that the effects of interdepedence *on the United States* have been inversely related to the extent of its dominance of the international economic system.

The growing assertiveness and solidarity of the Third World and the challenge posed by its demands for a New International Economic Order can also be viewed as a partial function of the decline of American power. To be sure, the pressures for a global redistribution of wealth and power were initially set in motion by the processes of decolonization and state formation that began in the immediate postwar years and culminated in the early 1960s. These pressures would no doubt still be operative even if the United States had been able to maintain its superordinate economic position. What is of interest from our perspective is that it is the international economic order created under the aegis of the United States (while it was at the apex of its hegemony) that is currently under attack. It is precisely those norms, rules, and institutions that comprise the infrastructure of the American-created order that the New International Economic Order seeks to alter. Krasner extends this line of reasoning and argues that Third World countries have actually coopted the international institutions initially created by the United States and are currently utilizing them to promote structural change:

> By taking advantage of the autonomy that the hegemonic power, the United States, was compelled to confer on international organizations during the period of regime formation at the conclusion of World War II, Third World countries have been able to alter regime characteristics during the period of American hegemonic decline.[3]

Again, we do not mean to give the impression of a crude and parochial reductionism that regards the mounting Third World demands for structural transformation of the international economic order as a mere byproduct of the erosion of American hegemony. Rather, we are asserting that the systemic changes summarized under the rubrics of "interdependence" and the "Third World challenge" can be adequately comprehended only when viewed in the context of an international system within which a hegemonic power is in decline. Our argument can be summarized in the following three propositions: (1) The form and substance of ongoing systemic changes in international capitalism derive in large part from the nature of the liberal order that was successfully organized under the auspices of U.S. hegemony; (2) the velocity of these changes has been and is being accelerated by the decline of American power; (3) these changes raise complex and unique problems for the United States as it adjusts (or fails to adjust) its international economic interests and policies in accordance with its diminished international position.

What is at issue is determination of an appropriate role for the United States in a substantially altered global environment. Ambivalence and uncertainty about this role are currently manifest in a number of specific policy areas including, *inter alia*, national security, trade, money, energy, food, and foreign aid. In many of these areas, it is fair to say that American economic policies, both domestic and international, are out of phase with the structurally changing world economy. Perhaps this disjunction will appear in historical retrospect to be but a momentary phenomenon, a temporary hiatus in an otherwise orderly transition from hegemon to ordinary country. Perhaps the United States, in a burst of creative energy and innovation, will be able to regenerate the capabilities and leadership necessary for a second *Pax Americana*. At this point in time, neither of these scenarios seems a likely prospect. While the decline of American power is widely recognized among scholars, policy makers and the American public, there is scant appreciation of the international systemic context within which this decline has occurred and little agreement concerning the likely consequences of decline for American interests and policies.

This volume, representing a variety of scholarly perspectives, seeks (1) an explanation of the rise, exercise, and decline of American hegemony; (2) a realistic grasp of the implications of hegemonic decline for American interests and policies; (3) an understanding of the organization and process by which U.S. international economic policies in the period of decline are formulated and implemented. An explicit premise of the book is that these objectives cannot be attained with an exclusive reliance on any single level of analysis. That is, either a broad systemic orientation or a focus on U.S. internal policy-making machinery, when employed in isolation from the other, will produce a partial, underspecified explanation.[4]

The systemic level of analysis abstracts from intranational sources of state behavior and instead emphasizes the constraints and incentives that the international system poses for its constituent national units. Variation across states in terms of their attributes, goals, and decisional processes, which might be expected to result in variation in state behavior, is subordinated in the systemic mode of explanation to the stimuli and forces exerted by the structural configuration of the whole system of states. In other words, the constituent parts of the system are "blackboxed," that is, assumed to be more or less homogeneous with respect to their goals and internal characteristics. The systemic approach has demonstrated considerable explanatory power in application to a variety of international relations questions, especially in those multipolar situations in which the homogeneity assumption can be regarded as tenable. Under these circumstances, it is possible to deduce likely state responses to systemic forces and thus to generalize or preduct patterns of state behavior. But this assumption is less than apposite in reference to international systems characterized by a unipolar distribution of capabilities (a precondition for hegemony). The would-be hegemon possesses extraordinary capabilities in relation to all other states in the system and, therefore, is confronted with a contemporaneously unique set of systemic incentives and constraints. The manner in which the unipolar state responds to these constraints and incentives, and thus the nature of the hegemonic *system*, cannot be deduced from systemic characteristics alone. Rather, it is also necessary to examine closely certain key factors that are internal to the hegemonic state, for example, the relative strengths of international and national capital, popular sentiments favoring internationalism versus those favoring isolationism, the objectives of key decision makers, and the ability and willingness to adjust to shifting systemic conditions.

At the same time, however, hegemony is a genuinely systemic phenomenon in the sense that the hegemonic power is instrumental in establishing and maintaining *systemwide* order and stability. Moreover, responses of other states in the system—support and nonsupport, compliance with or challenge to the hegemon—are crucial to the nature and duration of the hegemonic order. Once created, the order and its various constituent regimes often exhibit their own dynamics that do not derive directly from the preferences of the hegemonic power. For these reasons, the national level of analysis is also far from sufficient in and of itself.[5]

Our contention that the two levels of analysis must be employed in a complementary fashion (for the attainment of scholarly, as well as policy-making, objectives) is manifest in the form and substance of this volume. The contributions to part 1, representing several different perspectives on hegemonic systems, address the questions of the extent and nature of structural changes in the postwar global political economy and the consequences of these changes for American interests and policies. The diverse analyses therein are complemented by the contributions to part 2, which offer alternative approaches to understanding the organization, process, and content of U.S. international economic policy.

SYSTEMIC PERSPECTIVES: HEGEMONY, LEADERSHIP, ORDER, AND STABILITY

In the first two chapters of part 1, Stephen Krasner and Robert Keohane bring similar perspectives to their analyses of different policy dimensions involved in the postwar rise and decline of American hegemony. Krasner's analysis focuses on trade and monetary policies, while Keohane scrutinizes in depth three cases of American hegemonic leadership in the international petroleum arena. Both authors stress that hegemonic leadership is predicated not simply on an overall preponderance of power but also on command of a diversity of power resources—economic, political and military—that can be brought to bear in a range of different situations and issue areas. Both also emphasize that hegemony is a political *and* an economic phenomenon. For Keohane, economic hegemony is a function of "comparative advantage in goods with high value added, yielding relatively high wages and profits," while political hegemony requires a state that "is powerful enough to maintain the essential rules governing interstate relations, and willing to do so" (page 50). He asserts that the United States met both of these conditions, at least until 1963. (The other authors in this section implicitly agree, though they differ as to when and if to analytically terminate the period of hegemony.) Krasner's table 2.2 (Indicators of U.S. Power Capabilities) demonstrates the preponderant extent and the multidimensionality of American power at the outset of the period, and also provides a concise and graphic summary of the relative erosion of specific American capabilities from 1950 to 1976 (page 38). Though it would be simplistic to directly equate the efficacy of American hegemony with the decline in specific power indicators (the uneven rate of decline across indicators makes such an assessment even more problematic), the information in the table presents an unequivocal picture. The United States no longer possesses the extraordinary capabilities it once exercised to influence or control the outcome of specific issues or situations and applied to broader system-maintenance activities.

Their emphases on American provision of system-maintenance functions in the formation of the postwar international economic order is another important area of convergence in the Krasner and Keohane chapters. Both authors argue that only a hegemonic power has sufficient capabilities and incentives to make those investments in systemic infrastructure that are necessary to undergird an open international order based on liberal tenets. Thus, a defining feature of hegemonic *leadership* is the willingness to *invest* resources toward the provision of systemic order and stability rather than use of the hegemon's superordinate position to *extract* or *consume* resources from the rest of the system. We might qualify this distinction by postulating that the hegemon need maintain a sufficient margin (or surplus) of investment over consumption so as, on the one hand, to create and maintain the norms, rules, institutions, and general conditions requisite for a stable and open international regime; and on the other hand, to sustain the legitimacy of its leadership by avoiding the perception of exploitation among other members of the system (whose cooperation is also necessary for the operation of hegemonic order).[6] Pursuit of a policy of investment by the United States thus entailed at times the sacrifice of short-term, tangible economic interests for the attainment of longer-term, systemwide political goals. This is not to suggest that American behavior was motivated by a selfless altruism nor to imply that the United States did not derive substantial economic benefits from its hegemonic position. Rather, and this is a key lesson of collective goods theory, the United States, as the economically largest, most prosperous, and most competitive member of the system, had the greatest stake in long-term stability and order and, hence, also the greatest incentive to invest in and sacrifice for the creation and maintenance of a stable and open international regime.[7]

As evidence of American willingness to sacrifice immediate economic interests, Krasner offers the prominent examples of the Marshall Plan, American encouragement of European integration, tolerance of Japanese protectionism, and promotion of Japanese admission to General Agreement on Tariffs and Trade. In the monetary realm, Krasner posits that the American commitment to a fixed-rate regime and tolerance of an overvalued dollar into the early 1970s constituted a form of investment in systemic order that more than offset the benefits accruing to the United States from the dollar's key currency role.

It follows that with the relative decline of American capabilities, the United States has been less willing (and domestically less able) to subordinate specific national interests to the more diffuse goal of global order. Stated more generally, behavioral change (in the form of American policy) has followed from structural change (the systemic alteration in the distribution of capabilities). Krasner points out that concomitant with the abrogation of its hegemonic role, U.S. international economic policy has increasingly reflected pressures for satisfaction of particularistic economic interests. In the area of commercial policy, the United States has acted to protect a growing number of industries threatened by foreign competition, has vigorously promoted American exports via the use of subsidies, and has shown increasing tolerance for departures from an open international trade regime. In monetary affairs, the Nixon administration's devaluation of the dollar and the eventual transition to a flexible-rate regime in the early 1970s effectively ended the institutional arrangements governing international finance originally established at Bretton Woods. Those events signaled an American retreat from its hegemonic role and objectives and the advent of policies more suited to a large state seeking to maximize its national economic welfare.

Keohane's recent works have performed the important function of differentiating the effects of ascending and declining hegemony on different issue areas and their associated international regimes.[8] His chapter in this volume extends this line of analysis to the cardinally topical area of oil. As Keohane notes, "Since oil is the source of crucial American weakness in the 1980s, this emphasis may also help us understand the sources of our current dilemmas" (page 51). Keohane's careful use of State Department archival data illuminates the evolution of American hegemonic leadership over three specific cases: successful efforts to gain control over Saudi Arabian oil between 1943 and 1948, the sterling-dollar problem in 1949–50, and the Emergency Oil Life Program in 1956–57.

Keohane argues that efforts to consolidate American control of Saudi oil during the 1943–48 period represented prehegemonic pursuit of strictly national interests: "establishment of dominance preceded exercise of American leadership" (page 56). Once having established this dominance, however, American oil policy subsequently reflected a concern for the welfare of Western European allies. The sterling-dollar problem arose in 1949 when British attempts to stem the outflow of dollars involved discrimination against American oil companies; at issue was the problem of who was to absorb the costs of adjusting to oversupply in the world oil market. Under pressure from the oil companies to defend their interests, the U.S. government eschewed various proposed solutions that would have discriminated against the oil companies, endangered the financial position of Great Britain, or benefited the United States and Britain at the expense of other allies. Though the problem was eventually resolved by the boom in oil markets that accompanied the outbreak of the Korean war, American policy balanced national objectives (defense of private American interests) and broader systemic objectives (concern for the economic viability of other members of the system). The Eisenhower administration's Emergency Oil Lift Program most clearly illustrates, in Keohane's view, the exercise of American hegemonic leadership. Egypt's blockage of the Suez Canal in 1956, following the invasion of Egypt by British, French, and Israeli forces, threatened to produce a severe oil shortage in Western Europe. The U.S. government was able to marshall its considerable and diverse resources to halt the multilateral invasion of Egypt, to prod recalcitrant American oil companies to increase production, and to coordinate the logistics of transporting sufficient American oil to Europe. In short, American power was used effectively to resolve a multidimensional crisis involving domestic and transnational interests, as well as the interests of other members of the Western alliance.

An additional and intriguing finding that emerged from Keohane's archival research is that a handful of State Department officials were sufficiently prescient in the 1945–47 period to advocate maximal use of abundant and low-cost Middle Eastern petroleum and the corresponding conservation of American oil reserves. While such a policy was doomed in the face of myopic but powerful domestic producers intent on maximal exploitation of American reserves, it is interesting to speculate on the U.S. international position in the 1980s if a "drain-America-first" policy had not been followed. In sum, Keohane's major conclusion from the three case studies is that the United States was able to utilize its preponderant economic, political, and military resources to establish dominance and then to exercise a benign form of hegemonic leadership in the petroleum area. The brevity of American hegemony, however, is in large part attributable to the failure of domestic interests to make those adjustments necessary in the long-term to maintain America's hegemonial capabilities. The resulting exhaustion of American oil reserves is plain evidence of Keohane's assertion that "in the longer run, the hegemonic leadership strategy was self-liquidating; rather than perpetuate the conditions for its success, it permitted their demise" (page 70).

In contrast to the postwar focus of the Krasner and Keohane contributions, the chapters by Christopher Chase-Dunn and George Modelski bring a much longer historical perspective to their analyses of the dominant position of the United States in the political economy of the postwar world. Both view the occurrence of American hegemonic leadership[9] as an element in the contemporary replication of a transcendent global historical process. For both authors, this process involves the cyclical rise and decline of hegemonic core states (in Chase-Dunn's terminology) or world powers/lead economies (in Modelski's), coupled with a cycle of formation and deterioration of global political order. While they share a longer temporal domain, and thus attempt to bring "lessons of history" to bear on the current American situation, there are considerable differences in their analytical approaches and, hence, also in the lessons that they derive. Examination of political and economic dynamics are dovetailed in each of the two chapters, but it is clear that the authors assign different relative weights to political and economic factors in their respective premises and explanations. Modelski builds upon his previous emphasis on political-strategic aspects of the global system by integrating world economic factors into his long cycle framework. He regards the political and economic spheres as relatively autonomous but also interactive; neither is treated as an endogenously determined function of the other. In contrast, in Chase-Dunn's formulation, the transcendent logic of global capitalism subsumes interstate political machinations and thus serves as the world system's motor force.

Chase-Dunn sets out to compare the American hegemony with two historical antecedents, seventeenth-century Netherlands and nineteenth-century Great Britain. All three hegemonies are identifiable as situations in which "military power and economic competitive advantage in core production are concentrated in a single state" (page 81).[10] Periods of hegemony can be analytically partitioned into three overlapping stages based, successively, on competitive advantage in and export of mass consumption goods, capital goods and services, and central place functions (transportation, finance, insurance). Hegemonic periods alternate with periods in which military and economic resources are distributed more evenly across the core of the world economy (i.e., periods of multipolarity and classical interstate power balancing). The three hegemonies have been associated with international openness with respect to movements of goods and capital, as the hegemonic powers have promulgated the ideology of free trade, and provided its infrastructural basis, in order to exploit maximally their various competitive advantages. Multipolar periods, in contrast, have tended toward closure as the competing core states turned toward mercantilistic policies in efforts to increase their national wealth and power vis à vis their rivals. Moreover, the competition in multipolar arrangements among relatively equal core states has engendered more conflict and war than is typically found in periods of hegemony, during which the hegemon has had the means as well as the incentives to impose comparative stability and order on the rest of the system.

Chase-Dunn's objective is to account theoretically and empirically for the dynamics of this process by which systemic structures and their associated properties alternate. He approaches this question, the "cycle of core competition," by inventorying the "causes and conditions of the rise and fall of hegemonic core states" that have been common to the Dutch, British, and American hegemonies. In the economic realm, the problem is one of understanding "the formation of leading sectors of core production and the concentration of these sectors . . . in the territory of a single state" (page 80). In brief, Chase-Dunn finds that the three ascending core powers have shared the following attributes: geographic centrality, an innovative and sophisticated technological base, relatively abundant investment and human capital, diversified capital intensive agriculture, cheap raw material inputs, and relatively large home markets. Emphasis is given to the large size of the hegemon's home market since its existence, in addition to facilitating several of the other conditions, enables the hegemonic state to offer access to its attractive home market as an incentive for other core states to accede to the hegemon's preference for an open international trading system.

Political conditions for hegemony begin with the existence of preponderant political (and presumably also military) power relative to other states. Also of fundamental importance is the ability of the hegemon to gain and maintain the strong support of the class coalition that comprises its domestic political regime (recall that this factor, though not cast in "class" terms, was of decisive importance in Keohane's analysis). The three hegemonies have also exhibited relatively egalitarian and pluralistic domestic political arrangements, a circumstance that has been instrumental in the creation and expansion of effective demand in the aforementioned home markets.

Conditions leading to the relative decline of hegemonies have generally entailed systemic processes, in contrast to the catalogue of national attributes associated with ascent. First and foremost is the diffusion of core production to other states. This diffusion (and to some extent autonomous emulation) of production techniques, skills and expertise, and the capacity for technological innovation, produces a systemic leveling of capabilities that diminishes the hegemon's superordinate position within the global division of labor and thereby erodes its competitive advantages in leading sectors of core production. There is an ironic dialectical logic at work here in the sense that the very mechanisms of free trade and unrestricted capital movements, established and championed by the hegemon, serve as the channels through which the essential elements of hegemony are diffused.[11]

Chase-Dunn also points to the "turnover time of fixed capital" as a related factor in hegemonic decline. While the hegemonic powers reaped the benefits of their initial technological and productive lead, other core states have adopted later-generation infrastructural components and capital equipment. Thus, as the hegemon's industrial base undergoes "economic aging," rival states are seizing the competitive lead in key sectors of core production. As wages and social overhead costs rise in the egalitarian hegemonic state, there is reduced incentive for capital accumulated within the hegemon to remain within its national boundaries; the hegemonic state, owing to its commitment to liberal economic ideology and its alliance with internationalist segments of its class coalition, can hardly attempt to constrain the mobility of capital. In this fashion, the phenomenon of economic aging has contributed to the demise of hegemonies directly, through the immediate loss of competitive advantage, and indirectly, via its interaction with the rising wage and social costs of labor, by encouraging the exit of capital.

As the hegemonic state's original competitive advantages have shifted, Chase-Dunn argues, the solidarity of its supporting class coalition has fragmented. Krasner demonstrates for the American case that the forces of national capital—especially those industries and labor groups threatened by foreign competition—demand protection and more state attention to national welfare rather than support for continuation of the state's system-maintenance activities. Moreover, and at some cost to the international legitimacy of its hegemonic role, the hegemon's commitment to liberal, free trade principles is undermined in the process.

Finally, perhaps as the cumulative result of these developments, the hegemonic state (or at least key political forces within it) tires of the hegemonic role and becomes unwilling to bear its attendant system-maintenance costs. In Keohane's and Krasner's terms, support for *investments* in international order deteriorates and demands mount for use of the hegemon's resources to augment *consumption*.

Chase-Dunn's comparative discussion of the Dutch, British, and American hegemonies illustrates that his generalized conditions of hegemonic rise and decline fit these periods with a convincing, though variable, degree of precision. The discussion should also serve to dispel any notions that the problems of contemporary American (and world) capitalism are unique:[12] An antiquated industrial base, declining productivity and international competitiveness, spiraling wage and social overhead costs, rising foreign competition, and demands for protection are all familiar themes in the litany of current American economic woes. There are, of course, unique features associated with every historical era, but the value of Chase-Dunn's contribution lies in its demonstration of transcendent historical patterns and regularities that inhere to the world-system of capitalism taken in its entirety.

In his previous work on long cycles, Modelski has shown that the global political system has exhibited regular cyclical fluctuations between (1) periods in which a single *world power* has assumed responsibility for provision of systemic order and security and (2) situations that lack the leadership of a single world power and in which order-keeping functions are either collectively managed by major states in an ad hoc manner or neglected altogether.[13] His chapter in this volume links this long cycle of global politics with the rise and fall of *lead economies* and corresponding fluctuations in global economic order and stability. Modelski posits that Kondratieff waves (cyclical price fluctuations with a period of about sixty years) serve as the coordinating mechanism between the processes of global politics and economics and produce alternating periods of political and economic innovation.

Whereas Chase-Dunn identified three periods of hegemony, Modelaski argues that there have been five long cycles of global politics, each associated with the world leadership of a particular state: sixteenth-century Portugal, seventeenth-century Netherlands, eighteenth-century Great Britain, Great Britain again in the nineteenth century, and the United States in the twentieth century.[14] In contrast to Chase-Dunn's emphasis on core production as the main ingredient of hegemony, Modelski's world powers have attained this status by virtue of their "ready access to the ocean based on secure insular or semi-insular positions, command of the sea, and suitable political and economic resources and organizations" (page 98).[15] Each world power has also been an innovative lead polity in the sense that "its political system served as a political example and functioned therefore as a model for political development for other states" (page 100). At the global level, world powers have generated a series of strategic and diplomatic innovations (as summarized in Modelski's table 5.2, Major Political Innovations Linked to World Powers) (page 101).

Each long cycle has contained four phases: global war, world power, delegitimation, and deconcentration. In brief summary, interstate struggle over world leadership is resolved by global war, with the winner emerging as the "world power" and leading the system through a phase of stability and order. But order is subject to entropy and thus tends to decay over time. With this decay, the legitimacy of the world power is assailed, its international coalition fragments, and the strategic power of global reach is dispersed. Other major powers contend for world leadership, and the cycle is renewed by another global war fought to resolve the problem of succession.

Modelski argues that this long cycle of the global political system is connected to world economic processes through two principal linkages. The first link is the identity between world power and lead economy; each world power has also been a lead economy, with the latter defined in terms of the creation of leading industrial sectors, extensive participation in world trade and foreign investment, an advanced agricultural sector, and provision of global transportation and communication services.[16] The second link stems from the fact that world powers have constructed the framework of the global economy (by performing what we have earlier termed system-maintenance and infrastructural functions or, following Keohane and Krasner, by "investing in order").

Because of these linkages Modelski expects "fluctuations in the political process to be coupled to changes in the global economy, and vice versa" (page 106). His attention then turns to the processes that govern the relationship between global political and economic instabilities: How are the long cycles of global politics coordinated with fluctuations in global economic activities? Modelski finds the answer to this question in the price (rather than output) version of the Kondratieff wave, a cyclical movement of prices with a period of approximately sixty years. Thirty-year "up" phases of rising prices (signifying relative scarcity of basic resources, i.e., food and raw materials) alternate with thirty-year "down" phases of falling prices (indicating relative abundance of basic resources). He then relates the Kondratieff wave to alternating periods of political and economic innovations and to the long cycle of world leadership. In short, up/scarcity phases of the Kondratieff are associated with periods of political problems and innovations and down/abundance phases with periods of economic innovations (i.e., technological breakthroughs and the creation of new leading sectors). Pairs of Kondratieffs are then matched with each long cycle of world leadership (see his table 5.5, on page 111). Hence, in Modelski's formulation, the "global war" and "delegitimation" phases of the long cycle are periods of political innovation and are coupled with up/scarcity phases of the Kondratieff wave. The "world power" and "deconcentration" phases are periods of economic innovation and are coupled with down/abundance phases of the Kondratieff.

How does Modelski's long cycle framework portray the period in which the United States has been the "world power" and "lead economy"? According to Modelski's model, the United States emerged from World War II as both world power and lead economy, ending a 1914–46 global war phase of the long cycle and a corresponding up/scarcity phase of the Kondratieff. The United Nations was the principal political innovation to result from this phase. The 1946–73 period is quite plausibly posited as a down/abundance phase of the Kondratieff and as the stable, orderly world power phase of the long cycle; economic innovations included the creation by the United States of new leading sectors in electronics, computers, nuclear energy, aerospace technology, travel, education, and health. The OPEC embargo of 1973–74 signaled the onset of another up/scarcity phase of the Kondratieff and the delegitimation phase of the long cycle.

In summary, the chapters in this section individually and collectively demonstrate the utility of "grand theory" in application to contemporary problems of American international economic policy. Though there are numerous points of divergence, there is also considerable convergence insofar as all employ variants of a rather parsimonious theory. Stated simply, variations in global order and stability are attributed to variations in the systemic distribution of power resources and capabilities, with a unipolar/hegemonic distribution associated with higher levels of order and stability. Because the theory is cast at a high level of generality, it is better suited to the explanation of broad historical patterns and trends than to the prediction of outcomes of particular situations or specific sequences of events. This limitation results mainly from an ambigious area, a blind spot, in the theory (whether it is applied over replicative historical cycles or only to the American case). We have earlier discussed the idea that a systems-level theory should identify the set of specific constraints and incentives that the system poses for its constituent units. In addition, we argued that a system characterized by a unipolar/hegemonic distribution of capabilities proffers a unique mix of constraints and incentives to the hegemonic state. The blind spot arises in that the theory cannot predict or generalize as to how the hegemonic state will respond to these constraints and incentives. Nor can the theory predict how or if the hegemonic state will adjust to shifts in systemic constraints and incentives as structural change, in the form of alterations in the distribution of power resources, unfolds. Hence, the blind spot leads us, with some loss of parsimony, to the examination of factors internal to the hegemonic state. With the systemic parameters of the postwar rise and decline of American hegemony in mind, we now turn to analysis of the organization and process by which U.S. international economic policy is formulated.

NATIONAL PERSPECTIVES: ORGANIZATION, PROCESS, AND POLICY CONTENT

In order to *fully* complement the systemic perspective of the volume's first section, the national-level section would have to include analyses of the entire constellation of actors and interests—public and private, functional and regional, urban and rural, rich and poor, political, military, economic, and cultural—that comprise the whole of American society. While such a task is beyond the scope of this volume, the essays contained in this second section offer analyses of how this constellation of actors and interests is refracted through the prism of policy organization and process. By examining the governmental machinery that generates American international economic policy, the contributors explicate another, *internal* set of constraints and incentives that circumscribe the content and direction of that policy.

Though all the chapters take note of the fact that international economic policy is formulated in a global context of declining American economic power, only one (Paarlberg's) explicitly addresses the question of the direct effect of eroding hegemony on the content of American policy. This is not surprising since the organization and process of policy making has not been formally altered in response to America's changing world position; and there is of course no cabinet-level Department of Hegemonic Stability or Special Assistant to the President for Declining World Competitiveness. Nonetheless, as noted in the previous section, the longer-term phenomenon of decline is manifest in the form of a number of complex policy problems facing American decision makers. The manner in which policy makers, their respective institutions and associated procedures cope—or fail to cope—with these problems is the subject of this section. The five contributors shed considerable light on many of these problems that the beacon of grand theory is unable to illuminate.[17]

Robert Paarlberg's chapter provides a particularly appropriate transition between the two levels of analysis since he pits a systemic explanation (based on the theory of hegemonic stability) against national and transnational alternatives. His object of explanation is the post-1972 crisis in the world grain market, as manifest in volatile fluctuations in price, supply, and reserve stocks, failure to negotiate an international grain reserve agreement, and imposition of a grain embargo by the world's largest exporter (the United States) on the world's largest importer (the Soviet Union). The instability of the post-1972 situation contrasts sharply with the preceding two decades, which were characterized by steady growth, stable price levels, and relatively abundant reserve stocks for purposes of concessional food aid.

Acknowledging that some portion of the overall crisis is attributable to climatic and purely economic factors, Paarlberg asserts that the principal causes of the crisis are political in nature. He then develops three competing political explanations of the post-1972 destabilization. The first explanation is based on the now familiar logic of eroding hegemony. Prior to 1972,

> the United States, accepting the burdens of global leadership, acquired and managed a large and expensive grain reserve, thereby stabilizing world prices while providing a constantly available source of concessional food aid. Meanwhile, the United States ensured reliability of world markets by placing no restriction upon commercial free world access to its very large grain supplies (page 122). . . .

These actions by the United States allowed less powerful grain exporters to promote their exports at the expense of U.S. trade. Exercising hegemonic leadership, Paarlberg observes, the United States tolerated such "free riding" policies in deference to its larger hegemonic interests in trade expansion, cold war concerns, and prosperity for its allies.

After 1972, however, instability in the market resulted partly from declining U.S. hegemony in the international system and the concomitant loss of ability to perform market-stabilizing tasks. Although grain price stability perhaps remained desirable.

> it could no longer be maintained, by the United States alone, at acceptable cost to larger international interests. In a weakened condition overall, the United States was now tempted to seek a different sort of advantage from its continuing strength in the world grain market. Self serving policies designed to maximize short-run gains for the United States replaced self-sacrificing policies geared to preserve long-run advantages for all (page 124).

Thus, when the USSR entered the grain market as a major buyer in 1972, the United States jolted the market "by suddenly disposing of very large quantities of grain . . . on credit and under subsidy, to the USSR" (page 125). Moreover, the United States delayed rebuilding its stocks, sharply curtailed the volume of its food aid, and emphasized bilateral trade agreements rather than continue the previous policy of open access to its grain supplies. The latter policy of bilateral agreements can "destabilize all portions of the market not covered by such agreements" (page 125) and reflected greater U.S. concern for stabilizing its own exports over stabilizing the world market.

An alternative explanation is transnational in that it focuses on the oligopoly exercised by five huge multinational grain trading companies.

Attention is drawn to these companies because of their role in the 1972 Russian grain sales, which damaged the domestic American economy. This line of argument suggests that these transnational firms, operating beyond the control of any single government and according to an exclusively private calculus, were able to sell off U.S. grain reserves and thereby contributed to the post-1972 price destabilization. Acknowledging that "it is seldom the intention of an effective oligopoly to introduce instability into its own operating environment...," Paarlberg reasons that the major grain companies probably lost some control over the market "by the entry of an aggressive new competitor, Cook Industries, into trade with Russia" (page 133). Cook was responsible for large, destabilizing sales to Russia at a time when it was in the long-run interests of the trading companies to restrain exports.

Paarlberg finds neither the eroding hegemony nor the transnational explanations adequate for understanding the instability in the grain market after 1972. He dismisses the former largely on the basis that American leadership was actually an epiphenomenon of domestic policies: "A large grain surplus was accumulated by the United States not for the purpose of promoting stability or security in the world market, but rather to satisfy internal political demands for high and stable farm income" (page 127). He finds even less support for the transnational explanation, demonstrating that the grain trading companies serve primarily as "middlemen" and lack control over such key factors as production and supply, transport, pricing, and destination. Paarlberg thus attributes crisis in the world grain market to a third explanation: the concatenation of uncoordinated national grain policies.

He argues that "the world grain market has no systemic logic of its own at the world level," that it reflects "little more than the combined external effect of many separately determined national grain policies, each undertaken according to a separate logic at the 'unit' level, with little regard for external conditions or external consequences" (page 135). Unlike the world oil market, the relatively small volume of grain trade does not comprise "the principal market through which most needs are satisfied" (page 135). Instead, destabilization in the grain market resulted largely from separate political actions taken by the United States and the Soviet Union. Specifically, the American decision to liquidate expensive grain reserves and "delay the return of idle cropland to full production" in combination with the Soviet decision to pursue, at all costs, its ambitious program to expand livestock herds, " ensured that the world grain market would suffer through a period of serious instability and insecurity following the bad [Russian] harvests of 1972" (page 136). Further, actions by the European Community and Japan to protect internal food prices exacerbated the market instability already set in motion by U.S. and Soviet actions. Paarlberg stresses that all these decisions derived more from preoccupation with internal concerns than international ones. Within the United States, he points to the Nixon administration's desire to reduce costs to the Treasury of maintaining grain reserves and the election-year influence of farm state and agribusiness interests in raising farm prices. He concludes: "What the logic of national politics hath wrought, the international system, which lacks a confident hegemonic leader, now must seek to manage" (page 142).

Paarlberg's conclusion that national policies better explain the world grain crisis leaves unanswered the question of how such policies are made. Stephen Cohen addresses this subject in a comprehensive survey of the alternative modes of policy making in the formulation of American international economic policy. Prior to elaborating the multiple modes and supporting them with a number of illustrative case studies that demonstrate the impact of organization and process on policy content, Cohen performs several useful definitional and conceptual tasks. First, he points out that "international economic policy can be viewed as an intersection where domestic economic, international economic, domestic political, and external political concerns meet" (page 148). Second, he disaggregates the concept of international economic policy and shows that it actually consists of a heterogeneous and disparate range of governmental actions. Third, Cohen enumerates the enormous number of bureaucratic and legislative actors involved at various points in the policy process. Finally, he convincingly argues that, given the diversity of concerns embraced, the range of actions included, and the number of actors involved, no single model or theory of international economic policy making can possibly suffice. In sum,

> All the major models utilized in the foreign policy decision-making process can be shown, both in pure form and in variations, to be applicable in international economic relations. At this time, it does not seem possible to predict *a priori* exactly which model will be relevant for any given problem or issue. Nor is the interrelationship among these models fully explainable (page 151).

Cohen then proceeds to explain the rationale and demonstrate the applicability of various models of executive branch and executive-legislative policy making, including presidential fiat, shared images and perceptions, multiple advocacy, bureaucratic politics, single agency domination, the personality factor, executive-legislative interaction, and other residual models. Cohen's exposition of the advantages and drawbacks of each of the multiple modes of policy making, along with his careful use of case study material, thoroughly maps the terrain and renders further summary unnecessary. What remains to be accomplished, and Cohen cautions that it is a formidable task, is development of a unified theory capable of predicting when and under what circumstances each of the policy-making modes is operative and explaining the linkages among them.

Roger Porter's chapter narrows our focus to presidential decision making in the international economic policy area. Given the enormous range of demands that press on Presidents' time and energies, there is obvious need for the provision of coherent and objective advice and counsel if effective presidential decisions are to be regularly made. Porter sees two major organizational obstacles to the consistent formulation of a decisional agenda in which policy alternatives are clearly drawn: the substantive interrelatedness of international economic issues and the fragmentation of organization and authority within the executive branch. The problem thus becomes one of *integration* of multiple and complex issues into an integral overall policy and *coordination* of the different perspectives, preferences, and objectives of the various individuals and executive-branch organizations involved in international economic policy formulation.

The picture that emerges, however, from a survey of the institutional arrangements through which the integrative and coordinating tasks have been attempted over the past three decades is one of impermanence, lack of continuity, and uneven efficacy. Porter concludes that these institutional arrangements have been characterized by the absence of an international economic analogue to the National Security Council (NSC); continual creation and re-creation of separate cabinet-level entities to deal with international and domestic economic policy issues; continual creation and re-creation of issue-specific cabinet committees; informal relations among leading officials rather than effective formal arrangements; and the relative lack of presidential reliance on the advice of White House international economic policy staff compared to such reliance in national security and domestic affairs.

Porter weighs the pros and cons of four alternative organizational solutions to the problems of integration and coordination: the consolidation of functions in a "super department"; formal designation of single cabinet officer as a "super secretary" for economic affairs or *de facto* delegation of economic policy responsibility to a "czar" (e.g., Treasury Secretary John Connally in the Nixon administration); a centralized White House staff similar to the Nixon-Kissinger NSC; and cabinet-level council combining the principles of multiple advocacy and collegiality. Reflecting his own executive branch experience, Porter argues for the multiple advocacy approach.

Although admittedly a difficult system to operate, he enumerates several organizational guidelines that can help ensure its effectiveness. First, the council must be seen as a vehicle of the President if departments are to take it seriously. Second, an honest broker should manage the council, with requisite abilities and temperament to pull "the strands of a problem together into a balanced presentation . . . using advocacy as an instrument of brokerage" (page 187). Third, the staff should be capable of preventing officials from circumventing the council. And finally, it should meet regularly at the cabinet level to enable its members "to speak authoritatively for their department or agency" (page 187). Porter concludes by cautioning against the establishment of a separate international economic policy channel to the President and advocates linking foreign economic policy issues to the domestic economic, rather than national security, policy machinery.

Karen Mingst examines the manner in which the content of U.S. commodity policy is circumscribed by what she terms the liberal economic paradigm. She argues that the range of alternative commodity policies that are in principle available are in practice truncated by virtue of policy-makers' adherence to the ideology of liberal, free trade economics. Mingst develops a typology of commodity policies that then serves as a dependent variable; she shows that the type of policy chosen (and not chosen) is a joint function of the liberal economic paradigm, the mode of decision making employed at the micro level, and factors relating to the characteristics of the specific commodity in question.

The typology delineates four categories of policy that

> reflect different temporal sequencing between an event or set of conditions and a policy. *Reactive* policies attempt to reduce damage or detrimental side effects of conditions after these effects are being experienced. . . . *Regulatory* policies seek to avoid potentially damaging outcomes before the evidence is clear. . . . *Confounding* policies result from logically inconsistent or uncoordinated policies, usually emanating from either the reactive or regulatory mode. . . . *Anticipatory* policies are designed to provide a decision algorithm before problems arise (page 201).

Mingst provides examples of each type with reference to a variety of mineral and agricultural commodities. She suggests that reactive and confounding policies are infrequent, and anticipatory policies are virtually nonexistent.

Mingst findings can be briefly summarized as follows. The first three types all fall within the parameters of the liberal paradigm, but "anticipatory policy by its basic nature is antithetical to the classical free functioning of the market" (page 202). The probability that a particular policy will be reactive or confounding increases with the number of participants involved in the policy process; consensus among decision makers that damaging outcomes are likely to recur is a necessary condition for adoption of regulatory policies. When American producers of a particular commodity are internationally competitive, policy tends to be reactive, especially reactive if the United States is a net exporter of the commodity. When domestic production is noncompetitive in world markets, policy tends to be confounding, more so if the United States is a net importer. Finally, Mingst relates her findings to the theme of hegemonic decline: "With U.S. hegemony eroding... it is logical to expect... reactive and confounding policies. Confronted with a declining economic position, policy makers react to protect entrenched and eroding markets" (pages 203–04).

The concluding chapter by Stephen Walker and Pat McGowan is a creative effort to render complementary the disparate insights of what they term neo-Marxist and neopluralist perspectives on foreign economic policy formation. Following a discussion of the fundamental epistemological, theoretical, and normative differences between the two approaches, the authors summarize the rudiments of each. The neo-Marxist perspective is explicated primarily in terms of the structuralist theory of the capitalist state, in which the function of the state is to ensure in the long term that the essential features of capitalist society are reproduced.[18] This role requires that the state be relatively autonomous from the pressures and demands of particularistic capitalist interests. State functions to shape, steer, and reproduce capitalist society are exercised through various "modes of structural determination,"[19] which establish "the outer parameters of change in American policy... and identifies the constraints that limit the range of variation and provides insights into the deeper structural changes that appear to be required to reshape U.S. foreign economic policy" (page 214).

The neopluralist perspective is developed in terms of Zimmerman's typology of foreign policy issues in which different types of issues (power politics, regulatory, distributive, and redistributive) are associated with different decisional processes.[20] In contrast to the broad structural focus of the neo-Marxist approach, the neopluralist perspective "sensitizes the analyst to the immediate surface causes of... short-run, incremental changes in U.S. foreign economic policy" (page 214).

The balance of the chapter interprets the findings of the previous four papers in terms of the insights provided by neopluralist and neo-Marxist perspectives. Zimmerman's issue typology is used to impose some order and predictability on the spate of policy-making models discussed by Cohen, and various examples and relationships from the other papers are recast as modes of neo-Marxist structural determination. The value of the chapter lies in its demonstration that the neo-Marxist and neopluralist perspectives ask different kinds of questions and that the answers to these questions can be combined to provide a more comprehensive understanding of the process and content of American international economic policy.

The contributions to this volume demonstrate that both systemic and national levels of analysis are necessary for understanding American international economic policy. Knowledge of the many domestic factors that the shape the process and content of that policy is inadequate without some prior understanding of the larger world economic system and the changing U.S. position within it. Neither perspective, however, exhaustively covers the full range of issues pertinent to the U.S. global economic role. Nor do the perspectives enable us to predict the substantive direction American policy will take as U.S. policy makers grapple with these issues. They do provide us with a variety of important insights into U.S. international economic policy, offer some prescriptions, and suggest some lines of future inquiry. It is to these concerns that we will turn in the concluding chapter.

NOTES

1. For a summary of the debate over interdependence and a systematic application of the concept, see Robert O. Keohane and Joseph S. Nye, *Power and Interdependence: World Politics in Transition* (Boston: Little Brown, 1977).

2. For a useful overview of the NIEO's component issues, see Branislaw Gosovic and John G. Ruggie, "On the Creation of a New International Economic Order: Issue Linkage and the Seventh Special Session of the UN General Assembly," *International Organization* 30 (Spring 1977); Stephen D. Krasner's, "North-South Economic Relations: The Quests for Economic Well-Being and Political Autonomy," in *Eagle Entangled: U.S. Foreign Policy in a Complex World*, ed. Kenneth A. Dye, Donald Rothchild, and Robert J. Lieber (New York: Longman, 1979) convincingly differentiates the NIEO's political and economic dimensions and the policy problems each dimension poses for American policy.

3. Stephen D. Krasner, "Transforming International Regimes: What the Third World Wants and Why," *International Studies Quarterly* 25 (March 1981): 143.

4. See J. David Singer, "The Level of Analysis Problem in International Relations," *World Politics* 14 (October 1961), for a seminal treatment of the analytical implications of relying on either the national or systemic level of analysis.

5. For an emphasis on domestic sources of international economic policy, see Peter J. Katzenstein, ed., *Between Power and Plenty: Foreign Economic Policies of Advanced Industrial States* (Madison: University of Wisconsin Press, 1978).

6. The cross-time ratio of a hegemonic state's *investment* and *consumption* might serve as an indicator of its leadership (and also to distinguish between *hegemonic leadership* and *imperialism*, with a ratio in excess of unity suggesting the former and less than unity the latter). It may be that other state's *perceptions* of this ratio is the more crucial variable. In either case, operational definition of the ratio would be difficult. Though in this chapter we stress the hegemonic state's incentives and behavior, the incentives (and changes in them) for lesser states in a hegemonic environment should not be overlooked.

7. For an explication of hegemonic leadership from a collective goods standpoint, see Charles P. Kindleberger, *The World in Depression, 1929–1939* (Berkeley: University of California Press, 1977), chap. 14; and "Systems of International Economic Organization," in *Money and the Coming World Order*, ed. David P. Calleo (New York: New York University Press, 1976).

8. For the distinction between "overall power structure" and "issue/regime specific" variants of the hegemonic stability theory, see Keohane and Nye, *Power and Interdependence*, chp. 3; for application of the theory to the monetary, trade and oil issue areas, see Robert O. Keohane, "The Theory of Hegemonic Stability and Changes in International Regimes, 1967–1977," in *Change in the International System*, ed. Ole R. Holsti, Randolph M. Siverson, and Alexander L. George (Boulder, Colo.: Westview Press, 1980); and "Inflation and the Decline of American Power," in *The Political Economy of Domestic and International Monetary Relations*, ed. Raymond Lombra and Willard Witte (Ames: Iowa State University Press, 1981).

9. Both Modelski and Chase-Dunn would quarrel with our use of the term *hegemonic leadership*. For Modelski, *hegemony* carries derogatory connotations. Chase-Dunn employs the term hegemony, but, it is safe to say, he does not view *leadership* as its principal feature.

10. Note that Chase-Dunn's concept of "economic competitive advantage in core production" is essentially similar to Keohane's definition of economic hegemony.

11. For the argument that foreign investment was the major channel through which the hegemonic advantages of nineteenth-century Great Britain and the postwar United States have been diffused, see Robert Gilpin, *U.S. Power and the Multinational Corporation: The Political Economy of Foreign Direct Investment* (New York: Basic Books, 1975).

12. One important difference between American and previous hegemonies is its shorter duration, which Chase-Dunn attributes to the world system having reached certain "ceiling effects" (see his discussion pages 90–91).

13. George Modelski, "The Long Cycle of Global Politics and the Nation-State," *Comparative Studies in Society and History* 20 (April 1978); and "The Theory of Long Cycles and U.S. Strategic Policy," in *American Security Policy and Policy-Making* ed. Robert Harkavy and Edward A. Kolodziej (Lexington, Mass.: Lexington Books, 1980).

14. Modelski's inclusion of sixteenth-century Portugal and eighteenth-century Great Britain as world powers and long cycles stems from his stress on the strategic-military requisites of world-power status. Chase-Dunn excludes these as replications because they fail to meet the criteria for "hegemony of core production" (see Chase-Dunn's discussion, page 86).

15. Cf. Chase-Dunn's assertion that hegemonic "success relied more on economic competitive advantages in the production of the material commodities than on military superiority, although both were important" (page 89). Modelski, though emphasizing strategic-military factors, assigns "high saliency" to economic as well as political processes and acknowledges that "a lead economy built upon a global flow of activities is a *sine quo non* of world power" (page 104).

16. Note the substantial overlap between Modelski's definition of lead economy and Chase-Dunn's preconditions for economic hegemony.

17. The editors' tasks of summary and comparison in this section of the introductory essay are lessened considerably by the comprehensive overview of modes of international economic policy making provided in Cohen's chapter and the integrative survey and synthesis in McGowan and Walker's concluding chapter.

18. For an overview of Marxist theories of the state with a thorough discus-

sion of structuralist versions, see David A. Gold, Clarence Y. H. Lo, and Erik Olin Wright, "Recent Developments in Marxist Theories of the State," *Monthly Review* 27, nos. 5 and 6 (1975).

19. The notion of structural determination is elaborated in Erik Olin Wright, *Class, Crisis and the State* (London: New Left Books, 1978).

20. William Zimmerman, "Issue Area and Foreign Policy Process," *American Political Science Review* 67 (December 1973).

PART I

Systemic Perspectives: Hegemony, Leadership, Order, and Stability

2

American Policy and Global Economic Stability

Stephen D. Krasner

For the world economy, the 1970s was a period of turmoil compared with the 1950s and 60s. Prices for the world's most important commodity, oil, quadrupled. Prices of other raw materials fluctuated sharply. Major foreign corporations in primary commodity industries were nationalized in many Third World countries. Foreign manufacturing subsidiaries were subject to a much wider array of controls. Nontariff trade barriers, such as orderly marketing agreements and unilateral quotas, became more widespread. Exchange rates fluctuated. Rules for the international monetary regime lost precision. Slower growth rates were accompanied by higher rates of inflation. The Third World more vigorously pressed for a new international economic order.

What accounts for these changes and what do they augur for the future? The most optimistic interpretation points to errors in policy, particularly self-indulgence on the part of the United States. If these errors are corrected, the world economy may once again be set on the golden path to growth. Others see the 1970s as a period of abrupt but noncontinuous changes, such as the quadrupling of oil prices and the growth of manufactured exports from some LDCs (Less Developed Countries). Once adjustments are made, stability will return.

The majority of observers believe that the changes of the 1970s are not transient. Nevertheless, they remain hopeful that the policies of the 1960s can be reestablished in the 1980s. The basis for this optimism is the assertion that the benefits of an open international economic regime are so great that its collapse would be intolerable. We are all in the same boat, and if it capsizes, we will all drown. Since this prospect is discomforting, everyone will bail or row, depending upon the circumstances and their particular talents. The concept of interdependence, the shibboleth of the 1970s, is based on this image of mutual benefit and mutual loss.

This prevailing liberal image rests on the basic belief that international economic order is ultimately sustained by economic wants. Actors cooperate because it is in their economic self-interest to do so. Since underlying wants—high employment, rapid growth, price stability, technological innovation—have not changed, there is no inherent reason why the world economy cannot be returned to a stable liberal path. What is required is sufficient will. (Economists assume, although less so than in the past, that they can provide the wisdom.)

While the importance of economic self-interest cannot be ignored in any effort to understand international economic behavior, the prevailing interdependency view ignores the fundamental contribution that political power, more specifically the power of the United States, has made to the creation and maintenance of the postwar international economic regime. An emphasis on American power suggests that the conditions of the 1960s cannot be re-created in the 1980s because one of the fundamental factors that determines the nature of the international economic regime, the distribution of power among states, has altered.

The decline of American power has two implications for the world economy. First, the international economic order is becoming messier. Different issues are being handled in different ways. Behavior is increasingly being determined by *ad hoc* calculations of interests rather than rules and norms. Some areas are becoming more open, others more closed. In part this change reflects an alteration in American goals from an emphasis on long-term global political objectives to an emphasis on specific national economic interests. This change in turn is intimately related to the loss of America's hegemonic position, for only a hegemonic state can afford to sacrifice clear national interests for long-term and often ill-defined systemic objectives.

Second, the decline in American power makes the present system more fragile. Even for a well-established regime, political power is necessary to absorb unexpected shocks. An effective leader may act as a lender of last resort for the financial system, a market for redundant commodities, a provider of scarce resources, a guarantor (by force if necessary), of responsible behavior by individual actors. Such effective political action is much easier when there is a hegemonic distribution of power in the international system than when there is a multipolar one.[1] While all states in a multipolar world may see their interest in maintaining an open regime, they will not necessarily be willing to accept the costs needed to sustain it. Some great shock under conditions of rising uncertainty can, like the last play in a sequence of prisoner's dilemma games, lead actors to cheat against the system in favor of their own short-term self-interest. If one believes the system is doomed, continued sacrifice is foolish at best. Such insecurity is much less likely in a hegemonic world because the leading power has the capability to act, and in its pursuit of long-term objectives, can be relied upon not to destroy the system for its own short-term economic interests.

Neither messiness nor fragility imply that the system is doomed to collapse. Protection in one area does not necessarily mean protection in others. Over some thirty years of increasing openness, powerful domestic groups have become heavily involved in international economic transactions. Their economic self-interest provides a strong but brittle mortar for the present system. The global economy may, with good fortune, be spared the kind of trauma that would require the effective exercise of political power. Absent a powerful external shock, the edifice will remain standing.

AMERICAN POWER

The central structural characteristic of the immediate postwar period was the overwhelming power of the United States. American power was dominant not only in overall terms but also over a wide range of specific issue areas. U.S. leaders did not often have to worry about the difficulties of linkage (i.e., utilizing resources in one issue area to secure desired outcomes in others). This peculiar situation was a result not simply of the human and natural resource base of the United States but also of the destruction wrought by the Second World War on all other major world powers. While the United States had become the world's leading producer of manufactures before 1900, and the world's most important source of credit after the First World War, only after 1945 did America assume such extraordinary structural dominance.

Comparison with the nineteenth-century is instructive. Nineteenth-century Britain has frequently been regarded as the functional equivalent of twentieth-century America, both economic hegemons of their respective eras. Nevertheless, at the peak of its power in 1860, Britain's gross national product (GNP) exceeded that of its nearest European rival, Russia, by only 12 percent. By contrast, in 1950 America's aggregate economic output was 173 percent greater than that of the Soviet Union, the second-largest economic actor, and 327 percent greater than that of Great Britain, the third-largest actor.[2]

Influence in the international system is a function of particular capabilities, not just overall size. The GNPs of Japan and the Soviet Union are now about equal, but it would be foolish to equate the power of these two countries. In some areas, such as advanced nonmilitary technology, Japan has superior resources; but in others Japan is markedly inferior to the Soviet Union. Power resources that are useful in one area may be ineffective in others. Japan's steel production would not impede an invasion unless it had been transformed into ships, tanks, guns, and planes. The world price of wheat cannot easily be regulated through sales of petroleum. Britain's naval power and financial resources could not deter a German attack on France in 1914. Linkage across different issue areas can be attempted only under certain conditions and even then will not necessarily succeed.[3]

The unique character of American power in the postwar world was a manifestation not just of overall capabilities but also of the exceptional diversity of U.S. resources. The United States enjoyed not just overall structural dominance but also issue-specific dominance.[4] In a world characterized by varying degrees of currency nonconvertibility until 1958, the United States held most of the world's foreign exchange reserves. In the late 1940s the United States accounted for three-quarters of foreign capital investments and for almost one-third of the world's exports. It produced more than 50 percent of the world's petroleum, more than 40 percent of its steel, and about 20 percent of its wheat. The United States was the major source of foreign aid and food aid. In the early 1960s American research and development expenditures accounted for more than 50 percent of the expenditures of seven major countries (United Kingdom, France, West Germany, Canada, Japan, Soviet Union, and the United States). During the Korean war, U.S. military expenditures were equal to 50 percent of the world total. The United States held a commanding lead over the Soviet Union in strategic weapons and open-ocean naval capability.[5]

When the United States was threatened by one kind of power resource, it often had a similar resource at its own disposal. In Korea, military force could be met with military force. After the 1967 Middle East War, an Arab oil embargo could be frustrated by an increase in the production of American oil. When American policy makers did not have similar resources at their disposal, successful links were frequently accomplished. Lend-lease settlements and loans were used to influence British commercial policy immediately after the Second World War. Foreign aid funds were used to alter European monetary policy in the 1950s. The threat to retract support from the British pound was used to induce Britain to withdraw from Suez in 1956. Covert intervention and military assistance was used to restore the Shah to power in 1953 and contributed to Arbenz's downfall in 1954. American leaders were able to bring into play a very wide range of resources with few opportunity costs for the United States. American threats were credible because the United States would not lose much if they were carried out. American leaders could usually construct a link that would enable them to compel other actors to alter their policy.[6] Inducements could be offered because the United States had resources that others needed much more than they were needed by the United States.

AMERICAN POLICY

A state can use its power capabilities to pursue a wide range of objectives. As Robert Keohane points out in his essay in this volume, until 1947 American policy makers pursued specific and concrete objectives. The International Monetary Fund Articles of Agreement reflected American fears of inflation rather than British desires for a well-endowed un-restrictive source of capital. In 1945 and 1946 the United States used lend-lease and a large loan to try to force Britain to abandon imperial trade preferences, which impeded U.S. exports. Non-American com-panies were successfully excluded from the oil riches of Saudi Arabia.

However, once the extent of British weakness became apparent, and the hope of conciliation and cooperation with the Soviet Union faded, the basic orientation of American policy shifted. From 1947 into the 1960s emphasis was consistently placed on broad and often diffuse political objectives rather than specific economic and strategic interests. American leaders pursued what can be termed a policy of *investment* rather than consumption. They moved to create an international structure, including an international economic order, that would provide returns over the long run. American economic policy was primarily oriented toward general long-term global, rather than tangible national, economic goals.

The United States was the prime mover in the creation of a more open international regime for trade. The fundamental purpose of this re-gime was to facilitate the movement of goods and factors across interna-tional boundaries. These movements were to be controlled by private corporations. All this was consistent enough with national, group, and noncommunist bloc interests. America and its corporations had much to gain from an open system. Such a system was also consistent with Amer-ican political goals not only because such a trading regime would be in-formed by liberal principles but also because trade was associated with growth, political stability, and anticommunism.

There were, however, many tradeoffs between political objectives associated with regional welfare and specific national economic interests. As long as American central decision makers could free themselves from pressures from particular groups in the United States, they resolved such conflicts in favor of broad political interests. American willingness to sacrifice specific economic interests for long-term political goals was man-ifest in the active promotion of European integration and the toleration of discrimination against the United States by both Europe and Japan. American leaders believed that a unified Europe would integrate Ger-many and resist Soviet aggression or communist infiltration. Marshall Plan aid, dispersed through the Organization for European Economic Cooperation (OEEC) required joint arrangements. The 1950 OEEC Code of Liberalization was directed at the reduction of quantitative bar-riers within Europe but not with the United States. The European Pay-ments Union, for which the United States provided reserves, encouraged intra- rather than extra-European trade. The European Coal and Steel Community received a GATT waiver because of U.S. backing, despite its violation of a rule which requires that customs unions cover virtually all products. The Treaty of Rome was also vigorously supported by the United States, even though the establishment of associated states violated

GATT articles and could only harm American trading interests. As a result of the proliferation of regional integration schemes, the percentage of trade that took place under unconditional MFN (Most Favored Nation) conditions fell from 90 percent in 1955 to 77 percent in 1970.[7] While these blocs may have furthered global welfare through trade creation, they were trade diverting for the United States.

The United States also tolerated Japanese protectionism to further more general political goals. By the late 1940s American leaders had concluded that it was critical to rebuild the Japanese economy, for reasons similar to those that led them to encourage European unification. They accepted a high degree of protectionism in Japan during the 1950s and '60s. The Japanese tariff structure was designed not only to develop new industries but also to lessen the social dislocation of openness by protecting high-employment industries even if they were declining. The peace treaty with Japan provided for special access to the U.S. market. As a result of American prodding, European countries continued discriminatory practices even after Japan was admitted to GATT in 1955. Only in the early 1970s did U.S. policy makers begin to push Europe to accept more Japanese goods.[8] The consequences of these policies are suggested by the table 2.1, which gives the percent of U.S. and EEC imports from Japan divided by Japan's percent of world exports. If trade were equally distributed, the figure would be 1.00.

TABLE 2.1 **Japan's Trade with the United States and the EEC**

	1948	1951	1960	1970	1976
U.S.	5.75	2.41	2.05	2.12	1.65
EEC	.22	.35	.27	.40	.50

Source: Derived from figures in IMF, *Direction of Trade, Annual*, 1970–76; UN, *Yearbook of International Trade Statistics*, 1960.

Until the 1970s, the United States was importing more than twice as much from Japan as would be expected on the basis of Japan's share of world exports; and the EEC less than half as much. American policies allowed Japan to enjoy the benefits of an open system while lessening many of the costs of adjustment. Japan became the world's third-largest industrial power, with consequences not altogether favorable for American trading interests.

Analytically, the American treatment of Japan as opposed to Europe more clearly demonstrates the primacy of long-term political and economic objectives. The overvaluation of the dollar, which American policy makers accepted from the late 1950s until August 1971, hurt the U.S.

trade balance but made it less expensive (in terms of dollars) for American firms to establish European subsidiaries, a clear benefit for a specific group. The Japanese, however, continued to impose tight restrictions on direct foreign investment until the early 1970s. The Japanese secured a great deal of their technology at very low cost through indigenous development of nonproprietary transfers. When they had to pay for foreign technology, they opted for licensing rather than accept direct investment.[9]

In sum, during the postwar period the United States did not try to fully exploit all of its commercial advantages. Free trade was accepted in areas where the United States did not have a comparative advantage and discrimination was tolerated where American products did have an advantage. The liberal order was not symmetrical; U.S. markets were more open to foreign products than foreign markets were to American. One study of the postwar trading system concludes "that postwar trade liberalization has been a beneficial exercise for America's trade partners, and that if any country could be said to have 'lost' within our given time horizon it was the United States itself."[10]

Until the late 1960s, American international *monetary* policy also focused on the general political interests of the noncommunist world rather than national economic goals. The American dollar was the key currency. The size of the American economy assured a capital market in which large transactions could be made without affecting interest rates. The relatively low involvement of the United States in the world economy (the ratio of U.S. exports plus imports to GNP was about 8 percent) made it unlikely that international pressures would force American policy makers to alter currency values. Stability, liquidity, confidence— the major prerequisites for a key currency—were easily met by the dollar. In the absence of such an asset, which could serve as both a reserve and transactions currency, the world economy could not have grown as rapidly in the postwar period.

The reserve currency role of the dollar did enhance the national economic interest of the United States in several ways; it was a consumption as well as an investment good. The United States was able to prolong its deficit because foreigners were willing to hold dollars; uncomfortable choices could be postponed. The United States derived seignorage from the fact that average interest payments on its foreign debts were lower than they would have been had dollars not been regarded as international reserves. The reserve role of the dollar also provided special benefits for U.S. financial institutions because American banks had easier access to dollars, at least before the growth of the Eurodollar market.[11]

Nevertheless, these benefits of being the key currency country should not be exaggerated. After the 1950s U.S. policy makers did not fully avail themselves of additional policy flexibility because of the fear that the dollar overhang would collapse. Foreign holdings complicated American monetary policy making, which was forced to anticipate movements of these assets. Often these predictions were incorrect. During the 1960s the Federal Open Market Committee generally let foreign considerations take precedence over domestic ones in setting monetary policy.[12] As foreign dollar deposits grew, the United States was compelled to pay higher interest rates to lessen the possibility that they would be converted into gold or other national currencies. Thus, the direct national economic effects on the United States from the key currency role of the dollar were mixed.

The emphasis that American policy makers placed on noncommunist bloc, rather than national, welfare is more clearly shown by their commitment to a fixed-rate regime and toleration of an overvalued dollar for at least a decade, and possibly two, than by their endorsement of the key currency role of the dollar. *Ceteris paribus* large countries should prefer flexible-exchange-rate systems, and small countries should prefer fixed-exchange-rate systems. Empirically, large countries are less involved in international trade than small ones. The ratio of trade (imports plus exports) to GNP for the United States is now about 16 percent. For small countries such as the Netherlands and Belgium this ratio exceeds 75 percent. With a fixed-exchange-rate system a country can only rectify a balance of payments deficit by deflating relative to its trading partners. For a large country only a relatively small proportion of these price changes affect the balance of payments; nevertheless, the whole economy must be deflated. But with a flexible-rate system, a large country can tackle a deficit by changing its exchange rate, and thus also changing the relative prices of traded and nontraded goods; overall, this is a less painful process. For a small state, on the other hand, fixed rates are preferable because they insulate the economy from continuous price changes emanating from the world economy; virtually all small states have, in fact, maintained fixed parities against the currencies of their major trading partners since 1973. The American endorsement of a flexible-rate system after 1973 was, therefore, in keeping with the kind of system that would normally be preferred by a large state primarily concerned with its national economic welfare.

More important than the adoption of a fixed-rate system in assessing the motives of American foreign economic policy was the overvaluation of the dollar. From 1946 to 1949, the United States enjoyed a large balance-of-payments surplus, and American leaders forced the European countries and Japan to devalue their currencies. Some of these devaluations were massive. Britain and Sweden devalued by 30.5 percent, Belgium by 12.3 percent, Canada by 9.1 percent. By 1949, the German mark had lost over 90 percent of its prewar value, the Italian lira 63.9 percent, and the Japanese yen 98.4 percent. These devaluations, as much as the Marshall Plan, spurred European and Japanese recovery and encouraged investments in export-oriented industries that competed with American producers.

These devaluations also had an immediate impact on the American balance of payments. The trade surplus, which had been $5.3 billion in 1949, fell to $1.1 billion in 1950. On the official reserve basis, the overall balance of payments showed a $3.3 billion deficit in 1950. From 1950 until 1974, the United States had an overall surplus only in 1957 and in 1968–69. American deficits were not produced by trade flows, which did not show a deficit until 1968, or by direct foreign investment, where repatriated earnings consistently exceeded capital outflows, but by government expenditures for military purposes and foreign aid. Between 1949 and 1964, U.S. military and aid payments were equal to between 48 and 63 percent of the American export earnings that had to service them.[13]

Thus, America's monetary policy, like its commercial policy, was heavily guided by long-range political concerns associated with the well-being of the noncommunist world rather than specific American economic interests; by investment, not consumption. The deficit was the result of large official transfers that could not be offset by private commercial or capital flows given the exchange rates that had been encouraged by the United States. These exchange rates were themselves a function of the desire of American leaders to encourage European and Japanese recovery.

Only an extremely powerful state would pursue such policies, for a chronic balance-of-payments deficit will eventually force uncomfortable choices even for reserve asset countries; and political leaders do not relish having choices forced on them by external events. Only an extremely powerful state could encourage the growth and development of its allies without weighing carefully the consequences for its own position in the international system. Only an extremely powerful state could rationalize its policies with a set of beliefs about the relationships among economic development, political development, democracy, and policies toward the United States that rested upon a series of untested, indeed untestable, assumptions.[14]

Investment is not the normal pattern of behavior in international politics. Usually countries must weigh policy options against constrained resources. Given the uncertainties of the international environment, they must place a high discount rate on future returns. Countering present threats to specific interests is usually far more compelling than reacting against future dangers. Only its exceptional structural domination freed the United States from many of the constraints normally imposed by the international system. The territorial and political integrity of the United States was not threatened. U.S. economic preeminence appeared beyond challenge. From 1947 into the 1960s American policy makers enjoyed that rare luxury of being able to emphasize creating rather than reacting to the international environment. Because American power was so great, they could invest rather than consume.

For the international economic regime the consequences of an American policy of investment rather than consumption were extremely salutory. The burdens of openness were eased for America's allies. Decision makers in the United States compromised liberal principles to facilitate West European and Japanese sales abroad. An overvalued dollar also promoted exports for America's trading partners. The domestic costs of openness were alleviated by U.S. tolerance of protectionism in other countries. Free riders in the economic sphere were accepted, for American policy makers were most concerned with political objectives. The international economic regime was stable because one state willingly accepted most of the costs.

THE DECLINE OF AMERICAN POWER

The United States has lost the unique position that it held in the immediate postwar period. This is reflected not so much in aggregate terms (the American GNP is still more than twice as large as Russia's and Japan's, its nearest rivals) as in a loss of power resources relevant to specific issue areas. This uneven pattern of decline, particularly striking in the 1970s, is suggested by table 2.2

TABLE 2.2   **Indicators of U.S. Power Capabilities: Ratio of U.S. to World Total**

	1950	1960	1970	1976
National income[a]		.45	.39	.31
Crude petroleum production	.53	.33	.21	.14
Crude steel production	.45	.26	.20	.17
Iron ore production	.42	.19	.13	.10
Wheat production	.17	.15	.12	.14
International financial reserves	.49	.21	.16	.07
Military expenditures	.32	.48	.35	.27
Exports	.18	.16	.14	.11
Foreign aid[b]		.58	.45	.32

Sources: Derived from figures in UN, *Statistical Yearbook*, various years; OECD, Development Advisory Committee, *1979 Review*, pp. 286–87; SIPRI, *Yearbook* 1968/69, pp. 200–201, and 1977, pp. 222–23.

[a] Only market economy countries.

[b] Only members of OECD, Development Assistance Committee

The figures in the table are only suggestive. The relationship between power capabilities and the actual ability to alter outcomes can be assessed only by examining the relative opportunity costs of change in specific situations.[15] Still, the table does not indicate that the United States has become a second-rate power. In a wide range of activities it continues to be the world's most prominent actor. In some areas, such as agriculture, its global position has hardly changed in the postwar period. Nevertheless, the enormous slack accorded the United States through the 1950s by the absence of any serious threat to minimalist political goals or specific economic interests was gone in many issue areas by the 1970s.

The change in American power has brought a change in the goals of American foreign economic policy. While the need to accommodate the demands of specific economic groups has remained a constant feature of American policy, goals associated with national as opposed to global economic welfare have become more important. American leaders have hardly abandoned commitments to a stable international order. Indeed, American rhetoric continually emphasizes the identification of national interests with global interests. Nevertheless, when there is conflict, American policy makers have increasingly opted for clearly identified national goals rather than more ambitious and more ambiguous global objectives whose relationship to American interests are uncertain.

In the area of *trade*, the shift in American objectives is reflected in several ways. First, U.S. central decision makers have more vigorously pursued particularistic interests associated with protecting import-competing industries and promoting exports. In the past the United States has acted to shield many industries threatened by imports—dairy products beginning in 1954, petroleum and textiles in the late 1950s, steel in 1967. While the level of protection has varied, the fragmented nature of the American political system has made it impossible for central decision makers to ignore interest-group pressures. The scope and depth of such protection has increased in the 1970s, however, as more sectors have been subject to foreign competition.

The United States has also begun to press more vigorously for greater export opportunities. Funding for the Export-Import Bank has sharply increased in the last decade. The average annual value of exports supported by Exim programs increased from $2,863 million for the 1965–69 period to $9,026 million for 1975–77.[16] In September 1978 the administration initiated an export promotion program that provided for a $500 million increase in Exim direct-loan authorizations for FY 1980 (the above figures cover several programs other than direct loans), a $100 million loan guarantee program for small business, and additional funds for State and Commerce Department export promotion programs.

The United States has also been the moving force behind OECD negotiations to reach an agreement on regulating the terms governing export financing. American leaders have become increasingly concerned about European arrangements that leave American exporters at a relative disadvantage. (One highly publicized case involved credit arrangements for the sale of the European Airbus to Eastern Airlines.) Initial agreement was reached in March 1978, but shortly after concluding another agreement in October 1978, American policy makers demanded more stringent restrictions on interest rates and wider coverage of products. It has been difficult to reach a final accord; the United States has threatened a general policy of matching foreign credits and has already, on a case-by-case basis, offered export financing at rates as low as 4 or 5 percent to counter foreign offers.[17]

A second manifestation of a more interest-oriented American trade policy is an increase in the willingness to tolerate departures from the rules of a liberal international economic regime. Such departures have always existed, but there has been some attempt to both cover over and bracket them. The various textile agreements, for instance, while providing for overall guidelines on export growth, have been implemented through bilateral agreements, a clear violation of the most-favored-nation principle. But by placing these arrangements outside GATT, and making them subject to some international rules, textiles could be bracketed off from the modal liberal practices prevailing in the rest of the trading system. The various voluntary export restraint arrangements, which the United States began negotiating in the late 1960s, have covered a wide range of products including steel, shoes, and television sets. In the Tokyo Round, provisions in a number of the codes violate nondiscriminatory treatment. The Government Procurement Code, which the United States has strongly supported, essentially follows the principle of conditional most-favored-nation status. If a country does not grant concessions to the United States, it will in turn not be granted concessions, even if the same concessions have been given to other countries.

The Trade Act of 1974 also reflects a concern with more specific American interests. While endorsing a continued commitment to free trade, the act dictates a more interest-oriented, even protectionist, set of policies. The act increases the role of Congress, altering a pattern of greater presidential autonomy initiated by the Reciprocal Trade Agreements Act of 1934. By changing the definition of injury, the act makes it easier for a domestic group to secure relief through escape-clause actions. By mandating that the Treasury make a decision on countervailing duty cases within twelve months after a complaint has been brought, it precludes long delays that had, during the 1950s and '60s, given the executive a way of circumventing U.S. countervailing duty laws.

The main purpose of the Trade Agreements Act of 1979 was to bring American domestic legislation into line with the agreements concluded during the Tokyo Round. The act endorses liberal principles. However, with the exception of injury standards in antidumping and subsidy cases, the Act is likely to make it easier for American firms to secure protection. It sets more stringent time limits for assessing antidumping duties and countervailing duties against subsidies. When a preliminary finding of dumping is made, importers will now have to deposit sums equal to dumping duty estimates. In the past they were required to obtain less expensive Customs bonds. The Commerce Department and the U.S. Trade Representative (USTR) must assist U.S. firms in their efforts to secure information, including information from foreign sources. For both subsidy and antidumping investigations, the new law makes tentative negative findings but not tentative positive findings, immediately subject to judicial review, a provision that makes it relatively easier for domestic industries to move their case into the judicial system when administrative decisions are negative.[18]

Along with passage of the Trade Agreements Act, Congress forced the President to reorganize the trade functions of the American government. This reorganization is generally described as an effort to increase efficiency and coherence. The reorganization plan is better understood as a manifestation of the general movement toward a more vigorous defense of specific American economic interests.

The central feature of the plan is that it upgrades the roles of the U.S. Trade Representative, formerly the Office of the Special Trade Representative, and the Department of Commerce. It downgrades the roles of the State Department and the Treasury Department. The USTR is now given the lead responsibility in formulating trade policy for both agriculture and industry. This portfolio previously was held by the Department of State. Commerce becomes the main agency for implementing actions related to trade. Antidumping and subsidy investigations have been transferred from the Treasury Department. U.S. commercial attaches will be transferred from the State Department to the Commerce Department.

While this reorganization plan does involve some consolidation, particularly the linking of policy formulation and functional negotiation in the USTR, it hardly streamlines the U.S. policy structure. Major responsibility will still be divided among the USTR, the Commerce Department, the International Trade Commission, and the Agriculture Department. What the reorganization does do is to lessen the role of the two departments with the strongest general political concerns and commitments to free trade—State and Treasury. The State Department incorporated foreign trade policy within a general political framework. Given the opportunity, Treasury generally construed the law in ways that would minimize American countervailing duties.[19] Given Commerce's more limited portfolio and closer relations with particular sectors and industries, it is more likely to interpret legislation in ways that favor American producers seeking import relief.

In sum, in specific sectors, export promotion, international agreements, national legislation, and bureaucratic organization, American trade policy has become more oriented toward specific national objectives. While in the 1950s and '60s such goals were often sacrificed when they conflicted with global political objectives, the opposite is the case today.

The shift in American policy toward more clearly identifiable national objectives is also apparent in *monetary affairs*. Beginning in the late 1960s, American leaders adopted policies that altered the two aspects of the postwar system that were most detrimental to clearly identifiable national economic goals—the overvaluation of the dollar and fixed exchange rates.

Initially, American concern was focused on the international value of the dollar. Optimistic assessments about a natural reversal of the balance-of-payments deficit, which had been made in the early 1960s, had to be rejected as American inflation accelerated with the Great Society and the Vietnam war. In 1968 the Nixon administration adopted a policy of benign neglect, which was designed to force other countries to revalue their currencies by refusing to check the American deficit. This approach did have some success; in early May 1970, the Germans felt compelled to allow the mark to float upward.

But benign neglect did not work fast enough. The overall deficit continued, and more important, the United States suffered its first postwar deficit on the trade account in 1970. The dollar now appeared overvalued not only if both political and purely economic transactions were considered but even if purely economic transactions were considered: American exports not only failed to cover imports, aid, and military expenditures; they could not finance imports alone. Between January and August 1971 the United States lost $3.1 billion in foreign exchange ($1.1 billion in the first half of August) and drew down $2.4 billion in swap arrangements. On August 15, 1971, Nixon suspended convertibility of the dollar.[20] Bretton Woods was ended. The suspension was accompanied by a number of other measures including a 10 percent surcharge on all imports. The major spokesman for the administration's policy, John Connally, projected an extremely nationalistic image. In both style and substance, August 1971 represented a watershed in the postwar economic policy of the United States; it indicated that American leaders were no longer prepared to sacrifice clear national interests, in this case accepting the costs of rectifying the deficit under the existing monetary regime, to preserve global economic welfare.

August 1971 initiated a series of changes that culminated in a flexible-rate system. The fixed-exchange-rate system was restored with the Smithsonian Agreement of December 1971, which provided for an 8.5 percent devaluation of the dollar in exchange for the termination of the 10 percent import surcharge, and an increase in the permissible range around which currencies could move before official intervention took place from plus or minus 1 percent to plus or minus 2.25 percent.

Smithsonian did not last. The pound was devalued in 1972. In February 1973 a further 10 percent devaluation of the dollar followed an $8 billion capital flight. In March speculation was renewed, and the Europeans and Japanese closed their foreign exchange markets. In the middle of the month, the major countries failed to reach agreement on new fixed rates. *De facto*, a floating-rate system came into existence. This situation was ratified by the Jamaica accords revising the Articles of Agreement of the International Monetary Fund, which in essence recognized existing practices. There are now no agreed-upon guidelines for intervention in international monetary markets or liquidity creation. The dollar retains a major role in the system more by default than design. While there is no indication that American policy makers saw August 1971 as a step toward a flexible-rate system, they did not resist this new system as it came into being.[21]

In sum, as American power has declined, American objectives have changed. Increasingly, greater emphasis has been given to specific national goals; broad Western bloc objectives play a less prominent role in American policy. In trade, the United States has more vigorously defended the interests of specific industries, has more aggressively promoted exports, and has more strongly protested foreign practices that injure domestic markets or prejudice foreign sales. In monetary affairs, American policies have contributed to the devaluation of the dollar and the end of a fixed exchange rate system. All these policies can be identified with specific national economic interests. This shift in emphasis is not a temporary aberration; it is a reflection of a fundamental change in the global political position of the United States. Only an extremely strong country can consistently pursue long-term political objectives, can invest rather than consume. The globally oriented rhetoric of policy makers has not changed, but the substance of policy has already returned to the course more frequently followed by states.

PROSPECTS

What is the prognosis for a world economy more firmly rooted in particularistic calculations of interest? One consequence is already apparent. The regime is becoming messier. Given American toleration of various forms of discrimination, the postwar order in its heyday was in many ways more open than it was liberal; many departures from liberal practices did not surface because the United States did not challenge them as long as the norm of increasing international economic activity was promoted. As American policy makers have become more oriented toward national economic interests, departures from prevailing rules have become both more frequent and more visible. The United States now routinely challenges the practices of others, and at the same time endorses and sometimes initiates violations of liberal rules. There is no state whose international economic policy can be explained by adherence to a consistent set of principles. Rather, *ad hoc* calculations of interest increasingly determine national behavior. The result is a more confused and complicated international economic system.

In the area of trade there has been more openness in some arenas and more closure in others. While tariff reductions have continued, progress in removing nontariff barriers has been limited. In some sectors restrictions on the movement of goods have been lessened; in others, increased. For instance, despite the highly politicized nature of the aircraft industry, a code liberalizing trade in this area was concluded at the Tokyo Round of tariff negotiations. But at the same negotiations not much progress was made in altering the fundamentally discriminatory nature of world trade in agricultural products. While the proportion of trade subject to restrictive measures has increased in the 1970s, there has been no significant downturn in the global movement of goods if changes in overall economic activity are taken into account.

Similarly, in the international monetary arena the relative neatness of the fixed-rate gold exchange system has given way to much more diverse international practices. As of the middle of 1978 the IMF listed 42 countries as tying their currencies to the dollar, 5 to the British pound, 14 to the French franc, 15 to the SDR, and 31 to some other unit of exchange. Fifty countries were listed under the heading "exchange rates otherwise determined," which included those countries that described their regimes as floating, those that adjusted their regimes on the basis of a set of indicators, and "certain other members whose regimes are not otherwise described in this table." When major countries, including the United States, are placed in a residual category in a table that has eight headings, it is some indication that things are not simple. Amidst this diversity of national practices, however, the U.S. dollar has maintained its central position as a reserve currency. For data from 76 countries reported by the IMF the dollar constituted 80.9 percent of official reserves in 1970 and 81.2 percent in 1977. This reserve currency role persisted through a period when official reserves increased nearly fivefold and the trade-weighted value of the dollar fell by more than 10 percent.[22]

Can such a disorderly global economic order be stable? Conventional liberal perspectives offer an analysis on the one hand, and policy prescription on the other, that are strained if not contradictory. Analytically, national economies are seen as enmeshed in a web of economic interest; the costs of breaking relations would be exceedingly high. Even the United States, the most self-sufficient of the Western countries, would experience severe dislocations if the system veered sharply toward closure. *A fortiori* this is held to be true for other countries including major Third World states. If interdependence so closely binds the world's national economies, one would have to conclude that there is not too much to worry about.

The liberal policy prescription is, however, much more cautious and demanding. For policy purposes, decision makers and analysts in the

United States tacitly see the world economy in a state of permanent disequilibrium: Failure to progressively eliminate restrictions invariably leads to regression. The world is seen poised between the slippery slope of protectionism and the verdant meadow of liberalism. One step along the slope leads to others because of intranational and cross-national dynamics: If one industry within a country gets protection, others will make the same demands; if one country's products are discriminated against, it will discriminate against others.

The analysis and the policy prescription do not sit comfortably together. If the web of interdependence is so powerful, why are protectionist breaks so likely to unravel the entire system? The history of the postwar order provide more support for the contention that interests can be a powerful binding force than for the assumption that the system cannot tolerate inconsistency.

The postwar experience offers little evidence for the slippery-slope hypothesis. The regime has been peppered with exceptions to liberal principles including agriculture, textiles, Japanese protectionism, and the associated states of the EEC. There is no logically necessary relationship between protection for one sector and protection for another, at the national or international level. Within a country, appeals for protection based on government consistency are only one of many arguments that an industry can use. Other factors—the industry's size, employment level, geographic concentration, and political organization—are likely to be far more important. The American shoe and textile industries have not gotten the same level of government support. In the international system the ability to retaliate against protectionist measures depends on the relative opportunity costs of change for the parties involved. Those countries that are now most likely to be the targets of protectionism—Japan and newly industrializing LDCs—are not in a position to retaliate because the costs of a trade war would be much higher for them than for importing countries.

The analytic position preferred by conventional liberal analysis, the binding force of interests, has more merit. Particularistic calculations of interest, either at the sectoral or national levels, impart great inertia to a well-established international economic order. After three decades of increasing openness, powerful groups in all advanced market economy countries have become deeply involved in the world economy. In the United States, multinational corporations, large banks, technologically sophisticated industries, and agriculture derive a major part of their earnings from international transactions. Such interest groups do not want to see the system closed. In other countries, which are even more heavily involved in world trade (the ratio of imports plus exports to GNP was 17 percent for the United States in 1975, versus 26 percent for Japan, 51 percent for Germany, 39 percent for France, 54 percent for the UK, and 48 percent for Italy), a calculus based on particular group interests is likely to be even more heavily weighted in favor of sustaining a basically open international economic regime.

This is not to deny that there are many sectors threatened by imports. The list of technologically conventional industries, many with global over-capacity, includes shoes, textiles, steel, shipbuilding, and consumer electronics. Pressure groups associated with these sectors have gotten some form of protection in virtually all major industrialized countries.[23] Still, the balance of particularistic calculations of interest is almost surely on the side of those that want to preserve the existing order. In the clash of narrow interests, protectionist forces will have to be mollified but they will not, in the absence of a major economic depression (no small caveat this, but one that goes well beyond international economic questions alone), be able to move the national policies of the major trading countries to an endorsement of closure and protectionism. In the United States, for instance, the Multifibre Agreement, trigger prices for steel, and orderly marketing agreements for shoes will continue in one form or another, but Burke-Hartke will not pass.

Thus, an interest-based analysis of the global economy does suggest that the system is not inherently unstable. The liberal emphasis on interests as the underpinning for a regime can offer an accurate analysis for a well established international economic system, one in which there are many groups with a stake in the regime's stability. But this conclusion also weakens any assertion based on the assumption that policy consistency is essential to prevent a regression to protectionism.

There is, however, one critical caveat that must be amended to this conclusion: Interests are an effective cement only if actors believe that the global economic regime will endure. This belief limits completely self-centered, short-term behavior. Many international economic conditions offer the temptation to cheat, provided that others do not follow suit. The country that can impose an optimum tariff is better off if its trading partners do not retaliate. The country that can throw the burden of currency stabilization on to others may ease some difficult domestic choices. The cartel member that can sell under the table gains additional revenues, provided that its partners do not drive the price down by following the same strategem. Such cheating is generally limited if all of the parties believe that they are involved in a continuing game in which misconduct will be discovered and punished. The belief that the game will endure is essential if interest-motivated behavior is not to lead to a breakdown of the system. If interest-motivated actors conclude that the economic order is about to undergo dramatic change, they will scramble to save what they can, fearing always that if they do not act first (whether it is a country imposing trade barriers or a bank declaring default), others will leave them stranded.

As we have seen, confidence is not likely to be shaken by cross-national or intranational protectionism generated from within the system.

It could, however, be undermined by external shocks. If such shocks occur—another oil embargo and production cutback, defaults in several borrowing countries, simultaneous crop failures in major grain-producing areas, a communist electoral victory in France or Italy, turmoil in the Arabian peninsula—political leadership would again become essential for the stability of the regime; for such shocks can quickly change confidence into fear and panic. Shocks can be absorbed most effectively by a leader that is willing and able to defend the order as a whole. Such a leader can bail out the monetary system. It can provide goods that are in short supply. It can employ its ideological, economic, and military resources to entice or cajole groups or countries to resist the temptation to jump first. The absence of leadership does not mean any necessary change in the basic shape of the vessel—the body of rules, norms, and behavior that constitute the global economic order—but it does imply that the vessel has become more fragile, more likely to be suddenly shattered. If a shock does occur, confidence could dissipate precipitously, and cheating could quickly become widespread.

Thus the liberal interest-based analysis is convincing only as long as things go on much as they have in the past. But if there is some sudden externally caused disequilibrium, the absence of political power would be keenly felt, for the American adoption of policies directed more toward clearly identifiable national economic interests means that there is no effective leader in the present system. Appeals for greater political will and wisdom will not change this basic fact, for American behavior is not a function of short-sightedness or chauvinism but of a fundamental change in the world political position of the United States. The United States is acting like an ordinary power. A world of ordinary powers, as opposed to one of hegemonic leadership, has historically been the most common condition of world politics. In this sense we are returning to normalcy, but normalcy in international politics is much less stable than the world we have known for the last thirty years.

NOTES

1. Two major recent expositions of this argument are Charles Kindleberger, *The World in Depression, 1929–1939* (Berkeley: University of California Press, 1973); and Robert Gilpin, *U.S. Power and the Multinational* Corporation (New York: Basic Books, 1975).

2. Paul Bairoch, "Europe's Gross National Product: 1800–1875," *Journal of European Economic History* 5 (Fall 1976), table 4; World Bank, *World Tables 1976*, p. 282.

3. Arthur Stein, "The Politics of Linkage," *World Politics* 33 (October 1980).

4. For a discussion of overall structural and issue structural models, see Robert Keohane and Joseph Nye, *Power and Interdependence* (Boston: Little Brown, 1977) pp. 42–53.

5. For sources, see table 2.2.

6. See Stein's "The Politics of Linkage," pp. 65–69, for a discussion of coerced linkage and Kenneth Oye's "The Domain of Choice," in *Eagle Entangled: U.S. Foreign Policy in a Complex World*, ed. Kenneth Oye, et al. (New York: Longman, 1979), pp. 13–17, for a discussion of backscratching.

7. Gerard and Victoria Curzon, "The Management of Trade Relations in the GATT," in *International Economic Relations of the Western World 1959–1971*, ed. Andrew Shonfield (London: Oxford University Press, 1976), 1:229, 243; and Gilpin, *U.S. Power*, chap. 4.

8. Curzon and Curzon, "The Management of Trade," pp. 254–55; I. M. Destler et al. *Managing an Alliance: The Politics of U.S.—Japanese Relations* (Washington D.C.; Brookings Institution, 1976), p. 37.

9. Gary R. Saxonhouse, "The World Economy and Japanese Foreign Economic Policy," in *The Foreign Policy of Modern Japan*, ed. Robert A. Scalapino (Berkeley: University of California Press, 1977), pp. 286–89.

10. Curzon and Curzon, "The Management of Trade," p. 200.

11. Benjamin J. Cohen. *Organizing the World's Money: The Political Economy of International Monetary Relations* (New York: Basic Books, 1977), pp. 67–73.

12. C. Fred Bergsten, *The Dilemmas of the Dollar: The Economics and Politics of United States International Monetary Policy* (New York: New York University Press, 1979), pp. 258–259; Karen Orren, "Liberalism, Money, and the Situation of Organized Labor" (mimeo, UCLA, February 1979), p. 37.

13. Sidney E. Rolfe and James L. Burtle, *The Great Wheel* (New York: McGraw-Hill, 1975), pp. 67, 68, and 73.

14. For an excellent explication of American beliefs about the relationships between economic development, political development, and international politics, particularly with regard to the Third World, see Robert Packenham, *Liberal America and the Third World* (Princeton: Princeton University Press, 1973), p. 1.

15. Albert Hirschman, *National Power and the Structure of Foreign Trade* (Berkeley: University of California Press, 1945), p. 1.

16. Derived from figures in United States, Export-Import Bank, *Annual Reports* 1974 and 1977.

17. *World Business Weekly*, 15 December 1980, pp. 6–7.

18. Mathew Marks, "Recent Changes in American Law on Regulating Trade Measures," *The World Economy*, 2, 4 (February, 1980).

19. For an illuminating illustration of Treasury's liberal inclination, see Robert L. Meuser, "Dumping from 'Controlled Economy' Countries: The Polish Golf Car Case," *Law and Policy in International Business* 11 (1979).

20. Rolfe and Burtle, *The Great Wheel*, pp. 97–101.

21. Ibid., pp. 114–15; Tom de Vries, "Jamaica, Or the Non-Reform of the International Monetary System," *Foreign Affairs* 54 (April 1976): 609.

22. Data from International Monetary Fund, *IMF Survey*, 22 May 1978; pp. 155–57.

23. Susan Strange, "The Management of Surplus Capacity: or, How Does Theory Stand up to Protectionism 1970s Style?" *International Organization* 33 (Summer 1979).

3

Hegemonic Leadership and U.S. Foreign Economic Policy in the "Long Decade" of the 1950s

Robert O. Keohane

In the 1950s Henry Luce's short-lived "American century' was at its height. The United States was by far the world's most powerful country, economically as well as militarily; and it was willing to exercise leadership to realize its vision of the future. The "long decade" of the 1950s can be dated from 1947, the year of the Truman Doctrine and Marshall Plan, to 1963, the year of the test-ban treaty and the Interest Equalization Tax. During those sixteen years, the cold war coexisted with active and successful efforts by the United States to reconstruct an open, dynamic, world capitalist system.

It is hardly any wonder that American students of international political economy often seem to view the 1950s with nostalgia. In those years, it is argued, foreign economic policy was harnessed to responsible world leadership rather than to the search for petty and often ephemeral gains at the expense of one's allies and trading partners. During the "long decade," the United States used its own vast political and economic resources to construct the basis for a strategy of "hegemonic leadership"— in which the United States provided benefits for its allies but also imposed constraints upon them.

This paper explores what American leadership in the world political economy actually meant in the period between 1947 and 1963. How did the United States exercise leadership, what were the preconditions for such activity, and what were the results? America's successes and failures in the 1950s may shed some light on the problems facing the architects of U.S. foreign economic policies during the 1980s.

To assess the meaning of American leadership in the 1950s, it is necessary to have a clear understanding about the material base from which that leadership was exercised, that is, to explicate a conception of "hegemony." Hegemony in the world political economy is twofold, resting both on economic advantages and on political dominance.

Immanuel Wallerstein has defined hegemony in economic terms as "a situation wherein the products of a given core state are produced so efficiently that they are by and large competitive even in other core states, and therefore the given core state will be the primary beneficiary of a maximally free world market."[1] This is an interesting but poorly worked out definition, since under conditions of overall balance of payments equilibrium, each unit—even the poorest and least developed— will have some comparative advantage. The fact that the United States in 1960 had a trade deficit in textiles and in basic manufactured goods (established products not, on the whole, involving the use of complex or new technology) did not indicate that it had lost hegemonic status.[2] Indeed, one should expect the economically hegemonic power to import products that are labor-intensive or that are produced with well-known production techniques. An economically hegemonic power can better be defined as one with a comparative advantage in goods with high value added, yielding relatively high wages and profits. These may well be goods on which there is some sort of monopoly, deriving, for instance, from political power or from technological advantages. In this case, the hegemonic power will be a price maker, and its partners, by and large, will be price takers.

Politically, a hegemonic power can be defined as one that "is powerful enough to maintain the essential rules governing interstate relations, and willing to do so."[3] Not every country that would be considered hegemonic on an economic definition could be considered politically hegemonic, as the examples of Holland in the 1640s and (perhaps) Japan in the 1980s or '90s will indicate.[4] The United States in the 1950s met both these conditions, at least for the world capitalist system, as fully as any state has done in the modern era. Even at the end of the decade, U.S. gross domestic product was double the sum of the GDPs of Britain, France, Germany, and Japan combined; and the United States had trade deficits only in the categories of food, crude materials, minerals, petroleum, basic manufactured goods, textiles, and footwear.[5]

Fred Hirsch and Michael Doyle define hegemonic leadership as follows: "This label implies a mix of cooperation and control; economic relations, created by political and economic means, have been mainly cooperative; and political relations, solidified by economic means, have been cooperative-hegemonic."[6]

The dominant power provides positive incentives for cooperation, as well as persuading its allies that they should join in a common cause. To a considerable extent, the hegemonic power focuses on "milieu goals" rather than "possession goals"; it seeks a favorable order even at the expense of foregoing attempts to maximize its short-term advantage.[7]

At the same time, hegemonic leadership does not prevent the dominant state from pursuing its own interests, within limits. It may even use coercion and pressure to set the boundaries of legitimate action by its allies; within these limits, it may place reliance on persuasion and positive inducements. Under hegemonic leadership, the leader invests tangible resources in building stable and favorable international arrangements, but at the same time, it may extract resources from particular areas of its domain, and it can be expected, within limits, to look after the interests of its own nationals and its own firms.

Hirsch and Doyle argue, on the basis of evidence about trade and monetary policies, that after 1947 the United States followed a hegemonic leadership strategy. I concur with this argument. Yet the "long decade" rested not only on stable money and nondiscriminatory trade but on cheap oil from the Middle East provided largely through American companies for America's allies in Europe and Japan. Between 1943 and 1954, the United States, through state action by using its international oil companies, assured itself of control of Saudi oil resources and a large share of control of oil in Iran and Kuwait.[8] These policies led not only to actions in the Middle East—with which this paper will not deal extensively—but to repercussions in relations between the United States and its European partners. The nature of American "hegemonic leadership" will become clearer if we refer not only to familiar work on money and trade but also discuss oil issues in some detail. Since oil is the source of crucial American weaknesses in the 1980s, this emphasis may also help us understand the sources of our current dilemmas.

The main body of this paper attempts to show what American hegemonic leadership meant by exploring how it worked in the areas of money, trade, and oil. For the reasons given above, we will focus on oil. Three petroleum cases will be discussed in detail: American efforts to ensure control of Saudi Arabian oil between 1943 and 1948; the sterling-dollar oil problem of 1949–50; and the Emergency Oil Lift Program in the wake of the abortive Anglo-French invasion of Egypt in 1956. The concluding sections of the paper address the question of how hegemonic leadership can be established and how it can be maintained in the long run by discussing the preconditions for American exercise of such leadership and the failure of American policies to recreate the conditions that made hegemonic leadership viable.

THE OPERATION OF HEGEMONIC LEADERSHIP

The story has often been told of how, in 1947–48, the United States readjusted its monetary and trade policies in response to the Soviet threat (as perceived by decision makers) as well as the failure of Britain's attempt to restore sterling convertibility in the summer of 1947. As Hirsch and

Doyle point out, this did not represent an abandonment of earlier policy objectives:

> The United States—by providing massive additional *financing* and accepting trade and payments liberalization by *stages*—saved rather than abandoned its earlier objective of ultimate multilateralism in 1947–48. Such a policy was then possible because of the fundamental characteristic of the international political economy of the time: United States leadership on the basis of only qualified hegemony. The strategy, as is well known, was a major success: the moves toward progressive regional liberalization, undertaken by European economies that were strengthened by the aid injections, paved the way for a painless adoption of multilateralism at the end of the 1950s, with the moves to currency convertibility and the ending of trade discrimination against dollar imports.[9]

With respect to Europe, the United States during the 1950s made short-term sacrifices—in financial aid, or in permitting discrimination against American exports—in order to accomplish the longer-term objective of creating a stable and prosperous international economic order. Except where domestic politics interfered—as, most markedly, on trade policy, particularly in agriculture—the United States was quite successful in using its tremendous economic resources to provide incentives to European countries to subscribe to the American vision of a restructured world economy.[10]

The most striking and far-reaching example of United States leadership is perhaps provided by American efforts, dating from 1949, to assure most-favored-nation treatment for Japan. From the autumn of 1951 onward, Japan sought, with American support, to be allowed to join the General Agreement on Tariffs and Trade (GATT). The struggle was long and difficult: Britain in 1951 even opposed allowing Japan to send an official observer to GATT; in 1953 it was finally agreed that Japan could participate in GATT without a vote; and in 1955 Japan became a Contracting Party. Even then, other members that accounted for 40 percent of Japan's exports immediately invoked Article 35, making GATT's non-discrimination provisions inapplicable to their relations with Japan. For a decade the United States helped Japan persuade other GATT members to disinvoke Article 35, thus ending discrimination against Japan; this was accomplished for all major trading partners by the mid-1960s. American policy was based on a combination of political and economic calculations. If Japan were to prosper, it would need to trade with other industrialized countries; hence American markets must be open to Japanese exports. Given this politically determined necessity, discriminatory restrictions imposed on Japan by other nations would result in a heavier burden placed on the United States: Goods not imported by others would have to be absorbed by the American market. Since the United States, as leader, was resolved to keep Japan in the American-led system, it had strong incentives to persuade or pressure its allies into helping out. "Free world interest" combined with U.S. interests to mandate a leadership strategy.[11]

American success in exercising hegemonic leadership was greatly facilitated by the existence of a perceived threat from the Soviet Union, and by the economic conditions fostered by the Korean war and rearmament policies in the early 1950s. Historians of various schools have emphasized the importance of the cold war for the British loan and the Marshall Plan. Harry Truman is reported to have said that the Marshall Plan and the Truman Doctrine were "two halves of the same walnut."[12]

As noted above, we shall consider three cases of American hegemonic leadership in oil. The first of these—American efforts to establish control of Saudi Arabian oil between 1943 and 1948—illustrates the lengths to which the U.S. government was willing to go to assure that it, or at least U.S. companies, retained exclusive possession of these petroleum resources. The ability later of the United States to dispense oil to its allies, or to assure them of supplies despite their own lack of military power, depended on the success of this initial effort at self-aggrandizement. The sterling-dollar oil incident provides a revealing glimpse into the cross-pressures under which American policy makers were operating in the period before the Korean war as they sought to protect American interests in the Middle East, to defend U.S. companies against discrimination, and also to build a cooperative alliance system under Washington's leadership. The Emergency Oil Lift Program illustrates the tremendous capabilities that the United States commanded at the height of its dominance in the mid-to-late 1950s, and the ability of the U.S. government, in a crisis, to mobilize those capabilities even against formidable domestic resistance.

The major theme of these cases is the efficacy of American action. The United States had so many resources—economic, political, and military—that it was able to attain its essential objectives in each of these situations. Hegemonic leadership rested on the deployment of tangible as well as intangible assets. The minor theme of these cases, most evident in the events surrounding the Anglo-American Petroleum Agreement in 1944–45 and those having to do with the emergency oil lift in 1956–57, concerns the impact of domestic politics in thwarting certain governmental initiatives and shaping others. As we shall observe at the end of this chapter, the fragility of American hegemonic leadership—reflected in the fact that it lasted, in full force, for a "long decade" rather than a century —can be accounted for in good measure by the refusal of domestic interests to adjust, or to sacrifice, for the sake of the long-term power position of the United States.

SECURING SAUDI OIL: 1943–48

Concern about future domestic oil shortages, and information about the vastness of Saudi Arabian reserves, led planners in the U.S. government in 1943 to pay attention to the problem of how to assure continued American control of the Saudi concession, held jointly at the time by Standard of California (Socal) and the Texas Company (Texaco). At first, worry centered on British designs, although "nowhere in the accessible British archives is there any evidence of a British plan in the 1940s to actually displace the American concessionaire."[13]

Having recognized the importance of Saudi oil in the postwar world, American planners moved vigorously to secure it for the United States. The first attempt, led by Interior Secretary Harold Ickes, centered on the development of a government-owned Petroleum Reserves Corporation (PRC). This extraordinary enterprise was to purchase all the stock in the California-Arabian Standard Oil Company (Casoc), then owned by Socal and Texaco; its board of directors was to consist of the secretaries of state, interior, war and navy. Although Ickes pushed hard for this plan, the State Department was always lukewarm at best. Eventually, negotiations for the purchase of Casoc were terminated as the result of pressure brought to bear on Ickes by Standard Oil of New Jersey (Jersey) and Socony-Vacuum (Socony).[14] The PRC later attempted to make arrangements for a government-owned pipeline from the Persian Gulf to the Mediterranean, a scheme that was also blocked by competitors of Socal and Texaco.[15]

Meanwhile, the State Department was urging a different route to secure control of Saudi oil: a petroleum agreement with Great Britain. The Anglo-American Petroleum Agreement was negotiated and signed first in 1944, and after severe criticism from the oil industry, renegotiated with industry participation during 1945; but it was never ratified as a treaty by the U.S. Senate. The complex story of the fate of the agreement has been well told elsewhere,[16] so a brief review will suffice.

The original agreement, signed in 1944, would have in effect established a government cartel for the management of world oil supplies. The joint Anglo-American Petroleum commission would "recommend production and exportation rates for the various concession areas in the Middle East [to prevent] ... the disorganization of world markets which might result from uncontrolled competitive exploitation."[17] Middle Eastern production would be managed and markets guaranteed. Yet this proposal came up against a formidable coalition of interests. Members of the Senate Foreign Relations Committee had insisted successfully from the outset that the agreement be submitted to the Senate as a treaty. In a sense this sealed its fate, since the governmental cartelization approach "ran counter to the vested interests of the American independents, the antitrust philosophy of the Department of Justice, the laizzez-faire ideol-

ogy of a remnant of New Deal opponents, and State's long-standing practice of not supporting one domestic interest group over another.[18] Even
had this not been sufficient to kill it, the proposal ran afoul of a fierce
bureaucratic battle for the control of oil policy between Harold Ickes and
the dominant forces in the State Department.

Having failed to secure Saudi oil either by direct government ownership or through international regulation, the U.S. government then
turned to a policy of support for the efforts of major American oil companies—Socal, Texaco, Socony, and Jersey in particular—to guarantee
their control of Middle Eastern oil. In 1946, Socal and Texaco found
themselves with prolific reserves of oil in Saudi Arabia and a joint ven-
ture, now named ARAMCO, operating there with a skilled production
team; but they also faced large demands for capital and uncertain markets for the huge quantities of oil that would be produced. Standard Oil
of New Jersey, by contrast, was chronically crude-short, and concerned
about being excluded from the richest, lowest-cost concession in the
world. Moved by the business conservatism of their leaders, and over the
strenuous objections of other company officials (at least in Socal), Socal
and Texaco decided, in early 1946, to invite Jersey to purchase a share in
ARAMCO. Eventually, Socony was also asked to participate, and
arrangements were made for a 30 percent purchase in ARAMCO by
Jersey and 10 percent participation for Socony.[19]

Yet to consummate this deal it was necessary somehow to nullify the
restrictions of the Red Line Agreement of 1928. This agreement had required the partners in the Iraq Petroleum Company (IPC) to produce or
purchase oil within the Red Line Area (including Arabia as well as Iraq,
but not Iran) *only* through the IPC. In other words, IPC member companies were not to compete with the IPC itself within the Red Line Area.
By 1946 the IPC companies were Anglo-Iranian (23.75 percent), Shell
(23.75 percent), Compagnie Francaises des Petroles (CFP, 23.75 percent), Socony (11.875 percent), Jersey (11.875 percent), and the Gulbenkian interests (5 percent). Socal and Texaco, not being members of
the IPC, were not restrained from producing in Saudi Arabia; but Socony
and Jersey were. For these companies to join ARAMCO would constitute a violation of the Red Line Agreement.

In early negotiations, Shell assured the American companies that it
would participate in drafting new arrangements for IPC, and Jersey pla-
cated Anglo-Iranian with an agreement to purchase large amounts of
Iranian and Kuwaiti oil from it, over a twenty-year period, and to construct a new pipeline (never built) from Abadan to the Mediterranean.
CFP and Gulbenkian posed more serious problems. Fortunately for the
American companies, however, during World War II CFP and Gulbenkian had operated within Nazi-controlled territory and had in 1940 been
construed by a distinguished British barrister as having become "enemy
aliens," thus rendering the Red Line Agreement null and void. This

served as a sufficient pretext in 1946 for Jersey Standard and Socony to argue that the agreement was legally dissolved and to open negotiations for a new agreement free of the restrictive clauses of the earlier one.[20]

Not surprisingly, CFP objected strenuously. Not only were its leaders presumably insulted by being labeled "enemy aliens" as a result of the defeat of France; they feared that the effect of the ARAMCO deal would be to reduce production from Iraq, where CFP shared an interest. CFP therefore sought participation in ARAMCO itself, along with Jersey and Socony. In addition, the French government protested strongly, holding the U.S. government responsible, and threatening to take direct action in France against Jersey in retaliation for its actions.[21]

The companies and the State Department recognized the seriousness of French protests. Negotiations ensued, with the State Department providing "firm diplomatic support" for the companies.[22] The negotiations actually took place among the companies concerned, and with Gulbenkian personally, but were followed closely by the interested governments.

CFP's proposal for participation in ARAMCO was blocked by King 'Abd-al-'Aziz of Saudi Arabia, who declared that he would not agree to the sale of any part of ARAMCO to a non-American firm.[23] In February 1947 officials in the State Department proposed that Socony purchase the 11.875 percent holding of Jersey in the IPC and withdraw from the ARAMCO deal.[24] Had this been done, the Red Line Agreement would not have been violated. This scheme was not accepted by the companies, however.

The terms worked out dissolved the Red Line Agreement but did give the French the right to draw larger shares of oil from IPC production than their proportionate holdings in IPC would have allowed, and involved a commitment by Jersey and Socony to support increased IPC production. Protracted negotiations took place with Gulbenkian, who reportedly told John C. Case of Socony that he simply would not respect himself unless he "drove as good a bargain as possible." Gulbenkian's ace in the hole was the fact that he had filed suit in London, threatening to open the complex affairs of IPC to the public; the day before arguments were to begin, the suit was settled.[25]

Although the U.S. government stayed in the background on the Red Line issue, it clearly supported its companies in their efforts to solidify their control of Saudi Arabian oil while they, and the United States, were strong relative to European firms and governments. As in financial and commercial policy, establishment of dominance preceded exercise of hegemonic leadership.[26] With respect to the objective of securing U.S. control over Saudi oil, American policy was consistent, vigorous, and successful: Resistance outside the United States could be dealt with from a position of strength. The vehicle for American policy, however, had to be adapted to the realities of American society: Plans for government ownership or control were abandoned in favor of support for the expansion of private corporations. U.S. policy was shaped both by the opportunities abroad for extension of national power and the constraints, as well as opportunities, engendered by the institution of capitalism at home.

THE STERLING-DOLLAR OIL PROBLEM

Even during the war the British government anticipated a shortage of foreign exchange during the postwar years and insisted, in negotiations on a petroleum agreement, on "the right of each country to draw its consumption requirements, to the extent that may be considered necessary, from the production in its territories or in which rights are held by its nationals."[27] In 1949 Great Britain decided to take such measures to save on dollar costs by discriminating against American-owned oil companies, contrary to agreements reached between the British government and U.S. companies in the 1920s and '30s. British measures not only affected imports into the United Kingdom but also reduced sales of American firms in countries such as Argentina and Egypt, with which Britain made barter agreements, providing oil in return for other goods. The British government also, in the spring of 1949, ordered British bankers

> to refuse to transfer funds in payment for American-supplied oil from sterling balances in London of countries outside the sterling area. Consequently, such countries as Finland, Sweden, Norway, and Denmark, which were so short of dollars as to require that all or part of their oil needs be purchased with sterling, were unable to draw on their sterling balances in the United Kingdom to pay for imports supplied by American companies. Consequently, they had to buy sterling oil.[28]

Since real money was at stake, the U.S. companies protested, claiming that Britain's actions were meant less to save dollars than to strengthen the position of British companies in the world oil industry at the expense of their American competitors.[29] The glut of oil that had emerged, at current prices, made it impossible for the companies to sell all the petroleum that they could produce; so the Americans' loss was the British firm's gain. Furthermore, a cutback in markets for U.S.-owned Eastern Hemisphere oil was seen in the State Department as having ominous implications for America's security interests:

> This situation raises serious security, political and economic problems in view of the fact that the foreign oil concessions, refining and marketing facilities and organizations of American oil companies depend upon the maintenance of foreign market outlets. If the American oil companies producing abroad are faced with the shrinkage in the market for their output they must necessarily curtail production. If the American companies are forced to cut back production at the same time the British companies are expanding their output, the former are placed in a dif-

ficult political and financial position which may in turn prejudice U.S. national security interests.[30]

An internal State Department memo in December focused directly on the implications of British policy for the U.S. position in Saudi Arabia:

> Loss of one-quarter annual revenue might stalemate Saudi Arabia progress while neighboring states advance, jeopardizing the unique cooperation and friendship now existing between U.S. and Saudi Arabia. Western orientation of Saudi Arabia, which counters Arab reaction to Western support of Israel, would suffer.[31]

Not everyone in the U.S. government saw the national interest and the interests of the ARAMCO partners as so closely linked. Oil was selling at several times its cost of production, yet neither the American nor British companies were seriously considering reducing prices as a response to stagnation in demand. The British financial situation was much more serious than the plight of already-wealthy American oil companies:

> The important interests of the United States would not be served if the dollar and other economic drain on the British is maintained at anywhere near the present or projected levels. $710 million in fiscal 1950 and well over $600 million in 1953 seems an impossible drain for anyone to contemplate. The absolute maximum savings of dollars and economic resources on the sterling area's oil accounts are desperately needed in view of Britain's present balance of payments and budgetary positions and the uncertain outlook for future ECA [Economic Cooperation Administration] appropriations. . . . It would sound very badly to have it publicized that the Government imposed serious burdens on the British economy, thereby nullifying part of the U.S. foreign aid program, in order to win for the five big American oil companies in the Persian Gulf the unique privilege denied to all American farmers and other American businesses of selling for sterling in third countries, on the ground of threat to the U.S. national interest, when the companies are selling Persian Gulf oil at a price between three and five times the cost of its production.[32]

The problem was essentially one of adjustment costs: Who should have to pay the costs of adjusting to a slacker oil market? Different possible outcomes were associated with different patterns of cost:

1. Intense price competition could have taken place, sharply reducing the cost of imported oil in Europe and elsewhere. Consumers would have benefited from this outcome, which would have facilitated European industrial recovery. Indeed, the ECA exerted some downward pressure on prices, leading to a fall in the per barrel "company take" in the Mid-

dle East from $1.52 in 1948 to $1.14 in 1949, but no general price war ensued.[33]

For obvious reasons, neither the British nor American companies wished to "solve" the problem of an oil glut by reducing prices precipitously. Nor did the governments display enthusiasm for this solution. Britain did not use sterling devaluation, in 1949, to encourage British companies to undersell U.S. firms, or to prevent British companies from increasing their profits from oil for which costs were incurred in sterling. Britain was presumably worried about the effects on its current account of reduced oil company profits, and repatriation of profits, as well as on those profits per se (which were shared by the government through its partial ownership of British Petroleum). Those American officials concerned with Saudi Arabia and other producing countries would not have been happy with the adverse effects of lower oil prices on relations with these states. Taken together, the vested interests arrayed against a market solution to the problem were powerful and well organized.

2. The United States could have accepted greater oil imports, thus reducing excess supply on world markets, at the expense of U.S. *domestic* production. American independent firms would have borne much of the cost of adjustment. Despite the fact that this arrangement would have been efficient, and would have permitted a continued (but slower) growth of U.S. domestic production, "a solution on this basis would be strongly opposed by U.S. independent producers, however, and it would probably not permit nearly as large an expansion of U.S. output in the Middle East as U.S. companies have been planning."[34]

3. Great Britain could have withdrawn its restrictions on American companies' operations. In this case the burden of adjustment would have fallen chiefly on the British economy, since the dollar drain would have not been reduced.

4. The United States and Britain could have *jointly* forced adjustment costs on to others by requiring purchasers of oil outside the United States and Britain "to pay at least the dollar cost in dollars of the oil supplied." This was the essence of a plan presented in November 1949 by W. L. Faust of the Socony-Vacuum Oil Company. This was a proposal for duopolistic action; as the U.S. Counselor for Economic Affairs in London noted, "Of course, many consumers would object, but if all American and British oil were marketed in this pattern they would have no alternative but to accept it." Nitze argued similarly that "it may be desirable for the Governments of U.S. and U.K. to attempt to regulate, on a formal or informal basis, the production and flow of oil products. Competition in the usual sense is unlikely and probably undesirable."[35]

5. Great Britain could have permitted U.S. companies to sell oil for sterling outside the sterling area, only converting into dollars the dollar cost of that oil; "unconverted pounds would be used by United States oil companies to purchase goods and services from the sterling area." This would have removed the discrimination against American firms (*vis-à-vis* British firms) while—according to Caltex a SoCal-Texaco company and American officials who supported the scheme—not increasing the dollar drain on Britain beyond what would be incurred by *British* companies increasing their production abroad.[36]

Solutions 1, 2, and 3 were vetoed by powerful actors: The companies resisted price-cutting, U.S. domestic interests prevented large increases in oil imports, and the British government's concern for its financial position stood in the way of unilateral British concessions. The Faust Plan was unattractive to many elements of the U.S. government since it would not alleviate the general dollar shortage but merely transfer part of the dollar crisis from Britain to oil-consuming countries, many of which were also subsisting on U.S. aid. Furthermore,

> The "third" countries, faced with paying a portion of the cost of petroleum in dollars, might demand similar treatment for their own exports of other commodities. . . . If this pricing policy became common we would be introducing an additional complicating element in international trade that seems clearly undesirable. Our general policy is in the opposite direction; for example, in our work on European integration our objective is to avoid the need for dollar settlements.[37]

The Faust Plan was essentially a proposal for a duopolistic imperial regime, which would extract resources from countries other than the United States and Britain for the benefit of U.S. and British oil companies. The U.S. Government could not accept it precisely for this reason: It conflicted too strongly with American policies in money and trade that emphasized hegemonic leadership and restabilization of the capitalist world economy. The great sympathy within the U.S. government, and in the Congress, for the oil companies seems to have inhibited the government from rejecting the Faust Plan out of hand, but the Caltex proposal (solution 5) was more congenial because it did not involve third-party complications and resulting threats to American milieu goals. Thus by December 1949 the Caltex proposal had essentially become the basis of the U.S. position:

> After extended interagency discussion, the U.S. Government has proposed to the British that American companies be allowed to sell part of their production to third countries against sterling payment. U.S. companies would be allowed to convert into dollars an amount equal to dol-

lar outlays British companies would have to make to replace equivalent existing U.S. production capacity.[38]

Acceptance of this proposal by the British would have ended the discriminatory advantages that British companies were then, according to the United States, gaining as a result of British governmental policy, and would have protected ARAMCO from unfair British competition:

> British companies are expanding at rates double normal estimates of increased demand and using surplus oil to displace United States oil through currency and trade restriction rather than through competition action such as price reductions, superior products, efficiency, etc.[39]

Yet the British government not only failed to accept this proposal but in December 1949 imposed new restrictions requiring affiliates of American companies to buy oil for import into the sterling area from British and British-Dutch companies rather than from American-owned firms (even members of their own group). "An American owned affiliate thereafter could import oil from sources owned by American companies only insofar as the volume of oil required to meet its needs was beyond what the companies having sterling status could supply. Jersey oil thus became marginal in its most important Eastern Hemisphere markets."[40] Jersey calculated that it would lose $85 million worth of sales during 1950 as a result of this regulation.

The American companies responded to this attack on their interests in two ways. First, they pressed the U.S. government to intervene more actively on their behalf. In January 1950 Tom Connally, then chairman of the Senate Foreign Relations Committee and a leading spokesman for petroleum interests (although especially for the Texas independents), advocated a cutoff of all Economic Cooperation Administration assistance to Britain. This was not done, but the ECA did suspend assistance to projects for expanding the British oil industry.[41] In April the State Department "presented a note to the British Government insisting on the right of United States companies to trade anywhere in the sterling area."[42]

At least some of the companies, of which Jersey is an example, also entered into direct negotiations with the British government. Having secured the support of the U.S. government,

> Jersey's Howard Page finally negotiated a complicated but satisfactory settlement directly with the British treasury in May 1950. The British agreed to end gasoline rationing, and Jersey undertook to supply all of the additional gasoline required by its British affiliates with payment in sterling. Instead of remitting profits to the United States in dollars, Jersey would use the sterling proceeds to purchase needed goods and equipment manufactured in Britain. Along with a series of similar agree-

ments worked out by Page in 1950 and 1951, this arrangement essentially solved the dollar oil problem.[43]

This solution was facilitated by the economic boom that took place after the Korean war broke out in June of 1950. Increased economic activity quickly eliminated the oil surplus and improved Britain's balance of payments position.

The sterling-dollar oil problem illustrates the combination of pursuit of narrowly defined self-interest and concern for alliance management that characterized U.S. hegemonic leadership. American companies were being discriminated against, and the State Department therefore came to their aid; but even before the Korean war broke out, the American desire to rebuild a strong Western Europe—reinforced and rationalized by the Soviet threat—inhibited the government from pushing the oil companies' case too hard. The United States was not willing to permit discrimination against powerful American interests under the guise of financial necessity; but its reaction was restrained. The outbreak of the Korean war, by stimulating rearmament and preventing a recurrence of serious recession, removed the initial economic difficulty of oversupply that had led to the issue in the first place. The intensity of the cold war after 1950 removed the major oil problem between the United States and Britain while reinforcing the inclination of both governments to settle their differences amicably.

THE EMERGENCY OIL LIFT PROGRAM, 1956–57

In July 1956 a series of disputes erupted between Egypt and the major Western powers, in particular the United States, Britain, and France. On July 19, the United States withdrew its offer to contribute $56 million toward financing the Aswan Dam; one week later, Egypt nationalized the Suez Canal. This led to an international crisis, the climax of which involved the invasion of Egypt by Israeli, British, and French forces in late October and the collapse of that invasion under pressure from the United States as well as resistance from Egypt and threats from the Soviet Union. As a result of the military actions, the Suez Canal, which at that time was the main route for oil shipments between the Persian Gulf and Europe, was suddenly blocked, leading to a potentially severe oil shortage in Europe.[44]

The reaction of the U.S. Government to this crisis provides a clearer illustration of hegemonic leadership in action. The United States used its great economic and political resources, and its links with major international oil companies, to cope successfully with the oil shortfall and achieve its own political purposes in the process.

Immediately following nationalization of the Suez Canal, the United States set up a Middle East Emergency Committee (MEEC), comprised of fifteen major U.S.-based oil companies, under the provisions of the Defense Production Act of 1950. The companies declared that they could not devise alternative tanker schedules for a crisis in any detail until it was known what the situation would be; but they established the organizational structure of the MEEC and acquired the requisite antitrust waivers from the government to allow them to coordinate among themselves. Planning was left to the companies: The role of the government, according to the director of the Office of Defense Mobilization, was to encourage voluntary agreements among the companies and to exempt them from antitrust laws.[45] In September the British, Dutch, and French governments sponsored the establishment of a parallel committee composed of the major European-based oil companies (Royal Dutch Shell, British Petroleum, and Compagnie Française des Petroles).[46]

In response to the British-French-Israeli invasion of Egypt, the United States suspended the operations of the MEEC, and it did not meet thereafter until December 3, 1956.[47] The U.S. government was clearly using the threat of an oil shortage to put pressure on Britain and France, during November, to withdraw their troops from Suez. By the end of November, however, it had become clear to American leaders that further pressure on the Europeans was unnecessary and would weaken the Atlantic alliance. President Eisenhower ordered reactivation of the MEEC to permit it not only to arrange tanker schedules but to enter into arrangements on a collective basis with the Organization for European Economic Corporation (OEEC), in order properly to plan for oil allocations. The Oil Committee of the OEEC established a Petroleum Industry Emergency Group from the industry (involving the United States as well as European companies), which advised the Oil Committee on procedures for allocation of scarce oil supplies among the European countries.[48] The United States insisted that the OEEC rather than the United States or the companies take the responsibility for allocating oil by country. One reason for this was to deflect Arab criticism of the United States, which would have been intense if America had aided Britain and France directly.[49]

Yet the United States played far from a passive role. It urged the OEEC to take immediate action to allocate supplies on a pro rata basis; and the MEEC reinforced the pressure to do so by deciding on December 28 not to cooperate on allocation arrangements in Europe without an OEEC decision, which was eventually forthcoming on January 7. Meanwhile, the MEEC approved tanker schedules allowing more efficient shipments of crude oil and refined products from Venezuela and the United States to Europe, replacing in good measure the long haul around the Cape of Good Hope for oil from the Persian Gulf.[50]

During the early phase of the crisis—between the closure of the canal and early January—the problem was essentially one of transportation: "not one of a shortage of oil but a shortage of the means of bringing it to

Europe."[51] If normal tanker patterns had been maintained, Europe would have received little more than 60 percent of its estimated needs. Yet reallocation of tanker patterns was remarkably easy; indeed, even before the MEEC was reactivated, international oil companies had increased their shipments from the United States to Western Europe from an average of 50,000 barrels a day to 370,0000 barrels a day, and had increased shipments to Europe by a further 224,000 barrels a day by increasing shipments from the Caribbean and diverting Middle Eastern crude from the United States to Europe.[52]

The more serious problem after the beginning of January was not tanker availability but the supply of crude oil. Increases in shipments from the United States were accomplished largely by drawing down stocks, which could not continue indefinitely. But the Texas Railroad Commission, which controlled production in Texas, refused to increase allowable production in January, and only increased it slightly in February, despite the European crises. The commission sought higher oil prices—an increase of 12 percent did take place in early January—and feared a later oil glut if supply were increased too rapidly. Independent Texas producers far from the coast opposed the supply increase since their output was effectively limited by transport problems, and they would benefit from higher prices. Furthermore, Europe needed heavy crude oil, but U.S. producers feared that as a consequence of increasing crude oil shipments to Europe, they would be stuck with large supplies of gasoline, which would depress the U.S. market. Thus there was what the *Oil and Gas Journal* called a "transatlantic feud" between the United Kingdom and the Texas Railroad Commission. The commission wanted the UK to end gas rationing and purchase gasoline from the United States in return for increased Texas production. European diplomats were pressuring the State Department for increased production, the assistant secretary of the Interior was calling for increased U.S. production, but the state regulatory agencies dragged their feet.[53]

Finally, President Eisenhower took a direct hand in the matter. In his presidential news conference of February 6, 1957, the following colloquy took place:[54]

William McGaffin, Chicago Daily News: The United States has been lagging on oil deliveries to Western Europe, one reason being that the Texas Control Board has not okayed a step-up in production in Texas. According to latest reports, Great Britain is down to about two weeks' oil supply. What do you intend to do?

President Eisenhower: Well, of course, there are certain powers given to the President where he could move into the whole field of state proration. I think the federal government should not disturb the economy of our country except when it has to. On the other hand, I believe that the business concerns of our country, the people that operate the tanker lines, the people that produce the oil, and all the other agencies, including those of the proration boards, should consider where do our long-term interests lie. Certainly they demand a Europe that is not flat on its back economically. . . .

Now all of this oil must flow in such a quantity as to fill up every tanker we have operating at maximum capacity. And if that doesn't occur, then we must do something in the way, first, I should say, of conference and argument and, if necessary, we would have to move in some other region or some other direction, either with our facilities or with others. But it must be done.

Faced with this barely veiled threat of federal action, the Texas Railroad Commission shortly thereafter increased the allowable production for March by 237,000 barrels per day over the February figure, to a point that was 380,000 barrels per day over pre-Suez levels. The big international firms favored the increase, and independents were now willing to go along because stocks had been reduced and prices had been raised during the first two months of the year.[55]

Once this had been done, the crisis evaporated quickly. With a mild winter, and more Gulf oil available, drains on stocks were arrested from February onward; tanker schedules were canceled on April 18, 1957, and the activities of the MEEC and its European partner organizations were effectively ended by May.[56]

The Emergency Oil Lift Program illustrates, in striking form, the paradox of external strength and domestic weakness that Stephen Krasner points to in his account of U.S. foreign economic policy.[57] The United States had overwhelming power internationally: It was able not only to stop the Anglo-French-Israeli invasion of Suez but, in the wake of that episode, to persuade European countries to decide on oil allocations and to use its own oil companies, with their tanker fleets, and its unused petroleum capacity at home, to supply Europe adequately with oil during the winter. Policy coordination between the U.S. government and the multinational companies, between U.S. and European companies, and between the U.S. and European governments was arranged harmoniously. The United States controlled immense resources that it could reallocate at little cost to itself; it was therefore able to exercise leadership *vis-à-vis* the Europeans, who had little choice but to follow. The key difficulties faced by the Eisenhower administration were internal—with the Texas Railroad Commission in particular. Federal-state policy coordination was so difficult that it required a threat of drastic action to achieve the desired results; U.S.-European coordination was easy by comparison. In this case, at least, the management of interdependence indeed depended on what happened at home.[58]

PRECONDITIONS FOR HEGEMONIC LEADERSHIP

Characteristic patterns of international economic behavior during the long decade of the 1950s seem to merit the labels of economic inter-dependence, or liberalism. Discrimination in international trade was gradually reduced, tariff barriers fell somewhat, and the international monetary system was reconstituted on the basis of pegged exchange rates with the dollar as international money. The volume of international trade, payments, and investment increased enormously. Concomitantly, economic growth was rapid, fueled by ample supplies of petroleum, the price of which was falling.

Politically, the decade could be described in terms of the growth of "complex interdependence," involving growing transnational, inter-governmental, and transgovernmental relationships among the advanced capitalist countries.[59] Force was banished as a direct, explicit means of influence among their governments; at the same time, the connections between domestic political economy and international political economy seemed to become more important—as illustrated by the Emergency Oil Lift Program of 1956–57. U.S. foreign economic policy fit the pattern of hegemonic leadership that Hirsch and Doyle describe: The United States both played a crucial role in bringing complex interdependence about, and adapted effectively to it.

Yet it would be mistaken to infer from these patterns of interdependence that power had been eliminated from international political economy. As Robert Gilpin has emphasized: "An economic system does not arise spontaneously owing to the operation of an invisible hand and in the absence of the exercise of power. Rather, every economic system rests on a particular political order; its nature cannot be understood aside from politics."[60]

Complex interdependence, and the relatively benign attention that the United States gave to the political economy of Western capitalism, rested on American industrial and financial dominance, as well as on American politico-military power. This is revealed especially well by examining U.S. policy, issue by issue, *before* American dominance had been achieved. In each case, the United States was less accommodating when it was seeking to establish its position of dominance than it later became after that position was secure.

In its first term the Roosevelt administration had been careful not to exercise international financial leadership; indeed, President Roosevelt virtually forced the adjournment of the London Economic Conference of 1933 with his famous message declaring that "the old fetishes of so-called international bankers are being replaced by efforts to plan national currencies with the objective of giving those currencies a continuing purchasing power."[61] As the 1930s depression continued and war grew closer, the United States became somewhat more accommodating, particularly in the

Tripartite Agreement of 1936, but this was only a very cautious step toward international cooperation. The Bretton Woods Conference of 1944 and the British Loan of 1945–46 marked a sharp change in American policy toward exercise of international leadership; but it is important to note that the terms offered by the United States for its cooperation were still very tough. At Bretton Woods, the United States stood for its interests as a creditor country, seeking to avoid becoming involuntary lender to the world.[62] According to revisionist historians, the U.S. government deliberately attempted to keep Britain just strong enough financially to be able to adopt liberal trade and payments policy but weak enough that it could not forego postwar U.S. credits.[63]

In part, this financial policy was a result of American commercial policy, which sought to ensure that Britain, and other capitalist countries, would dismantle preferential trade arrangements and cooperate in the establishment of nondiscriminatory international trade. The stringent terms imposed by the United States, in particular the Treasury Department, on the loan granted to Britain in 1945–46 reflected this aim.[64] As we have seen, only when British weakness had been revealed in 1947 was there a pronounced change in this policy. Although the long-run objective of assuring multilateralism remained, the conditions perceived by the United States had changed: Now it was clear that the United States was the dominant Western power and that it no longer had to fear the strength of its partners. Indeed, since their weakness had become the chief problem, it was appropriate to shift from a vigorous policy of breaking down trade barriers to one of combining support for rebuilding European economies, temporary acceptance of discrimination against American exports, and long-run moves toward liberalized trade.

In petroleum policy, as we have seen, vigorous actions to attain American objectives—whether through government ownership of oil reserves, a bilateral cartel, or support for enterprising American petroleum firms—also preceded the more benign phase of hegemonic leadership, as represented by the Emergency Oil-Lift Program. The United States sought control over crucial resources before it was willing to be generous in their disposition.

MAINTAINING THE VIABILITY OF HEGEMONIC LEADERSHIP

Any strategy that is viable in the long term has to re-create the conditions for its own existence. If the strategy requires maintenance of national strength, following the strategy must generate stength, or the strategy will eventually collapse. Any hegemonic leadership strategy, therefore, must seek to maintain the national base of resources upon which governmental influence, and leadership, rest.

Over the whole postwar period, U.S. policy has failed to assure this condition for long-term success. The United States has remained a major, although not dominant, factor in international trade, but during the 1960s and '70s its sectoral trade balances deteriorated severely in a number of major areas involving relatively advanced technology, such as motor vehicles; and concern was expressed about American advantages in such leading sectors as semiconductors and aircraft. American influence over international monetary regimes had rested during the 1950s on the stability of the dollar, and the confidence people had in it; stability and confidence both declined precipitiously in the wake of persistent American current deficits during the late 1960s and early '70s, and the refusal of the U.S. government, after 1973, to support the value of the dollar in international markets. In oil, the decline in American resources was even more dramatic: in 1956, the United States imported 11 percent of its oil consumption and had excess capacity of 25 percent for an overall surplus of 14 percent; by 1973, imports amounted to 35 percent of consumption (on their way to 45 percent +) and excess production capacity was a mere 10 percent of consumption by comparison.[65]

The failures to maintain American dominance seem to have had somewhat diverse sources. In trade, comparative advantage shifted as Europe and Japan recovered from the war and as formerly unindustrialized countries began to industrialize. In the monetary area, the United States attempted to fight the Vietnam war without making the requisite financial adjustments, and then continued, through much of the 1970s, to maintain an inflationary economy that continued to undermine the value of the dollar. Since the United States was the world's dominant financial power, it could refuse to adjust and at least temporarily shift the burden of adjustment onto others; but the eventual consequences for its currency and for its financial leadership were severe.

In petroleum, the sources of American weakness lay in the political power of domestic interests. As we saw earlier, the Anglo-American Petroleum Agreement was defeated by a coalition of interests led by independent domestic oilmen. In addition to securing U.S. control of Saudi oil reserves, planners in the State Department had sought to use the agreement to conserve domestic petroleum reserves by drawing down those of the Eastern Hemisphere. Acting Petroleum Adviser James Sappington argued in a memo of December 1943 that Middle Eastern oil should be "developed to the maximum and that supplies in this hemisphere be . . . conserved." Sappington even contemplated the possibility of Middle Eastern oil displacing domestic oil in the U.S. market, thus achieving "a further conservation of the reserves of [the Western] . . . hemisphere."[66]

In May 1945 the same objective obtained, although the State Department, in its public statements, was at pains to deny this. At that time, the head of the Petroleum Division, John A. Loftus, described the essential objectives of the Anglo-American Petroleum Agreement in a confidential memorandum as follows:

We want the operating policies of British private petroleum companies to be in reasonable conformity with our general policy objective of effecting a relative increase in the rate of exploitation in the Eastern Hemisphere (particularly Middle Eastern) petroleum reserves, and a relative decrease in the rate of exploitation in the Western Hemisphere. This is an objective which probably cannot be stated in precise or quantitative terms without provoking acute internal political controversy here; and even if precision were possible a quantitative agreement on petroleum production would sufficiently approximate a cartelization of the petroleum industry as to be subject to serious criticism in terms of our general economic foreign policy. Therefore . . . the best, if not the only, approach appears to be to obtain from the British an agreement upon certain broad principles governing petroleum development. In this case the principles would be of such a character as to permit and facilitate the expansion of Eastern Hemsiphere (Middle Eastern) oil production.[67]

By this time State Department planners probably realized that the aspiration to increase imports of petroleum into the United States, at the expense of domestic production, was unrealizable, but they continued to seek to limit the necessity for the export of Western Hemisphere petroleum to the Old World. Independent oilmen and senators from oil-producing states discerned the true purpose of the agreement, despite misleading statements from its proponents; they suspected correctly that "the object of the treaty is to permit the movement of petroleum from the Near East throughout the world and, if necessary, into the United States, rather than developing, or further developing, the oil resources of the United States."[68]

The defeat of the petroleum agreement, which was reported by the Foreign Relations Committee to the Senate in July 1947 but never voted upon,[69] illustrates once again the domestic Achilles heel of American foreign economic policy. State Department officials correctly foresaw the folly of "draining America first" while foreign oil could still be obtained easily and cheaply; but they could not prevail against domestic interests in a protected energy market. Defeat of the treaty was followed, in the 1950s, by the development of import quotas on oil, which further accelerated the exhaustion of American petroleum resources and therefore U.S. power resources in the world economy. The seeds of destruction of the hegemonic leadership policy had been planted before the policy itself had ever been implemented.

CONCLUSION AND IMPLICATIONS

The United States did indeed follow a hegemonic leadership strategy during the long decade of the 1950s. In the short to intermediate term, this strategy was a success: It assisted in the economic and political recovery of Europe and Japan, and maintained the milieu goals that the American government sought during the cold war. American leadership rested heavily on the dominance achieved by the United States, by 1947–48, in the major areas of foreign economic policy including finance, trade in manufactured goods, and petroleum. Stable money, nondiscriminatory trade, and cheap energy were the foundations for the American decade. The cold war legitimated U.S. leadership, but the resources used by the United States were derived from its own sources of political-economic strength.

In the longer run the hegemonic leadership strategy was self-liquidating; rather than perpetuate the conditions for its success, it permitted their demise. It is arguable that a decline in U.S. dominance was inevitable in trade; but the difficulties in finance and oil were more clearly of America's own making. The United States refused to adjust to a weakened financial position, in the late 1960s and '70s, instead resorting to financing its deficits and maintaining consumption through a process of disinvestment. In petroleum, special interest prevented the implementation of a farsighted strategic policy of conservation, which officials of the State Department were perceptive and public-spirited enough to envisage and support. In the crucial areas of finance and oil, American policy was crucially—indeed, fatally—weakened by the inconsistency of domestic policies with long-run international imperatives.

Thus the United States contracted a disease of the strong: refusal to adjust to change. Small states do not have the luxury of deciding whether or how fast to adjust to external change. They do not seek adjustment. It is thrust upon them, because they are not powerful enough to control the terms through which they relate to the international economic system. Powerful countries can postpone adjustment; and the stronger they are, the longer it can be postponed. Where adversity is temporary, this helps the powerful country to ride out the storm. But where adverse secular shifts are taking place, it merely postpones the inevitable, making it more difficult to deal with in the future. In this case, the ability to avoid costs in the short term simply gives myopic leaders, or institutions that yield myopic policy results despite leaders' preferences, the chance to dissipate their advantages. For Spain in the sixteenth century, discoveries of bullion in America had ultimately disastrous rather than beneficial effects: They contributed to the ruin of the economy and the crashing defeat of overextended Spanish armies.[70] For Britain in the nineteenth century, the existence of the Empire, into which it could retreat, fatally delayed a national reaction to industrial decline.[71] For the United States during the 1950s and '60s, its overwhelming economic superiority after World War II, buttressed by the deference that it received as the head of a cold-war alliance, also seems to have made it oblivious to the need for policy change.

It would be hard to argue that the United States has gone as far down the road toward economic oblivion as Spain had by the seventeenth century or Britain by 1914. Yet it seems clear that an enduring revival of

American influence will not be produced by the return of cold war (if such should happen) alone. Internal measures—to adjust to change, to build up industrial strength through investment and technological development to bring energy consumption and production more closely into balance—are necessary conditions for successful reassertion of U.S. leadership. As in the 1950s, interdependence can be managed only if the resources are available, if investments in national power, as well as in wealth, have been made. If capabilities are lacking, slogans about leadership will be to no avail.

NOTES

1. Immanuel Wallerstein, *The Modern World System II: Mercantilism and the Consolidation of the European World-Economy, 1600–1750* (New York: Academic Press, 1980), p. 38.

2. For the data, see Stephen D. Krasner, "United States Commercial and Monetary Policy: Unravelling the Paradox of External Strength and Internal Weakness," in *Between Power and Plenty: Foreign Economic Policies of Advanced Industrial States*, ed. Peter J. Katzenstein (Madison: University of Wisconsin Press, 1978), pp. 68–69.

3. Robert O. Keohane and Joseph S. Nye, Jr., *Power and Interdependence: World Politics in Transition* (Boston: Little Brown, 1977), p. 44.

4. For a discussion of Holland's "hegemony," see Wallerstein, *Modern World System*.

5. GDP data from Robert O. Keohane, "The Theory of Hegemonic Stability and Changes in International Economic Regimes, 1967–1977," in *Change in the International System*, ed. Ole Holsti, Randolph Siverson, and Alexander L. George (Boulder, Col.: Westview, 1980), p. 144. Trade data from Krasner, "U.S. Commercial and Monetary Policy."

6. Fred Hirsch and Michael Doyle, "Politicization in the World Economy: Necessary Conditions for an International Economic Order," in Hirsch, Doyle, Morse, *Alternatives to Monetary Disorder* (New York: McGraw-Hill for Council on Foreign Relations, 1977), pp. 27–28.

7. Arnold Wolfers, "The Goals of Foreign Policy," in Wolfers, *Discord and Collaboration: Essays on International Politics* (Baltimore, John Hopkins University Press, 1962), chap. 5.

8. For a lucid and concise general account, see Stephen D. Krasner, *Defending the National Interest: Raw Materials Investments and U.S. Foreign Policy* (Princeton: Princeton University Press, 1978), pp. 119–128, 188–215. New information on the period up to 1950 can be found in the thoroughly researched study by Irvine H. Anderson, *Aramco, the United States, and Saudi Arabia: A Study in the Dynamics of Foreign Oil Policy, 1933–1950* (Princeton: Princeton University Press, 1981). Anderson goes well beyond two other recent books on the subject: Aaron David Miller, *Search for Security: Saudi Arabian Oil and American Foreign Policy, 1939–1949* (Chapel Hill: University of North Carolina Press, 1980); and Michael B. Stoff, *Oil, War, and American Security: The Search for a National Policy on Foreign Oil, 1941–1947* (New Haven: Yale University Press, 1980).

9. Hirsch and Doyle, "Politicization in World Economy," pp. 31–32.

10. The literature on American financial and trade policies after World War II is voluminous. For a good overview, see Krasner, "U.S. Commercial and Monetary Policy." On monetary affairs, see Richard Gardner, *Sterling-Dollar Diplomacy* (New York: Oxford University Press, 1956); Fred Block, *The Origins of International Economic Disorder* (Berkeley: University of California Press, 1976); Alfred Eckes, *A Search for Solvency: Bretton Woods and the International Monetary System*, 1941–1971 (Austin: University of Texas Press, 1975). On trade, see E. F. Penrose, *Economic Planning for the Peace* (Princeton: Princeton University Press, 1953); Clair Wilcox, *A Charter for World Trade* (1949); Robert E. Hudec, *The GATT Legal System and World Trade Diplomacy* (1975) pp. 3–58; and Gardner, *Sterling-Dollar Diplomacy*.

11. For a discussion, see Gardner Patterson, *Discrimination in International Trade: The Policy Issues* (Princeton: Princeton University Press, 1966), pp. 271–305.

12. Walter LaFeber, *America, Russia and the Cold War, 1945–71* (New York: John Wiley, 1972), p. 53.

13. Anderson, *Aramco*, chap. 2.

14. Ibid.

15. Ibid., chap. 3.

16. Anderson, *Aramco*, has the most complete and detailed account. Stoff also discusses the agreement at some length, although he does not sufficiently appreciate the differences between the first draft and the second, or the loss of enthusiasm in the State Department for the redrafted version. See Stoff, *Oil, War, Security*, pp. 178–95; compare with Anderson, chap. 5.

17. Memorandum, "The Petroleum Division," October 1944, pp. 38–39 (Box 48, Harley Notter files, Record Group 59, National Archives); cited by Anderson, *Aramco*, chap. 3, note 76. It should be noted that for this paper, I have worked from the uncorrected galley proofs of Anderson's book, kindly lent to me by Sanford Thatcher of Princeton University Press. Page numbers for the text are therefore unavailable, and it is possible that final footnote numbers will be different from those given here.

18. Anderson, *Aramco*, chap. 3.

19. Ibid., chap. 5. Anderson has made a significant historiographical contribution by showing that Socal and Texaco took the initiative in offering part of ARAMCO to Jersey; it was formerly believed that Jersey pressed first for participation.

20. The essentials of the story in the last two paragraph can be found in the materials listed below, on which the first draft of this paper relied. The most comprehensive and solidly researched account, however, is in Anderson, *Aramco*, chap. 5. For the other materials, see *The International Petroleum Cartel* (staff report to the Federal Trade Commission, submitted to the subcommittee on monopoly of the Select Committee on Small Business, U.S. Senate, 22 August 1952; reprinted 22 April 1975); *Multinational Oil Corporations and U.S. Foreign Policy, Hearings of the Subcommittee on Multinational Corporations*, U.S. Senate, Committee on Foreign Relations (93–2), 1974, p. 8, Appendix 2; *Multinational Oil Corporations and U.S. Foreign Policy* (U.S. Senate, Committee on Foreign Relations, subcommittee on multinational corporations, 1975), chap. 2, "The 1947 Aramco Merger," pp. 45–55; John M. Blair, *The Control of Oil* (New York: Random House, 1976). For the draft contract between Jersey and the

Anglo-Iranian Oil Company, see National Archives (Record Group 59, Box 4231, file no. 800.6363/1-2847), material dated 20 December 1946, with a covering letter from a Jersey Standard official to the head of the Petroleum Division of the Department of State, indicating that this contract was the basic document in the transaction. See also Anderson, *Aramco*, chap. 5.

21. Dispatches of 14 and 20 January 1947 from the Embassy in London to the State Department (Record Group 59, Box 4231, file no. 800.6363/1-1447 and 800.6363/1-2047).

22. Anderson, *Aramco*, chap. 5.

23. Ibid.

24. Memo from Paul Nitze to Will Clayton, 21 February 1947 (National Archives, Record Group 59, Box 4231, file no. 800.6363/2-2147).

25. Anderson, *Aramco*, chap. 5. The Church subcommittee on multinational corporations alleged in 1975 that "although Exxon and Mobil eventually reached an IPC settlement the French never forgave the Americans for keeping them out of Saudi Arabia." *Multinational Oil Corporations and U.S. Foreign Policy*, p. 55. No evidence, however, is adduced for this assertion, of which no trace appears in Anderson's account. Indeed, certain pieces of evidence suggest the contrary. The U.S. Embassy in London reported on 14 March 1947 that the French seemed to like the idea that they could purchase more than their regular quota of oil from IPC (Record Group 59, Box 4231, file no. 841.6363/3-1447). On 29 May 1947, the Embassy reported satisfaction in London with "the only cloud on the I.P.C. horizon at the moment is the difficulty the major partners are having with Gulbenkian" (Record Group 59, Box 4231, file no. 800.6363/5-2947).

26. Linda Cahn argues that leadership strategies on commodity policy (wheat, sugar, tin) have been consistently followed by the United States only in situations where US hegemony was assured. See "National Power and International Regimes: United States Commodity Policies, 1930–1980" (Ph.D. dissertation, Stanford University, 1980).

27. Memorandum, "The Petroleum Division," October 1944, p. 35 (Box 48, Harley Notter files, National Archives, Record Group 59). Cited in Anderson, *Aramco*, chap. 3, note 73.

28. Henrietta M. Larson, Evelyn H. Knowlton, and Charles S. Popple, *New Horizons, 1927–1950*, vol. 3 of *History of Standard Oil Company* (*New Jersey*) (New York: Harper & Row, 1971), p. 706.

29. William Adams Brown Jr., and Redvers Opie, *American Foreign Assistance* (Washington, D.C.: Brookings Institution, 1953), p. 226. See also Larson et al., p. 707; *New Horizons*, and Anderson, *Aramco*, chap. 6.

30. Memorandum of Conversation of a meeting called by Paul Nitze of the Bureau of Economic Affairs, Department of State, on 9 April 1949, "to discuss the major aspects of the dollar-sterling oil problem and the views thereon of the interested offices of the Department" (Record Group 59, Box 4232, file number 800.6363/4-949).

31. "Working Paper, Near East Conference," 20 December 1949, p. 4 (Box 2, Records of the Petroleum Division, Record Group 59). Anderson also refers to this working paper, considering it as expressing "the basic State Department position for the duration of the "dollar oil" crisis. See Anderson, *Aramco*, chap. 6, note 94.

32. Personal memo of George Eddy of the Office of International Finance,

Treasury Department, referred to in a memo from Eddy to Henry Labouisse in the State Department, on 16 December 1949. (Record Group 59, Box 4232, 800.6363/12-1649). Eddy's personal memo had somehow fallen into the hands of the British, who were using it in their arguments with the American government. Raymond Mikesell, in the Department of State, also criticized high oil price policies: "I hope that some consideration will be given to the consumer, who thus far has been the forgotten man in this picture!" (Record Group 59, Box 4232, file no. 841.6363/7-649 CS/RA).

33. Brown and Opie, *American Foreign Assistance*, pp. 227–30. For the figures, see Hanns Maull, *Europe and World Energy* (London: Butterworth, 1980), p. 211.

34. Memo from Paul Nitze of the Bureau of Economic Affairs to the Secretary of State, 27 April 1949. (Record Group 59, Box 4232, file no. 800.6363/4-2749).

35. The quotes all come from documents in the National Archives of the United States (Record Group 59, Box 4232): (1) Memo of Conversation of meeting between B. Brewster Jennings, President, Soconoy-Vacuum Oil Company, Inc. and various members of the Department of State staff, 21 December 1949 (file no. 841.6363/12-2149; (2) letter of 2 December 1949, from Don C. Bliss, counselor for Economic Affairs of the United States Embassy in London to Henry R. Labouisse, Jr., Office of British and Northern European Affairs, Department of State (file no. 800.6363/12-249; and (3) Memorandum of Conversation of a meeting called by Paul Nitze of the Bureau of Economic Affairs, Department of State, April 9, 1949, "to discuss the major aspects of the dollar-sterling oil problem and the views thereon of the interested offices of the Department." Record Group 59, Box 4232, file number 800.6363/4-949.

36. For the quotation and the argument, see a memorandum to Ambassador Childs from R. Funkhouser, "Background on Current US-UK Oil Talks" (National Archives, Record Group 59, Box 4232, no file number, no date). It appears to have been written in September 1949.

37. Memorandum from Mr. Rosenson of the State Department Monetary Affairs Staff to Henry R. Labouisse, Jr., Office of British and Northern European Affairs (Record Group 59, Box 4232, file no. 800.6363/12-1349), 13 December 1949.

38. Working Paper, Near East Conference, 20 December 1949. (Record Group, Box 4232, no file number), p. 1.

39. Ibid., p. 3.

40. Larson et al., *New Horizons*, pp. 706–07.

41. Brown and Opie, *American Foreign Assistance*, p. 226. Within ECA, Walter Levy, ranking petroleum officer, had pointed out as early as February 1949 the difficulties posed for American companies by ECA plans to finance refinery construction in European countries by European firms (See National Archives, Record Group 59, Box 4232, file number 800.6363/2-1048, for E. L. McGinnes, Jr., memo on meeting of International Petroleum Policy Committee, 10 February, 1949).

42. The quotation is from Joyce and Gabriel Kolko, *The Limits of Power* (New York: Harper & Row, 1972), p. 461. In a meeting held on 9 December 1949 a representative of the Socony-Vacuum Oil Company, had "emphasized that

the oil companies were convinced that they would be unable to get anywhere with the British unless and until the State Department took a firm position with the British and insisted that a settlement of the matter be reached" (Memorandum of Conversation, Department of State, Record Group 59, Box 4232, file no. 841.6363/12-949, 9 December 1949), p. 2.

43. Anderson, *Aramco*, chap. 6.

44. For general accounts, see Robert Engler, *The Politics of Oil* (University of Chicago Press, 1961), pp. 260–63; Shoshana Klebanoff, *Middle East Oil and US Foreign Policy* (New York: Praeger, 1974), esp. p. 119; Paul Johnson, *The Suez War* (New York: Greenberg Press, 1957). The *Economist* (London) offered through coverage of the crisis throughout.

45. Testimony of Arthur Flemming, Director, Office of Defense Mobilization, U.S. Government, in *Emergency Oil Lift Program and Related Oil Problems, Joint Hearings before Subcommittees of the Committee on the Judiciary and Committee on Interior and Insular Affairs, U.S. Senate* (85th Congress, 1st sess.), 5–21 February 1957, p. 12.

46. Organization for European Economic Cooperation (OEEC), *Europe's Need for Oil: Implications and Lessons of the Suez Crisis*, (Paris, 1958), p. 21.

47. Engler, *Politics of Oil*, pp. 261, 307. *Emergency Oil Lift Program* hearings (henceforth *EOLP*), pp. 2543–48.

48. *Europe's Need for Oil*, pp. 28–29; *Petroleum Survey, "1957 Outlook," Hearings before the Committee on Interstate and Foreign Commerce, House of Representatives* (85th Congress, 1st sess.), February–March 1957, pp. 111–13; *EOLP*, p. 595. Eisenhower declared on 30 November 1956 that "the contemplated coordination of industry efforts will insure the most efficient use of tankers and the maximum availability of petroleum product." *Public Papers of the President*, 1956, p. 902.

49. For discussions of relations between the MEEC and the OEEC, see *EOLP*, pp. 1884–1931, 2451–52, 2538–49, 2583–89.

50. *EOLP*, p. 1983.

51. *Europe's Need for Oil*, p. 33.

52. Ibid., pp. 34, 29.

53. *Economist* (London), 12 January 1957, pp. 113, 133. *Oil and Gas Journal*, 21 January 1957, p. 74; 4 February 1957, p. 80.

54. *Public Papers of the President*, 1957, p. 124.

55. *Oil and Gas Journal*, 25 February 1957, p. 78.

56. *Europe's Need for Oil*, p. 38.

57. Krasner, "U.S. Commercial and Monetary Policy."

58. For a discussion of similar problems, see Peter J. Katzenstein, "Introduction: Domestic and International Forces and Strategies of Foreign Economic Policy," in Katzenstein, *Between Power and Plenty*.

59. Keohane and Nye, *Power and Interdependence*, chap. 1.

60. Robert Gilpin, *U.S. Power and the Multinational Corporation: The Political Economy of Foreign Direct Investment* (New York: Basic Books, 1975), p. 41.

61. Kindleberger, *The World in Depression*, p. 219.

62. Gardner, *Sterling-Dollar Diplomacy*, esp. p. 117.

63. Gabriel Kolko, *The Politics of War: The World and United States Foreign*

Policy, 1943–45 (New York: Vintage Books, 1968), p. 283. In his account of Bretton Woods and the British loan, Fred L. Block follows Kolko's version. See *The Origins of International Economic Disorder*, p. 59.

64. See the accounts of Hirsch and Doyle, (note 6), Block and Gardner (note 10), and Kolko (note 63).

65. Joel Darmstadter and Hans H. Landsberg, "The Economic Background," in *The Oil Crisis*, ed. Raymond Vernon, special issue of *Daedalus* (Fall 1975): 30–31.

66. Both quotes are from Anderson, *Aramco*, quoting "Memorandum on the Department's Position," Sappington, 1 December 1943, folder: "Petroleum Reserves Corporation Activities, 7/3/43-/1/144" (Box 1, Records on the Petroleum Division, Record Group 59). Other memos on the subject, according to Anderson, supported Sappington's reasoning.

67. Memo by John A. Loftus, 31 May 1945 (National Archives, decimal file 1945–49, Box no. 5849, file no. 841.6363/5-3145).

68. Question by Senator Robertson of Wyoming, *Petroleum Agreement with Great Britain and Northern Ireland, Hearings before the Committee on Foreign Relations, U.S. Senate* (80th Congress, 1st sess.), June 1947, p. 51. A principal opponent of the treaty by the time it came to the Senate, in its rather truncated form, was Harry F. Sinclair. See Davies testimony, *Petroleum Agreement* hearings, p. 117, and W. L. Connelly, *The Oil Business as I Saw It: Half a Century with Sinclair* (Norman: University of Oklahoma Press, 1954), p. 154.

69. *Congressional Record*, 80th Congress, 1st sess., records that the treaty was reported favorably by the Committee to the full Senate on 3 July 1947 (p. 8289). It was never debated; the only statement on the subject in the 80th Congress was a statement opposing it strongly by W. Lee O'Daniel of Texas. The State Department still supported it officially, if perfunctorily, as of 5 February 1948, when Willard L. Thorp included a paragraph about it in testimoney before a House committee. *Petroleum for National Defense, Hearings Before the Special Subcommittee on Petroleum, Committee on Armed Services, House of Representatives*, (80th Congress, 2nd sess.) 1948, p. 315. During 1948 the treaty simply dropped from view; during that year, it was not mentioned to any significant degree in the *New York Times* or the *Oil and Gas Journal*.

70. Perry Anderson comments, "If the American Empire was the undoing of the Spanish economy, it was its *European* Empire which was the ruin of the Hapsburg State, and the one rendered the extended struggle for the other financially possible." *Lineages of the Absolutist State* (London: New Left Books/Humanities Press, 1974), p. 74.

71. Marcello de Cecco comments: "Britain's retreat into Imperial markets, and her staunch defence of the privileges she enjoyed there, is one of the principal keys to an understanding of world economic history in (1890–1914)." *Money and Empire: The International Gold Standard, 1890–1914* (Totowa, N.J.: Rowman and Littlefield, 1975), pp. 28–29.

4

International Economic Policy in a Declining Core State

Christopher K. Chase-Dunn

This chapter develops the implications of the world-system perspective as elaborated by Immanuel Wallerstein (1979*a*) and others (Amin, 1975; Inkeles, 1975; Mandel, 1975) for the understanding of U.S. international economic policy options in the 1980s. The current position of the United States as a declining hegemonic core state is compared with that of earlier hegemonies in order to provide insights about possible futures.

The world-system perspective analyzes the behavior of states in the context of the structures and processes operating in the larger capitalist world economy. States are understood to be only one among many kinds of organizations competing with one another for dominance in terms of both military power and economic competitive advantage (Chase-Dunn, 1981). The structuring of the world division of labor into zones of core production and peripheral production (high wage production vs. low wage production) is reproduced over the long run expansion of the modern world-system while particular states may be upwardly or downwardly mobile in this politico-economic hierarchy. One of the long-run cyclical processes of the modern world-system is the rise and fall of particular core states (Chase-Dunn, 1978; Modelski, 1978; Bousquet, 1979). This I call the cycle of core competition.

Three states have been hegemonic in the capitalist world economy since its consolidation in the long sixteenth century—the United Provinces (Netherlands), the United Kingdom, and the United States. The periods in between these hegemonies were characterized by a *relatively* equal (multicentric) distribution of military power and economic competitive advantage among core states, and by high levels of conflict and competition within the core. These periods were also characterized by more bilateral and politically controlled relationships between the core and the periphery in which each core state attempted to monopolize exchange with its "own" colonial empire. Periods in which a single great power has been hegemonic have been characterized by relatively more free trade between different areas of the world economy (Krasner, 1976) as well as a more stable growth of production and exchange.

In order to understand the dynamic of the U.S. decline I have chosen for comparison the earlier hegemonies *within* the modern world-system. It may also be fruitful to compare the current situation to long-run cycles of expansion and contraction which occurred in precapitalist modes of production such as the rise and fall of the Roman Empire. Indeed this has been done in a recent study by Galtung, Heiestad and Rudeng (1980). They compare the decline of Rome in antiquity with what they call the "decline of Western imperialism." They find some similarities at the level of cultural processes, but I will argue that this comparison across qualitatively different modes of production is less apt than the comparison with earlier hegemonies within the capitalist mode of production.

The most obvious and important difference between the Roman world empire and the capitalist world economy is the organization of the state. In Rome a single overarching state apparatus came to encompass the economic division of labor, whereas in the capitalist world economy, which was born in Europe and Latin America in the sixteenth century, there is no single state but rather an institutionalized interstate system of unequally powerful and competing state organizations. The Roman world empire had a single center while the capitalist world economy is multicentric, albeit at various times there is a single most powerful (hegemonic) state. The main consequence of this structural difference is its effect on the dynamics of reproduction and growth in these two systems. In the Roman world empire economic competition was primarily mediated through a single-state apparatus, and although monetarization of the economy was extensive (Hopkins, 1978) a competitive price-setting market did not emerge to encourage increases in economic efficiency on the part of producers. The main way to gain and hold income was through obtaining access to political power. Roman property and contract law was quite "modern," but markets remained dominated by political power, and this power was centralized in a single apparatus. The main type of growth was *extensive* through the addition of control over lands and slaves. As Hopkins (1978:62) shows, the dynamic of the Roman economy was fueled by conquest. Roman military organization and transport technology, by far the most advanced in antiquity, eventually reached their spatial limits and territorial expansion halted.

The slave mode of production required new inputs as slaves were worked to death. Tribute as a form of surplus extraction was most remunerative in newly conquered lands. The ending of territorial expansion of the empire led eventually to a reversion to serfdom in the countryside and to ever-greater overhead costs of the political apparatus. The uniqueness of the Roman political constitution was its ability to incorporate oppositional groups into the state by the extension of citizenship. While the political system was always more oligarchial than the earlier Greek city-states (Anderson, 1974) the definition of membership was also much more flexible and allowed power to be shared with those in a position to mobilize effective opposition. The dynamic of cooptation of opposition led to changes in political forms—from republic to empire, and so on (Brunt, 1971)—but the necessity of integrating organizational forms within a single-state apparatus slowed the rate of organizational innovation and discouraged experimentation. Over time the weight of the political superstructure became greater than the underlying economy could bear. Because the Roman system was so centralized, the demise of Rome also meant the demise of the system. It was not possible for a new center to emerge to revitalize the mode of production and to allow it to restart its expansion on a new scale.[1]

By contrast, the capitalist world economy with its more decentralized polity allows for much greater economic *and political* competition. The existence of the price-setting world market, including national markets, while it is not a "perfect" market, does occasionally encourage investors to increase the efficiencies of production (to produce at lower cost) in order to gain a greater share of income. Thus technical development of productivity is encouraged by the fact that there is no central state that can impose monopoly control on the whole arena of economic competition. Similarly, the multicentric state system encourages the "export of capital" because political opposition to profitable investment and labor exploitation is mediated by the individual nation-states and often can be escaped by crossing state boundaries.

Political competition in the capitalist world economy is also much more dynamic than in earlier world empires. The interstate system allows different paths to "success" in the competition among states. Some may emphasize political-military expansion, while others combine this with a strategy of competitive commodity production for the world market. In such a decentralized political system, new forms of political organization can emerge unconstrained by any central state and thereby are free to compete with one another for dominance. What makes the modern world economy a *capitalist* world economy, however, is its unique combination of an interstate system with the institutions of commodity production for profit on a market and a high level of the commodification of labor power. These institutions are interwoven, along with the "private" nature of investment decisions, into a competitive interstate system; and it is the institutional combination of all these, along with the hierachical division of labor between core and periphery, that creates the qualitative uniqueness of capitalism as a system different from both earlier world empires and earlier world economies. This system has shown its flexibility over the 500-year period of its expansion and deepening. Unlike the Roman world empire, it has changed its center without going into devolution as a system. Thus the present period is most probably not a demise of "Western imperialism" but simply a demise of the hegemony of the United States. The main challenges to U.S. supremacy are posed by other core powers, not by the periphery. The possible outcomes, a new hegemony and continuation of the system, or real transformation of the capitalist world economy into a qualitatively different system, are options that bear only minimal similarities with the decline and fall of the Roman Empire.

CAUSES AND CONDITIONS OF THE RISE AND FALL OF HEGEMONIC CORE STATES

In this section a set of causes and conditions of the rise and fall of hegemonic core states is described. Then I present a rough overview of the series of hegemonies.

The rise and fall of hegemonic core states can be understood in terms of the formation of leading sectors of core production and the concentration of these sectors, temporarily, in the territory of single state, which hence becomes most economically and politically powerful of the core states. This process can be understood as a feature of the world economy as a whole insofar as it involves the interaction of systemwide variables such as the Kondratieff wave (Kondratieff, 1979), a business cycle with an approximate fifty-year period; the application of new technologies to production (Bousquet, 1979; Mandel, 1978; Rostow, 1978); and the usually violent reorganization of the state system (Modelski, 1978). The uniqueness of the world-system perspective is that it focuses on the systemwide dynamics of these cycles rather than on the exclusively national processes involved. The cycles that occur are the consequences of the relative overproduction in different periods of different types of commodities (core commodities and peripheral commodities) and the variable limits on effective demand that the political structures impose on consumption. During periods of the expansion of core production, labor and other politically organized interest groups increase their demands for shares of income. The expansion of core production increases the need for raw material inputs, many of which are produced in the periphery. The terms of trade between core and periphery shift in favor of the periphery enabling peripheral producers and the states they control to attain a relatively more favorable market position and to make more effective demands for a larger share of surplus value. This redounds on the struggle for shares in the core where wage increases (and the "cacaphony of equity demands") are less easily met by increased exploitation of the periphery. This dynamic leads to heightened class struggle within core countries and to increased competition among core countries for shares of a no longer growing world surplus value.

Nevertheless, although it would be preferable to present a model of the causes of this cycle of core competition in terms of variable features of the world-system as a whole, this author, like most others, has tended to think about such processes in terms of features of national societies. Thus the following discussion is couched primarily in terms of national comparisons, although the conceptual shortcomings of this type of formulation are acknowledged.

We may think about the cycle of core competition in terms of two alternating situations, one in which military power and economic competitive advantage in core production[2] are concentrated in a single state (hegemony) and one in which these features are spread more evenly across the core states. As has been said before, periods in which one state is hegemonic tend to be relatively peaceful regarding the level of conflict between core powers, whereas periods of a more equal distribution of power (economic and military) tend to be characterized by higher levels of conflict between core states.

Let us think about the causes and conditions of the rise and demise of hegemonic core states. In terms of the cities that became hegemonic world cities over the history of the modern world-system we may compare Amsterdam, London, and New York to peripheral cities and to other nonhegemonic core cities (Seville, Paris). Focusing first on the conditions that facilitate rise to hegemony we may focus on those that promote the development of production in key core commodities and those that facilitate the development of the necessary state strength to back up the expansion of world market shares.

Geographical location would appear to play some role in facilitating hegemony. Hegemonic powers are usually fairly central to the economic networks they come to dominate. This is obviously an advantage in terms of transport costs. Technology adequate to a breakthrough in competitive core production must be available, either from local inventors or by importation. All hegemonies, even the earliest, involve "industrial revolutions" in the sense that new, more economically efficient technologies were applied that allowed the production of mass consumption goods more cheaply than by competitors. Another necessary condition is the existence of investment capital sufficient to develop the new types of production in the hands of those willing to risk it in entreprenuerial ventures. Rising hegemonic powers have typically developed diversified capital intensive agriculture for home consumption and for export. They have relied on cheap imports of some staple commodities, most often produced in the periphery, which have allowed wages to be low and also have lowered the costs of raw material inputs to production. Human capital, that is, labor with skills relevant to the new type of core production, must be available, and at less cost than in competing areas. All these conditions in varying degrees contribute to the ability of an emerging core state to form a leading sector of core production that can serve as the basis for hegemony.

Hegemonies tend to have three stages. The first is based on competitive advantage in mass consumption goods that can penetrate the markets of other core producers and also can expand the absolute size of the market due to lower costs. The second stage is most often based on the production of capital goods for export, and the third stage is based on the export of services and the performance of central place functions for the world economy.

The political conditions of rise to hegemony are rather more complicated. A hegemonic state must be powerful vis-à-vis other states and must also have the strong support of the class coalition that composes its regime.[3] The quality and solidity of this class coalition are also important. It must strongly include classes with an interest in pursuing a strategy of profitable production for the world market. Although the ability of the state apparatus to extract surplus value through effective taxation is undoubtedly important (Tilly, 1975), the conception of state power I am using is not reduceable to the size of government income. A state is powerful if the classes that support it will grant it great support during emergencies (Tardanico, 1978). Its ability to extract surplus does not automatically show that it is strong in the sense that I mean here. The Dutch state could raise a navy overnight by convincing the Amsterdam merchants that their interests were at stake, whereas the French state, whose peacetime government revenues per capita were much greater than those of the British throughout the nineteenth century, could not raise so great a subscription during time of war.

The size of the state is also important, and as Wallerstein is fond of pointing out, it is possible to be too large as well as to be too small, especially if economic regions with contradictory interests are part of the same state. It may also be added that most hegemonic core states have a relatively egalitarian and pluralistic political system compared to those of their competitors. The pluralism allows rapid adaptation to changes in the interests of classes in the center coalition, as well as some flexibility to the demands of workers and farmers, and these can be advantageous in the world economy, at least during the period of upward mobility. The relative egalitarianism of the polity incorporates a larger percentage of the population into the development process and provides some (again temporary) solutions to the Keynesian problems of effective demand. Another way of saying this is to point out that upwardly mobile core states have relatively larger home markets than their competitors because of relatively more equal distributions of income.[4] Nation-building, the formation of a social solidarity at the national level, tends to be more advanced in emerging hegemonies. This contributes to political stability and to the expansion of the home market. It should be pointed out that these political qualities do not preclude the existence of a domestic underclass, but typically this is not so much a source of economic exploitation as much as an outcaste status group that reinforces the solidarity of the larger nation.

What, then, are the conditions that lead to the decline of a hegemonic core state? First it should be pointed out that core states do not decline absolutely. The entire world economy continues to grow, albeit at different rates. What happens is that core states *relatively* lose their hegemony. The most important cause of relative decline is the spread of the new types of core production to other areas of the core and to parts of the semiperiphery. Most emerging core states attempt to monopolize the new types of production, but unsuccessfully because of their inability to politically control the diffusion of techniques, skilled labor, and, eventually, investment capital. Competing producers in other states attempt first to win back their home markets, often employing political regulation of trade (protectionism) as well as the adoption of the new production techniques. Later they successfully compete with the hegemonic power in international markets.

Another factor that contributes to the loss of hegemony we may term the turnover time of fixed capital, especially investment (both private and public) in infrastructural inputs to the production system. This obviously operates at the level of heavy investment in technologies such as plant shells and expensive large scale machinery. Latecomers have an advantage in that they can adopt newer technical innovations, while earlier investors must wait to recoup initial investment. Steel plants in the United States and Japan are well-known examples of this. But the same problem may be seen in other investments in the built environment that are less obviously subject to the logic of profits, but that nevertheless have an effect on competitive production.

Transportation systems, urban structures, communications systems, and energy systems involve investments of resources that, once made, tend to be relatively permanent or not easily reorganized. The canal system of Amsterdam, more systematic and spacious than that of Venice, is a permanent feature of the city. The advent of other forms of transportation, more economically competitive ones, does not produce the rebuilding of Amsterdam, but rather the removal of some of its economic activities to other locations. Similarly, the location of cities on rivers is largely determined by the transport costs relative to a particular stage of transport technology. The advent of larger ships does not produce the removal of cities downstream, except in the sense that ports closer to the sea become the new centers of trade. At the level of nations, national transport systems, energy systems, communications systems, and the locations and division of functions between cities, as well as the types of technology utilized in factories, are all forms of investment subject to the turnover time of fixed capital. A second-running core state that is developing the new type of production can more easily incorporate the latest, most competitive techniques and features of overall social production than the already-invested hegemonic core state.

It can be asked why entreprenuers within a declining hegemonic core state do not invest *within* their national economies to revitalize material production and increase productivity. It may be that a particular steel company must wait for its sunk capital to be used up before building a new plant that uses more productive technology, but why don't other corporations make such investments? Here we may point out that the structure of national tariffs begins to play a role in the determination of investment locations. Tariff protection of national industries is on the increase in a period of slower growth as states seek to protect their national markets against international competition. It may be in the strategic and national interest to make new investments in steel, and indeed states occasionally adopt policies that subsidize such undertakings. But the purely profit-oriented logic of investment is unlikely to help a country which is losing its competitive position in the world market. Building a new steel plant next to the old plant means that the national market will have to be shared, while buying steel abroad from more competitive producers and investing in more immediately profitable enterprises located inside the tariff walls of other countries is the most likely strategy for private investors. Thus economic nationalism by itself might prevent the relocation of certain industries, but declining hegemonic core states are usually ambivalent on the choice between nationalism and internationalism. This reflects the interests of their "national" and "international" capitalists and the contradictions between producers and consumers (Hart, 1980). The road of state-sponsored "revitalization" advocated by those in hegemonic core states most concerned with the interests of national producers (both labor and capital) may be taken, but other competing states will also employ this strategy, and they are more likely to do it effectively because the coalition of classes that control these states are less dominated by those who have investments spread across the world economy as a whole. The international capitalists within a declining hegemonic core state can often convince consumers that it is better to try to hang on to centrality in world exchange and to benefit from low-cost imports than to adopt an expensive program of economic revitalization.

In addition, organizational features tend to have a certain inertia (or momentum if organization is a process). Once a national economy becomes organized in a certain way there is a tendency to crystallization around patterns which are then not easy to change. While organizational forms are much more malleable than are the infrastructural features discussed above (because material sunk capital is less malleable), social rigidities do form around these social institutions. Part of this is due to the opposition that successful capitalist accumulation creates. The very political pluralism and relative egalitarianism that was earlier a competitive advantage allows the formation of constraints on capitalist maneuverability and increases the costs of production. The most obvious example of this is the formation of political organizations that protect and expand the interests of workers. Wages, both direct and social, tend to go up in a successfully hegemonic core state. Similarly, other constraints on the continued revolution of production become politically articulated. The state begins to incorporate the interests of core workers, and these interests reduce the profitability of production within the country.

Another condition, one that often results from the last, is the export of investment capital. Capitalists respond to differentials in profit rates, and so the relative rigidity of the home economy produces the incentive to invest elsewhere, and thus the phenomenon of the export of capital. This means that fewer new investments in material production are made in the home economy, although new lead sectors do tend to emerge, especially in the provision of services to the larger world economy. Thus the world cities located in hegemonic core states typically become more important to the economic role of the country in the latter days of the hegemony. This is because the centrality in exchange that developed from the earlier centrality in production is an important resource for the national economy and for the functioning of the larger world economy.

It may be the case that, although benefiting from centrality to a certain extent, the hegemonic core state comes to bear too great a proportion of the costs of maintaining the overhead of the larger world economy (Szymanski, 1973). The smooth operation of the world economy requires the repression of deviance and the maintenance of order, as does any social system. The costs of maintaining this order tend to be borne by the hegemonic core state, and this taxation burden cannot easily be spread across the core as a whole. At some point the costs of centrality come to outweigh its benefits, usually after competing core states operating under the umbrella of the hegemonic state begin to effectively challenge its share of the world surplus value. This may be less a cause of decline than a symptom.

COMPARISON OF HEGEMONIES

We may roughly assess the generalizations of the previous section by reviewing the features of the three powers that have been hegemonic in the modern world economy (United Provinces, United Kingdom, United States) and by comparing them with the prior hegemony of Venice and with the powers that contended for hegemony but did not attain it. It should be remembered that in terms of the definition here employed, hegemony means first among many in terms of *both* competitive production and military power.

The Habsburg Empire (which included the core "dorsal spine" of the European world economy in the first half of the long sixteenth century)

(Bosquet, 1979) is seen as based primarily on political-military rather than economic centrality. The mercantile aggressiveness of the Portuguese (Modelski, 1978) served as the first wave of European expansion, but like the later centrality of Seville, it did not develop centrality in production.[5] The Portuguese expansion and the primitive accumulation of capital by the Spanish had important, although complicated, effects on the emerging European world economy (Wallerstein, 1974:67–84), but they did not lead to the development of core production in Lisbon or Seville. Somewhat like the case of France later on, Spain included areas with interests unconducive to the development of core activities, and the state was weighed down by the necessity of holding together centrifugal regions. The attempt to impose imperium on the not yet fully integrated capitalist world economy represented a precapitalist logic of domination partially reflected in the *wholly* mercantile model of exploitation that was the main feature of Portuguese and Spanish expansion to external arenas. These powers, while very important to the formation of the newly emerging system, were not themselves fully formed hegemonic core states of that system.

The United Provinces of the Netherlands fits our schema rather well. The Dutch Revolution created a republican federation in which the seafaring capitalists of Amsterdam held considerable power. The religious wars brought refugees to Amsterdam with their skills and what other capital they could manage to convey. Citizenship was to be had for the price of eight Florins (Barbour, 1963). Competitive advantage in production was first evinced in the herring fisheries, which captured a large share of this staple market in the Baltic and expanding Atlantic economy. Shipbuiling was another leg of Dutch core production that enabled merchants to outcompete Hanse and English pliers of the carrying trade. The cost-efficient Fluyt was easily adapted to many specialized uses and effectively manned by small crews (Wallerstein, 1980).

The Dutch state is often seen as small, but in terms of the notion of state strength employed in this discussion, it was estimable. Johan De-Witt could raise sufficient funds in a day on the Amsterdam bourse to defeat any sea power in the world. It may be argued that the state was split between the capitalist cities and the land-oriented house of Orange, but in comparison to the other core contenders, the capitalists had great sway indeed. During national calamities the princes of Orange rallied the populace to defend the nation, while during the peace the less patriotic urban capitalists had their way. The federation and the republican form of government enabled the state to adapt easily to changing economic and military contingencies and the changing interests of its center coalition.

The ideology of free trade and the rights of all nations to use of the seas were propagated by the Dutch intelligentsia during the period in which economic competitive advantage enabled the Amsterdam capitalists to undersell all competitors (Wilson, 1957). This did not prove incompatible with a policy of "armed trade" employed in the periphery to deprive the Portuguese of their monopoly of spices from the East Indies (Parry, 1966).

Barbour points out that in many respects Amsterdam is the last city-state. Its orientation toward the seafaring world economy was relatively unbridled by commitments to continental territorial aggrandizement. In this respect it was much like Venice, and the comparison is enlightening (Burke, 1974). The Venetian city-state, as argued above, was a hegemonic core state of a protocapitalist Mediterranean world economy. We can observe that the hegemonic core states are larger the larger is the system as a whole and that they contain more territory and a larger home market the more recent they are. It would be useful to attempt a comparison between the size of the home market of the hegemonic power vis-à-vis the size of the world economy as a whole to determine if there is an approximately constant ratio, or if this ratio is increasing with the cycles of the world economy. Lane (1973) observes that the Venetian ruling classes became land oriented during the period of their decline, and he interprets this as an attempt to form a nation-state that could compete with the larger states of the European world economy in formation. Yet we observe that the United Provinces (Netherlands) seem rather small in terms of land area and population size compared to the other states of Europe but nevertheless play the role of hegemonic core state rather effectively during the seventeenth century. The United Provinces may be seen as a kind of midpoint between Venice and England. The hegemonic state becomes increasingly a nation-state, and the size of the national market becomes larger and larger, with the U.S. national market being an immense share of the world economy it dominates. The Dutch decline exhibits the tendencies described in my description of hegemonic stages: the shift toward services, the export of capital, and the transformation of the capitalists from entreprenuers to rentiers (Burke, 1974).

The United Kingdom fits my stages of hegemony best, and this is no mystery because as inheritors of the sciences of development we know most about this "birthplace of modernization" and thus tend to generalize from it even though our overall perspective commands us to treat it no differently than the others. The three stages of hegemony can be seen clearly in the rise of cotton textile production, its replacement in the middle of the nineteenth century by the production and export of machinery and railroads, and the increasing importance of London in the later nineteenth century as a center of world financial services. The Dutch hegemony also matches rather well, although the middle period of export of ships, arms, and land reclamation projects tends to fit the notion of "capital goods" only loosely.

The English Revolution, like the Dutch, supports our notions of relative egalitarianism, pluralism, and the firm incorporation of diverse capitalist interests into a flexible state capable of mobilizing immense resources for international war while maintaining a somewhat sparse and inexpensive peacetime bureaucracy. It should be repeated here that we are describing features of the core of a larger capitalist system, not features of capitalism as a whole. We do not want to repeat the mistake of identifying capitalism as a system with the *laissez-faire* state.

The unity of the center coalition in the United Kingdom was not without contention, as can be seen by the history of the rise and fall of the Corn Law. But the agrarian capitalist landowners were much more integrated into successful production for the world market than were the aristocrats of France. France was a case of too large a nation-state in which the formation of the absolute monarchy was necessitated by the divergent interests of economic regions. The cities of the north were anxious to participate in the expanding Atlantic economy, while the older Mediterranean-oriented Occitania (Wallerstein, 1974:262–269; 1980) displayed the tendencies of downward mobility characteristic of other areas that had become semiperipheral to the system. The mercantilist and industrializing policies of Colbert were undercut by the focus on continental diplomacy and political-military aggrandizement (Lane, 1966). The "bourgeois revolution" was delayed until 1789, by which time England had stolen the march on the newly emerging types of core production. Paris became the cultural and diplomatic center of Europe, while London became the world city of a hegemonic core state.

The export of capital from England in the latter half of the nineteenth century is legendary. English capital went both to the periphery and to other core states. That this phenomenon was by no means new is shown by the earlier Dutch case. It must be seen less as a cause of the spread of the new types of core production to other areas than as a response to that spread. The discussion of the "climacteric" of British maturity (Phelps-Brown and Handfield-Jones, 1952) often alleges a loss of entreprenuerial spirit among business leaders, which reminds us of Pareto's foxes, but this, like the Dutch shift toward low-risk, steady profit investment, can be understood as a response to changing opportunities for investment. Risk capital did not disappear; it was sent abroad.

In the 1880s average incomes of workers in Britain began to rise (Emmanuel, 1972). This was undoubtedly the result of the successful organization of trade unions and political organizations of the working class, which allowed some of its interests to become incorporated into the British state. This new entry into the center coalition of the British state raised the cost of exploitation in Britain and created political resistance to the maneuverability of capital. These further encouraged the export of investment capital (McGowan, 1979).

The United States exhibits many of the general characteristics I have attributed to hegemonic core states. The semiperipheral position of New England's merchant capitalists in the eighteenth century created the potential for upward mobility, which was only realized by a series of political alliances and confrontations with the peripheral capitalists of the South. The development of core production was made possible by the creation of a state capable of defending fledgling core capitalists from competition with existing core industries abroad.

The final capture by core capital of the Federal state in the Civil War was possible because of an alliance with core labor (workers and farmers) on the issue of Western expansion (Chase-Dunn, 1980). It was at this time that the United States attained core status in the world economy.

Its further success and the attainment of hegemony was due to a combination of production for the home market and the international market. It is somewhat harder to identify a single mass consumption commodity that led to the development of a new sector around which economic hegemony was consolidated than for the earlier Dutch and British hegemonies. Agricultural commodities were important exports throughout the rise of the United States, as they still are. Agricultural commodities may be either core or peripheral products depending on the way they are produced. Slave-grown cotton was clearly a peripheral commodity grown for export to the capital-intensive English Midlands. Western wheat and other agricultural exports became more and more capital-intensive, such that now they are definitely core products relative to types of production occurring in the rest of the world economy.

The success of core production in the industrial North during the nineteenth century led to the early export of cotton textiles, and not long after, to the export of machinery. Electrical appliances and automobiles were important mass consumption exports, although many other industrial products shared in the U.S. competitive advantage in production. As discussed above, the home market played a much larger role in the early development of the United States than did the home market of earlier hegemonies. This was possible because of the successful and relatively egalitarian territorial expansion of the United States (egalitarian in the sense that land acquisition by small and middle-size owners was possible).

The U.S. hegemony may be instructively compared with the Dutch and British hegemonies. The size of the home market of the hegemonic core power relative to the size of the world market is approximately the same for all three hegemonies. All these hegemonies rose after competing core powers weakened themselves in intracore war. Their success relied more on economic competitive advantages in the production of the material commodities than on military superiority, although both were important. The maturation of hegemony brought increasing political and military centrality, as well as economic advantage (Barbour, 1963; Hobsbawm, 1968). Decline in each case has had more to do with the catching up of competing core powers than absolute decreases in levels of production and consumption.

The U.S. hegemony is different from the Dutch and British hegemonies in some important ways, however. The length of U.S. hegemony will probably be short, corresponding with the increasing frequency of other world-system cycles (Bergesen, 1980). Thus it does not make sense to simply extrapolate from the earlier cycles of core competition. Such an extrapolation based on the late nineteenth century would go as follows: The downswing of the Kondratieff, which began in 1873, could be compared with the period of the early 1970s. The United States would still have much centrality but would begin worrying about its economic competitiveness and ability to have its way in the world polity. A period of increased core competition would bring rising tariffs, increased colonial expansion, and division (and redivision) of the periphery. This period would be followed by the Edwardian Indian summer, the economic upturn which began in 1895. The world economy would appear to regain stability and growth, but war preparations and shifting alliances would result in a bid for political-military hegemony by an upwardly mobile power that had not succeeded in attaining much integration into the structure of world power (Germany in 1914, the Soviet Union in 2014). This extrapolation would predict the outbreak of World War III sometime after the turn of the twenty-first century, and a resulting reorganization of the world political structure that would allow a new hegemonic core power to emerge and a new period of capitalist accumulation to begin.

The apparently shortening period of world-system cycles may reveal imminent changes in the dynamics of the system which could alter the above scenario. Since the late nineteenth century the system as a whole has begun to experience the effects of certain natural and social upper limits. Previously the contradictory aspects of the logic of capitalist development have led to conjunctural reorganizations of the political structure of the system though intracore war. This is what has pushed the decline of old hegemonic powers and the rise of new ones able to operate on scales more appropriate to the expanded size and intensified nature of the system as a whole. These reorganizations have allowed the capitalist accumulation process to begin again on a new basis, that is, to adapt to the problems created by its contradictory nature, and to continue expansion and intensification. In the twentieth century, however, certain "ceiling effects" have been reached that create much deeper structural problems for the system than previously (Chase-Dunn and Rubinson, 1979). The inclusion of virtually all global territory and population into the capitalist world economy in the late nineteenth century eliminated the possibility of expansion to previously unintegrated areas. And the formal decolonization of the periphery, even though it has not eliminated (or even reduced) the hierarchical core-periphery division of labor, has increased the costs of exploiting the periphery. This reduces the amount of surplus value from this source available for resolving class conflicts within core countries and exacerbates other tensions.

How do these ceiling effects change the situation faced by the Dutch or the British in similarly late phases of their hegemonies? One possible difference is due to the increased density of political regulation of the capital accumulation process across the system. While most of this regulation is nationally controlled, and thus is more an increase in state capitalism than a change in the logic of the competitive accumulation process (Chase-Dunn, 1980), there are incipient forms of supranational economic regulation, and this provides a greater chance than ever before for the hegemonic core state to engineer a political solution to the trend toward increasingly bloody confrontation. The process of world state formation is unlikely to be realized in an effective monopoly of legitimate violence in the next twenty years, but this outcome has a greater probability of occurence than ever before. The hegemonic core state, and especially its ruling-class fraction with the greatest dispersion of investments across the globe, has the greatest interest in maintaining the present order and the global peace (Goldfrank, 1977).

From the point of view of this cycle of core competition, where is the United States presently? The U.S. hegemony in core production can clearly be dated from the 1920s (Chirot, 1977). After World War II the United States took on world political centrality, and this matured in the 1945–67 period of the Pax Americana. But economic hegemony began to decline from about 1950 on. In 1950 the United States produced 42 percent of world goods and services, by 1960 this had dropped to 35.8 percent and by 1970 it was 30 percent (Meyer et al., 1975:table 2). Financial centrality did not begin to slip until 1971, although signs of unrest due to balance of payments were seen earlier, as were pressures to engage in trade protection (Block, 1977). The defeat in Vietnam is often seen as an indicator of declining political and military centrality.

Thus the golden age of U.S. hegemony has clearly passed, but the United States will remain the largest national market and the most powerful military power for some time to come. The internal operation of the process of uneven economic development to be seen in the emergence of sunbelt cities will prolong the U.S. hegemony, as will the fact that U.S.-based corporations have advantages of scale that cannot be easily matched by the firms (private or public) of other core states. And, although the United States is dependent on raw material imports due to its high level of consumption, it is somewhat less dependent than many of its competitors because of remaining internal resources. Thus we can expect the United States to maintain its economic and political centrality in a world economy experiencing slower and less even rates of growth, but it can never recover the heights of hegemony reached during the score of years following World War II.

It would seem probable that the United States would attempt to organize a corewide approach to the problems of a contracting world economy because it still has the most to lose from increasing levels of core conflict. But this attempt is likely to be undermined by increasing intranational and international competition in a period of world economic stagnation (Kaldor, 1978). The relative harmony of labor and capital that has characterized U.S. class relations since the birth of the nation is likely to move in a direction more similar to other core states. Cross-cutting sectional differences are being evened out by the development of the sunbelt, and the U.S. party system will most probably come to reflect class interests in the way that European parties do. This change in the vocabulary of politics will probably not result in major changes in the U.S. class structure. Conflicting class interests over international economic policy will make it more difficult for the U.S. to engineer a corewide alliance. In the face of increasing competition for raw materials, the most likely strategy will involve the solidification of economic and political ties with some areas of the periphery. This would be the functional equivalent of a colonial empire, although the terms of the alliance are likely to be less exploitative for the peripheral areas than earlier colonial empires were. For one thing, formal recolonization is impossible (although it is interesting to think about why), and so trade agreements and military pacts must exhibit, at least on the surface, the formalities of a relationship between equals.

This tendency for core states to solidify relations with particular peripheral areas undercuts the tendency for violent conflicts among core powers to be fought out in the periphery. The export of violent confrontation to the less powerful areas of the globe has been the rule during a period of general economic growth in which any particular contested area is not so crucial for the core powers. But in a period of contraction, wars that break out in the periphery can easily become world wars.

This rough comparison of hegemonies reveals that most features of the three cases examined fit our general description of the causes and conditions of rise and demise. A clearer specification of the causes of this cycle of core competition and the use of systematic data to test the propositions of such a model will add much more to our evaluation of this approach. Such work has begun (for example, McGowan and Kordan, 1981). In the meanwhile, we may reflect on an interesting extrapolation of the cycle into the future. If the system does not go through a major transformation in the next decades such that a succeeding hegemonic core power is no longer a requisite of stability, we will be likely to see a coalition between two or more core powers fill this role. This is because, assuming the trend toward greater size of hegemonic core states continues, there are no extant states large enough to fill this role. Of course, the supranational union of two states would itself be a significant change in the state system, and this makes us wonder if some version of world government would be less probable. However, the obvious rationality of a collective international approach to the problems of stagnation and inequality has not found much political support even from the United States, the country with the most to lose from a period of disorder.

The United States should be likely to maintain economic internationalism longer than other core states, just as the British refused to adopt protection long after all other core states had. It should also be the biggest proponent of corewide cooperation because it has the most to lose from conflict. But these political thrusts could be successful only if combined with a realistic policy that seeks to redress the inequities of the core-periphery division of labor. This would mean support for programs that seek to create a more balanced development of the world economy.

The present international policy of the United States has been decidedly ambivalent. At the same time that the Trilateral Commission and some statesmen proferred a vision of intracore cooperation and free trade, the United States has moved toward protectionism and a solution to economic stagnation based on military expenditures. Most of the moves toward industrial revitalization have taken the weak form of "lemon socialism," bailing out large firms that could not continue without government subsidies. The structural contradictions within hegemonic core powers outlined above make moves in either policy direction ineffective. This is not to declare that decline is *inevitable*, and thereby to deny the existence of human freedom, but it is to argue that given the tendencies of the larger world-system a reversal of the decline is extremely unlikely.

What policy prescriptions follow from such a seemingly pessimistic analysis? First, I should point out that U.S. hegemony has not been a picnic for everyone. While some classes have benefited, others both within and outside the United States have not. Second, the hegemony of a particular state is less important than the dynamics of a socioeconomic system that produces both rapid and uneven development and extremely destructive wars that, under present conditions, could conceivably reduce the human species to a massive devolution. It is this system that should be changed rather than the preservation of a particular hegemony within it. But policy recommendations are utopian unless they come out of and can be realistically applied to the actual historical circumstances of relevance.

Within the realm of possibility it seems to me that the structural changes in the U.S. economy recommended by Carnoy and Shearer (1980) are the most viable form of "revitalization" in the sense that they constitute movement at the national level toward a system that would begin to eliminate the irrationalities of the capitalist world-system. Carnoy and Shearer recommend forms of economic democracy that would increase the collectively rational control of the U.S. economy. This would not prevent the United States from losing its military and economic hegemony in the world-system, but it would make possible an international economic and political policy oriented toward a similar reconstruction of the world economy. That is, it would be compatible with the support of a democratic world government that could control the anarchy of military conflict and promote a collectively rational approach to world economic development. While these ideas seem radical and even utopian given the present political climate within the United States, the recommendation of more limited directions would only reproduce the structures that create the negative consequences of uneven development and war.

NOTES

1. The survival of the Eastern empire centered in Constantinople does not represent the emergence of a new center that carried on the dynamic of expansion of the system that found its purest expression in Rome. Anderson (1974) argues that the Byzantine empire survived by a syncretism of Roman and less differentated monarchical political structures. The Western empire was far more dynamic in its period of expansion, and its contradictions were more purely articulated; thus its dramatic devolution.

2. Important to my definition of hegemony is the notion of core production. Core production is the production of commodities which employ skilled, high-wage labor and capital-intensive technology relative to periperal production, which is low-wage, labor-intensive. Core states are those in which core production is a high proportion of all production.

3. I shall call this class coalition the "center coalition" following Moore (1966). Other theorists of the state refer to it as the "power bloc" (Poulantzas, 1973).

4. André Gunder Frank (1979) points out that a relatively equal distribution of income, with a large home market for consumption goods, is a necessary, but certainly not a sufficient, condition for upward mobility in the world economy.

5. Frederic Lane (1979:15–19) shows that the Portuguese entry into the spice trade did not ever employ the lowering of prices to drive competitors from the market. The blockade of the movement of spices through the Red Sea and the Persian Gulf allowed the Portuguese to sell spices more cheaply than the Venetians, who continued to pay protection costs to the Soldan of Egypt. But the Portuguese blockade instead caused pepper prices to rise, even in Lisbon, and even when the Venetians again began meeting a large proportion of the demand. This illustrates the exclusive commitment of the Portuguese to the precapitalist economic strategy of administered monopoly prices, and partly explains their failure to develop core production. State power has always been used to facilitate capital accumulation in the capitalist mode of production but this has most usually taken the form of "protection rent" (Lane, 1979). Protection rent is the difference in costs of protection (both offensive and defensive) that returns to businessmen backed by more efficacious state power. The Portuguese relied exclusively on this form of profit-taking, however, even to the extent of not utilizing a price-lowering strategy when it would have led to greater returns. In this they inflexibly followed the tribute-gathering logic of precapitalist systems.

REFERENCES

Amin, Samir. 1975. *Unequal Development*. New York: Monthly Review Press.
Anderson, Perry. 1974. *Passages from Antiquity to Feudalism*. London: New Left Books.

Barbour, Violet. 1963. *Capitalism in Amsterdam in the Seventeenth Century*. Ann Arbor: University of Michigan Press.

Bergesen, Albert. 1980. "Long waves of colonial expansion and contraction." In Albert J. Bergesen (ed.), *Studies of the Modern World-System*. New York: Academic Press.

Block, Fred L. 1977. *The Origins of International Economic Disorder: A Study of the United States International Monetary Policy from World War II to the Present*. Berkeley: University of California Press.

Bousquet, Nicole. 1979. "Esquisse d' une theorie de l' alternance de periods de concurrence et d' hegemonie au centre de l' economie-monde capitaliste." *Review* II, 4: 501–18 (Spring).

Brunt, P. A. 1971. *Social Conflicts in the Roman Republic*. New York: Norton.

Burke, Peter. 1974. *Venice and Amsterdam: A Study of 17th Century Elites*. London: Temple Smith.

Carnoy, Martin, and Derek Shearer. 1980. *Economic Democracy: The Challenge of the 1980s*. White Plains, New York: M. E. Sharpe.

Chase-Dunn, Christopher. 1978. "Core-periphery relations: the effects of core competition." In Barbara H. Kaplan (ed.), *Social Change in the Capitalist World Economy*. Beverly Hills: Sage.

———. 1980. "Socialist states in the capitalist world-economy." *Social Problems* 27, 5:505–25 (June).

———. 1981. "Interstate system and capitalist world-economy: one logic or two?" *International Studies Quarterly*. 25, 1: 19–42 (March).

———, and Richard Rubinson. 1979. "Cycles, trends and new departures in world-system development." In John W. Meyer and Michael T. Hannan (eds.), *National Development and the World System: Educational, Economic and Political Change 1950–1970*. Chicago: University of Chicago Press.

Chirot, Daniel. 1977. *Social Change in the Twentieth Century*. New York: Harcourt Brace Jovanovitch.

Emmanuel, Arghiri. 1972. *Unequal Exchange*. New York: Monthly Review Press.

Frank, André Gunder. 1979. *Dependent Accumulation and Underdevelopment*. New York: Monthly Review Press.

Galtung, Johan; Tore Heiestad; and Erik Rudeng. 1980. "On the decline and fall of empires: The Roman Empire and Western Imperialism compared." *Review* IV, 1:91–154 (Summer).

Goldfrank, Walter L. 1977. "Who rules the world? Class formation at the international level." *Quarterly Journal of Ideology* I, 2:32–37 (Winter).

Hart, Jeffrey A. 1980. "The policy of the U.S. toward the NIEO." Paper prepared for the fifth annual Hendricks Symposium, "U.S. International Economic Policy in an Age of Scarcities," University of Nebraska-Lincoln, 10–11 April.

Hobsbawm, E. J. 1968. *Industry and Empire*. Baltimore: Penguin.

Hopkins, Keith. 1978. "Economic growth and towns in classical antiquity." In Philip Abrams and E. A. Wrigley (eds.), *Towns in Societies*. Cambridge: Cambridge University Press.

Inkeles, Alex. 1975. "The emerging social structure of the world." *World Politics* 27, 4 (July).

Kaldor, Mary. 1978. *The Disintegrating West*. New York: Hill and Wang.

Krasner, Stephen D. 1976. "State power and the structure of international trade." *World Politics* 28, 3:317–47.

Lane, Frederic C. 1973. *Venice: A Maritime Republic*. Baltimore; Johns Hopkins University Press.

———. 1979. *Profits from Power*. Albany: State University of New York Press.

Mandel, Ernest. 1978. *The Second Slump*. London: New Left Books.

McGowan, Patrick J., and B. Kordan. 1981. "Imperialism in world-system perspective: Britain 1870–1914." *International Studies Quarterly*, 25, 1:43–68 (March).

Meyer, John W.; John Boli-Bennett; and Christopher Chase-Dunn. 1975. "Convergence and divergence in development." *Annual Review of Sociology* I, Palo Alto, California.

Moore, Barrington. 1966. *The Social Origins of Democracy and Dictatorship*. Boston: Beacon.

Modelski, George. 1978. "The long cycle of global politics and the nation-state." *Comparative Studies in Society and History* 20, 2:214–35 (April).

Parry, J. H. 1966. *The Establishment of European Hegemony 1415–1715*. New York: Harper & Row.

Phelps-Brown, E. H., and S. J. Handfield-Jones. 1952. "The climacteric of the 1890's." *Oxford Economic Papers*, New Series, 4, 3 (October).

Poulantzas, Nicos. 1973. *Political Power and Social Classes*. London: New Left Books.

Rostow, W. W. 1978. *The World Economy: History and Prospect*. Austin: University of Texas Press.

Szymanski, Albert. 1973. "Military spending and economic stagnation." *American Journal of Sociology* 79, 1 (July).

Tardanico, Richard. 1978. "A structural perspective on state power in the capitalist world-system." Paper read at the annual meetings of the American Sociological Association, San Francisco.

Wallerstein, Immanuel. 1974. *The Modern World-System I: Capitalist Agriculture and the Origins of the European World-Economy in the Sixteenth Century*. New York: Academic Press.

———. 1979a. *The Capitalist World-Economy*. New York: Cambridge University Press.

———. 1979b. "Kondratieff up or Kondratieff down?" *Review* II, 4:663–674 (Spring).

———. 1980. *The Modern World-System II: Mercantilism and The Consolidation of The European World-economy 1600–1750*. New York: Academic Press.

Wilson, C. H. 1957. *Profit and Power: A Study of England and the Dutch Wars*. London: Longman.

5

Long Cycles and the Strategy of U.S. International Economic Policy

George Modelski

The long cycle is the process of change in the structure of politics at the global level; its essence has been the rise of nation-states to a position of world leadership and the competition that has followed. Running in tandem with it over the past five hundred years has also been the process of emergence, and subsequent decline, of lead economies. While the rise of world powers has been central to world politics, and the formation of lead economies has been fundamental to world economics, the relationship of these two processes to each other, an understanding of which is surely crucial to any serious conception of international economic policy, has rarely been subject to sustained analysis.

This chapter[1] advances the thesis that these two basic processes of the modern world system may be seen as linked in terms of a model of "alternating innovations" wherein, at the global level, generation-long periods of fundamental political innovation alternate with those of change in the industrial structure, bringing about fundamental shifts in the economy. The coordinating mechanism seems to reside in the sustained movements in prices known as the Kondratieff waves. A number of implications arise from this analysis for the strategy of U.S. international economic policy, the most important of which concern the definition of the contemporary world situation.

LONG CYCLES OF WORLD LEADERSHIP[2]

Central to the theoretical framework informing the present analysis are two concepts: world leadership and long cycles. We view them as the key to understanding the politics of the modern world system.

World leadership may be defined (for the modern world system) as the performance, by a nation-state, of the functions of ordering and maintaining global-level interactions. These functions have both political and economic dimensions. The political ones may be seen most clearly in the acts of instituting a world order *de novo*, as did the Portuguese; or by destroying an old one, as the Dutch did with English help to the Iberian; or by successfully defending it, as the British did, for instance, against Napoleon. The economic dimensions reside in the fact that a large portion of global interactions to be ordered concern international trade and other economic matters.

In the modern world such functions have in fact been undertaken and accomplished, on the whole, quite adequately by a succession of nation-states of defined characteristics. These characteristics included ready access to the ocean based on secure insular or semi-insular positions, command of the sea, and suitable political and economic resources and organization. States filling that role shall henceforth be called *world powers* and their names are shown in column 4 of table 5.1. Portugal, the first listed, displayed world leadership in moving the world system toward a higher degree of complexity by pioneering the Cape route to Asia and controlling the bulk of the world ocean for close to a century. The United Provinces of the Netherlands defeated Spain's attempt to take over that system on a monopolistic basis and reorganized the global system largely on their own terms. Britain succeeded them and for two centuries gave structure to oceanic interactions; she also successfully led several coalitions against attempts to impose imperial rule upon Europe, and by implication, also on the world. The United States assumed final responsibility for the structure of the global system in World War II, having provided the margin of victory and the ultimate leadership in the German wars of the twentieth century.[3]

World leadership thus refers to the structural arrangement for resolving the most pressing problems of world politics. Obviously it is not world government because it is a structure marked by high improvization, intermittancy, and crisis management. It is not a differentiated global institution but rather a set of functions performed by a nation-state that by dint of the right qualifications finds itself at the right moment doing the right things at the right place. But such a nation-state does not rule the world (or other nation-states) in an imperial manner nor exercise "worldwide domination"; rather, it orders aspects of global problems in a manner at the time regarded as legitimate. We need also to distinguish world leadership from hegemony by using the criteria of common interest and legitimacy. When a leading state acts in the public interest and its actions are thought legitimate, then its behavior cannot be described as hegemonial. On the other hand, we need not assume that nation-states in positions of world leadership can never act other than in the common interest or legitimately. All we do is not to adopt an initial presumption of hegemonial, that is, in the classical sense, tyrannical, behavior.

TABLE 5.1 **Five long cycles of world leadership**

Cycle	Duration	Global Powers[a]	World Powers[b]	Principal Challengers[c]	Global War
I	1517–1608	England, France, Portugal, Spain, U.P. Netherlands	Portugal	Spain	(Italian wars 1494–1516) Spanish wars 1581–1609
II	1609–1713	England, France, Spain, U.P. Netherlands	U.P. Netherlands	France	Wars of Louis XIV 1688–1713
III	1714–1815	Britain, France, Spain, Russia, U.P. Netherlands	Britain	France	Revolutionary and Napoleonic wars 1792–1815
IV	1816–1945	Britain, France, Germany, Italy, Japan, Russia, United States	Britain	Germany	World Wars I & II, 1914–18, 1939–45
V	1945–	United States, USSR	United States		

[a] Nation-states with significant capacity for global reach (sea power) in that cycle.

[b] Global power entering cycle with preponderant (50 percent or over) capacity for global reach.

[c] Global power acting as principal contestant in global war.

By choosing world leadership as a central concept of this analysis we also make it clear that we do not regard the modern world as some sort of anarchical society. To the contrary, our analysis clarifies the principles of order and authority that have governed that world for the past half millennium and that, while familiar to historians in each particular instance, have not been previously put together in quite this manner and have been generally unfamiliar to students of international relations. Anarchy could be in the eye of the beholder.

But world leadership, while a clear ordering principle, has also been marked by notable instability in its political process, and this instability is the basis of the second key concept of this analysis: the long cycle. Lacking a secure anchorage in a set of fully differentiated and legitimated institutions, world leadership has, over the long period of its currency, shown a tendency toward stimulating competition and generating a steady circulation in that position. Portugal and the Netherlands each had a golden age lasting about one century. Britain's sway extended over two successive cycles, each marked by severe challenge. The United States is well into one cycle. Each of these experiences merit the appellation of cycle because each contains the same characteristic sequence of events: a *global war*; a worldwide struggle of major proportions and consequences; an era of political and economic consolidation (*world power*); a mid-course period of political unsettlement and possible innovation (*delegitimation*); and a final sequence of rivalry and competitive disruption (*deconcentration*), setting the stage for another global conflict. (The italicized names are those that might be given to the four phases of the long cycle.) This is the simplest conception of the cycle as a pattern of recurrent events, but it can also be given a more technical meaning as a sequence of fluctuations in the output of order at the global level.

The long cycle therefore shows that ours is a pattern not only of leadership but also of competition for that position. Those powers that over the half millenium did contest that leadership, during prolonged bouts of warfare fought both on land and on the world ocean, we shall call 'principal challengers.'' Column 5 of table 5.1 shows them to be Spain, France, and Germany. (The question remains open for the fifth cycle.) They must be just as much part of our analysis as the world powers.

Weaknesses in the institution of world leadership including insufficient legitimation and information short-falls thus account for the long cycle. Yet its regularity has proved an important organizing feature of the world system, a major beat of its central circulatory process. It is in this sense, too, that the "nature" of world politics may be said to have remained unchanged for half a millennium, characterized in particular by the institution of war and especially by prolonged bouts of global warfare; and it is with regard to those latter periods that the "realist" (or pessimistic) interpretation of international politics is particularly appropriate. In that important sense the long cycle is a source of continuity in modern world politics.

But the modern world system has also been noted for a pattern of political evolution at both national and global levels. At both levels evolution has taken the form of *political innovation*, and the bulk of that innovation may be attributed to world leadership (see table 5.2). We note that each world power was, in its time, a "lead polity"; that is, its political system served as a political example and functioned therefore as a model of political development for other states. At this national level political evolution focused on the nation-state and on ways of moderating its tendencies toward centralization and power monopoly (through federalism, parliamentary government, democracy, and the rule of law). The nation-state rapidly consolidated its position in the world system and through several models became in the twentieth century the universal form of political organization.

The military evolution has reflected global political processes (especially oceanic exploration and the establishment of global networks) as well as the rise of the nation-state and has moved through ascending stages both of organization (intercontinental operations, new forms of infantry and artillery organization, standing and mass armies) and of weapon systems (land, sea, and airborne, from bronze cannon to nuclear missiles). The diplomatic arena has also been marked by successive increments in the degree of sophistication, beginning with the institution of residential diplomacy itself taking hold in Europe as a whole from 1500 onward (spearheaded by Spain drawing on Italian models). This was followed by the consolidation of a law of nations, initially in the Netherlands after 1600 (Grotius); the evolution of the theory and the practice of the balance of power by British statesmen and commentators at about 1700; the establishment of a Concert of Europe as a Great Power arrangement, under British sponsorship after 1814; a growing number of specialized international organizations, mostly European, later in the nineteenth century and leading up to the formation of a comprehensive system based on the United Nations, under United States leadership in 1945. While bearing all this in mind we must not ignore either the order instituted successively by each world power that too, in each century, amounted to a major political innovation.

TABLE 5.2 **Major Political Innovations Linked to World Powers**

Century	Lead Polity	Strategic/Military Innovations	Diplomatic Innovations
XVI	Portugal: first modern nation-state	The caravel, the *nau*, and the galleon; global operational networks	(Residential diplomacy)
XVII	Netherlands: federated republic	Professional navy; standing army	International law
XVIII	Britain I: parliamentary government	Battleship formation	Balance of power
XIX	Britain II: democracy	"Pax Britannica"; command of the sea	Concert of Europe
XX	United States: pluralist democracy	Nuclear deterrence	United Nations

Let us characterize these evolutionary changes as *waves of political innovation*, large-scale changes in the (hard and soft) technologies of the political (production) process that (though they also add to instability) generally conduce to the improvement in the performance and the effectiveness of political structures. Because of these evolutionary processes of innovation, the "utopian" (or optimistic) interpretation of world politics becomes more convincing. If in such a historically short period of five hundred years so much sophistication and refinement could be added to the conduct of affairs, then continued improvement cannot simply be ruled out of court as "unrealistic."

WORLD POLITICS AND WORLD ECONOMICS

As argued elsewhere,[4] the distinguishing characteristic of the modern world system has been the high saliency that the system equally accords to politics and to economics. One facet of that saliency is the high rate of innovation experienced both by politics (as just shown) and by economics over the past half millennium. In that the two structures are comparable, and in view of the close linkages between them, arguments about relative priority or which is the more basic of the two do not appear strikingly fruitful. That is also why we do not refer to the modern world as essentially or characteristically "capitalist" because that term is embedded in a conceptual framework of economic determinism, claiming uniquely high saliency for economics alone.

Politics and economics are not only equally salient but also closely linked in the modern system. The close linkage between world politics and world economics has assumed the following forms: (1) World powers have had lead economies; (2) world powers have constructed the framework of the global economy. These two basic formulations of international political economy we owe initially to Francois Perroux.[5] As a corollary to (1) we might spell out another generalization: (3) Principal challengers have had large economies.

"WORLD POWER" AND "LEAD ECONOMY"

The close link between the status of world power (or world leadership) and the role of "lead economy" is well understood in relation to nineteenth-century Britain and twentieth-century United States,[6] but it merits pointing out that a similar relationship also prevailed in relation to eighteenth-century Britain, seventeenth-century Netherlands, and sixteenth-century Portugal (until its temporary absorption into Spain in 1580),—in other words, to all the nation-states described as world powers.

Table 5.3 summarizes the relevant data and allows us to generalize that in the modern world system, each world power (defined by political criteria as the leading provider of order and as the principal source of political innovations for the world system) has at the same time also been a "lead economy," an "active zone," and the locus of major contribu-

TABLE 5.3 **World Powers and Lead Economies**

Century	World Power	Leading Sector's Share of World Industrial Production[a]	Agriculture and Food	Share of World Trade[a]	Share of Foreign Investment
XVI	Portugal	Exploration and discovery, shipbuilding	Grain imported from Baltic, also France, etc.	Lisbon world market for spices, gold	(Antwerp center of finance)
XVII	Netherlands	Shipping, textiles, fisheries	Baltic grain imports	Amsterdam world trade emporium	(Amsterdam center of international lending)
XVIII	Britain I	Shipbuilding, iron, agriculture, civil engineering	Net exporter until 1770s	1720:13% 1750:13% 1780:12%	(Amsterdam center of international finance)
XIX	Britain II	Textiles, railroads, shipping 1820:24% 1870:32%	Major importer	1800:33% 1820:27% 1870:25% 1913:16%	1870ca : 60% 1914:44% (direct plus portfolio)
XX	United States	Agriculture, electronics, nuclear industries, aerospace 1926–29:42% 1968:34%	Major exporter	1948:16% 1971:13% 1978:12%	1967:54% 1976:48% (direct only)

[a] Except for 1978, taken from Rostow, *The World Economy*, pp. 52–53, 70–73.

tions to international economic exchanges. To operationalize the concept of "lead economy" we emphasize not size (as it might be indexed by area, population, or GNP) but those indicators that bear on status as "active zone": the creation of leading sectors and the relative size of the industrial economy, and participation in world trade, both qualitatively (in goods of the leading sectors) and quantitatively (in shares of world trade or of foreign investment). We also note that each lead economy has been engaged in forms of advanced agriculture; while some have been substantial importers of foodstuffs (Britain, serving as the world's chief market for food in the second part of the nineteenth century), others have been exporters (Britain in the eighteenth century until the 1770s, and the United States in the twentieth); yet all have led in the organization of intensive food production (as Portugal, in cane sugar in the islands or in fisheries). Each lead economy has also been linked to basic innovation in global services relating to transport and communication as well as information.

Upon reflection, the linkage between world power and lead economy is not really surprising. A lead economy requires the political stability and international protection afforded by the services of the quality and the dimensions afforded by the world power. Each world power has been, in its time, the area of the greatest security of rights and entitlements, and of lowest transaction costs and superior global information services, and therefore also most frequently, the economy of refuge. On the other hand, world power is also costly and cannot be maintained without the support of an active and growing economy. Operations of global reach and global wars in particular cannot be conducted on the cheap. Hence a lead economy built upon a global flow of activities becomes *a sine qua non* of world power.

We might at this point insert a note about terminology. Perroux's initial characterization of the United States after 1945 was that of a "dominant economy." Later he distinguished between dominant position (a matter of size, wealth, and power) and leadership, that is, the ability to innovate and move ahead in the common interest.[7] The term "leading economy" came into use and we employed it in an earlier publication. But "leading economy" does not appear entirely satisfactory mainly because the term places emphasis on status ("ranking first") rather than function. That is why "lead economy"[8] seems preferable because "lead" used as adjective meaning "acting as a leader" or "going in front" more directly illuminates the functions we are attempting to analyze.

THE FRAMEWORK OF INTERNATIONAL EXCHANGE

We have just alluded to the benefits the lead economy derives from the framework of stability provided by each successive world power. That framework sustains not only the lead economy but also the global economy as a whole by giving the world power a leading role in the "fixing of the rules of the game" according to which international transactions are conducted.[9]

The basic relationship is that of the world power providing, among its range of political goods/services and through its own international economic policies and its initiatives in global arrangements, the political basis for global economic relations. The early world powers tended toward the regulation of intercontinental trade by rather crude devices of direct monopoly: Portugal by banning all trade without their permission; Spain by granting monopoly rights to Seville; the Netherlands by forming two large trading companies with monopolistic trading privileges and England following suit. More recently, the relationships turned more complex. World trade unfolds within a complex of trade and tariff rules, currency and credit regulations, and investment guidelines that have lost those simple monopoly features but still retain the strong influence of and some advantages for the world power (e.g., in the matter of international reserves). The basics of today's international economic order are still shaped by the issues debated and the decisions taken by wartime and postwar negotiators of the 1940s, in which the leading part was played by the United States.[10]

"PRINCIPAL CHALLENGERS" AND SIZE

A corollary of the proposition that "each world power has had a lead economy" is the generalization that no states other than world powers have had lead economies and, more particularly, that the principal challengers could not boast of lead economies. Is there anything more we can say about the economies and economic policies of the challengers?

We have earlier described the challengers as the world powers' competitors for world leadership and identified them in table 5.1. We observe that the characterization is *ex-post* because it hinges on participation in global war (the principal challengers being those states that fought a global war and lost, the world powers being those that won) and on issues of world organization.

As we look at the list (Spain, sixteenth and seventeenth centuries; France, seventeenth and eighteenth centuries; Germany, nineteenth and twentieth centuries), we would not describe any of these states as lead economies. They were not notable as centers of commerce or finance or for innovating industrial sectors. But that is not to say that they were economically insignificant. Spain explored large parts of the Americas and at about 1600 her silver mines were the envy of the world. France's natural wealth was always striking. Germany did indeed mount serious efforts in a number of fields in the late nineteenth century (see table 5.5). But none of them could properly be called lead economies in the sense that that description could be applied, say, to the Netherlands or Britain.

Spain's economy in the seventeenth century was a showcase of disaster.

The challengers' chief characteristic was the size of their economies. They all had economies that, brought together under unified political leadership, constituted large economic aggregates. Their population was invariably larger than that of the world powers; table 5.4 shows that clearly. Their territorial domain in the metropolitan areas was also larger. Their GNP, to the degree that it can be estimated for the earlier period, was of the same order of magnitude. Given such large economies, their tax bases were also substantial and could support considerable political aspirations. In summary we can characterize the economies of the challengers as large, territorially substantial, continentally significant if not dominant, for their time economically developed but uncommitted to strong intercontinental exchanges. They proved fully capable of mobilizing resources for large land campaigns but proved less adept at sustaining operations on the ocean.

TABLE 5.4 **The Relative Size of Principal Challengers**

World Population (million)	Year	World Power	Population (m)	As Percent of World Population	Principal Challenger	Population (m)
425	1500	Portugal	1.25	0.3	Spain	6.5
545	1600	Netherlands	1.5	0.3	Spain	8.5
610	1700	Britain	9.25	1.5	France	20.0
900	1800	Britain	16.0	1.8	France	29.0
3900	1975	United States	210.0	5.4	USSR	255.0

Source: Colin McEvedy and Richard Jones, *Atlas of World Population History* (New York: Penguin, 1978).

We might also, in parenthesis, comment on the notably small populations, in world proportions, of the world powers, as revealed by table 5.4. Portugal and Netherlands at less than, and Britain at somewhat over, 1 percent of the world total seem inconsequential. Even the United States, at 5 percent, belongs in the same order of magnitude. The significance of the world powers has not been in their size but in their capacity to accomplish global functions.

We have now established the nature of the nexus binding world politics and world economics, one that is crucially mediated by the role of world leadership and the process of competition for that role. Given that nexus, we would expect fluctuations in the political process to be coupled to changes in the global economy and vice versa. What might be the mechanism of that linkage?

THE KONDRATIEFF WAVE[11]

For several decades, students of economic fluctuations have been familiar with the Kondratieff. Nikolai Kondratieff formulated the concept of "long waves in economic life" between 1919 and 1926 and published his statistical findings and his explanations in monographs in Russian, parts of which were then translated into German and English. Joseph Schumpeter undertook a major interpretation of these cycles in the 1930s,[12] and in the past decade Kondratieff's work was taken up once again by, among others, Walt Rostow.[13] Yet, despite its general familiarity, the idea continues to be treated gingerly by many analysts, in part because of uncertainty as to the exact nature of the phenomenon and the precise subject of these fluctuations—"economic life" being a rather broad concept— but also because of the lack of a convincing explanation.

Concerning the nature of what is actually subject to flux, the uncertainty seems to revolve around the question: output or prices? Schumpeter's influential interpretation suggested the up and down movements to be those of production, of gross or net product, hence also periods of prosperity or depression. These movements would be propelled by waves of entrepreneurial innovation, technology, and hence growth. This would make them in fact fluctuations in output, in overall growth rates, and in economic progress, as measured by quantities of output per head of population. Kondratieff's own analysis was ambiguous on this point. It was conducted largely in terms of prices. Indeed his strong reliance on price data attracted unfavorable comment. But Rostow's more complex interpretation of long "trend periods" combines the consideration of the rise and sequencing of leading sectors in the Schumpeterian manner as waves of innovation with an account of periods of relative abundance or scarcity of food and raw materials giving rise to long-term movements in prices.

Similar uncertainty prevails about the explanation of the phenomena under study. The Kondratieff is still widely referred to as a process that requires explaining, even if it could be described well without being understood. One principal source of ambiguity relates to war. That wars indeed play a major part in the fluctuations observed has not escaped the attention of students of these matters; but their reaction has been either one of regarding wars as exogenous variables obviously affecting the economy but not in themselves part of the explanation of the process under study or one of claiming, as did Kondratieff himself, that such wars were caused by the economic process itself: "Wars and revolutions do not come out of the clear sky.... They originate from real, especially economic circumstances ... solely during the upswing of long waves ... [hence] wars originate in the acceleration of the pace and increased tension of economic life...."[14] Kondratieff's explanation inclines toward a monocausal, economic theory of war that by itself is unconvincing.

For the present analysis, we shall adopt the price (qualitative variant) of the Kondratieff and, broadly following Rostow, shall define up and down movements in terms of relative scarcity and abundance of basic resources of food and raw materials as reflected in price movements and appropriate changes in income distribution. Our periodization (as shown in table 5.5) corresponds broadly with Kondratieff's: His highs, starting *ca.* 1790, 1844–5, and 1891, correspond to ours at 1792, 1848 and 1914; and his lows, starting 1810–17, 1870–75, and 1914–20, match ours at 1815 and 1873. The only real divergence in this concept of long-term price movements of 30 years' length on the average concerns the period of the two world wars in the twentieth century. We see it decisively shaped by global warfare and the attendant scarcities.[15] This last comment points to the direction our analysis is taking: toward uncovering the mechanism governing the interplay of the global political and economic processes.

A SINGLE LOGIC FOR THE POLITICO-ECONOMIC PROCESS

Assuming, then, a world system in which the global polity and the global economy are doubly linked, and in which both are growing strongly, propelled by a stream of innovations, we might envisage that growth to occur in one of two ways: (1) by both politics and economics growing *jointly* and simultaneously, each such period of strong growth being followed by a period of lesser expansion in both, because no growth continues forever at the same rate; *or* (2) by *alternating* periods of expansion in the polity with periods of growth in the economy.

We assume these two structures of the world system to be related because they both draw on the same population and on the same global (hence, at any given point, finite) base of resources. The more goes for economic growth, the less is left for other social purposes. The more politics consumes by way of attention and resources, the less can be invested in wealth creation. These statements are, of course, subject to the general constraint that every social system absorbs (or requires) some minimum commitment to both politics and economics.

Assuming the complexity and the coordinating capacity of the world system to be high, and to be rising, we may perhaps envisage the first (i.e., joint) option to be more likely. Indeed we might want to specify the conditions and requirements needed for that option to be workable. But of the two alternatives, the second, the alternating model, appears to be simpler and thus more probable. For if we assume the stuctures of politics, and of economics, to be relatively autonomous, closed systems, hence separated by some boundaries, then the second option will require a lesser degree of intersectoral coordination than the first. In fact an alternation of periods of high-saliency politics with those of high-saliency economics would seem to offer an automatic manner of self-regulation, politics coming into play to deal with problems created by economics, or those economic progress has left unresolved and economics, in its turn, attending to the social system laid to waste by periods of excessive devotion to politics.

Given, then, a pattern of alternation, what may be regarded as the mechanism that brings this about, that is coordinating and synchronizing the movements both of politics and of economics? It might be suggested that the coordinating mechanism is the value system conceived in a broad fashion. The value system monitors, reflects, and adjusts the social priorities; and the price system as a whole reflects not just the state of particular markets but also the value judgments of the whole society. Thus the price system becomes one proxy for the value system, though by no means the only one or even the most important. But in a world system that assigns low saliency to culture at the global level, the value system will not function well and might indeed suffer from distortion, and in such case the price system might assume disproportionate significance, jointly with its political counterpart, the political-ideological priority system as expressed in demand for the political goods/services of order and justice.

It could be, therefore, that both global politics and global economics "listen to the same drummer": coordinated by the same value-price-priority system, both being affected by, and both responding to, the same movements in social valuations. When the demand for political goods/services (e.g., guns) and for particular political innovations rises, the scarcity of resources (including food and butter) will increase and the general price level is likely to rise. But then as the demand for guns goes down we would expect that to reduce pressures of an inflationary kind. For those reasons we must anticipate the demand for basic resources, hence also the general price level, to move in the same manner as the demand for political goods/services of world order. More broadly still, we would expect periods of high-saliency politics to be periods when attempts are made to improve the operations of politics through major innovation and the launching and establishing of new political industries.

The actual length of these phases is not immediately obvious but must have some relationship to the time needed to complete a political project of world proportions or to conceive, or to launch and consolidate, a leading sector. The relative length of these two major phases to each other may, in some sense yet to be clarified, reflect the respective strengths of politics and economics in the world system. But the requirements of rebalancing, of solving problems left unsolved in the previous phase, might in fact conduce to giving these structures a rough equality and the two phases comparable length.

But if we look beyond a mere alternation of periods of innovation we would also expect some additional longer-term "structure" to the system;

at the next higher level of complexity this could take the form, in every second "up" phase of global politics, of an extra strong upbeat: a major political overhaul. In the past this has been a global war, creating a new, however imperfect, world order. At that moment politics would be the stronger beat than economics, thus giving a century-long framework to world history and making the whole into a yet more complex and intricate pattern of instability.

This "alternating innovations" model of the long cycle in the modern world system therefore predicts the following:

1. Alternating, generation-long periods of resource scarcity and resource abundance, reflected in prices for food and raw materials and in the distribution of income;
2. Waves of political problems, and innovations, to coincide with periods of resource scarcities, and bringing the reordering of political structures and the rise of new regimes, states, and international organizations;
3. Economic innovations to move to fruition in "down" periods of relative abundance, finding embodiment in new leading sectors;
4. Some preponderance of political processes becoming evident in the fundamental changes associated with each second political "up" phase, leading to the establishment of a new world power.

ANALYSIS

Some reasonable evidence for the testing of these propositions is available for the period after 1763, that is, for the over two centuries since the onset of the Industrial Revolution (table 5.5).

1. Rostow's work[16] is our basic source for the trend periods of resource scarcities and abundance. He draws attention to several price revolutions, in particular those of 1799–1801, 1898–1900, and 1972–76, each of which inaugurated a period of food and raw material shortages and high prices. The prominent political transformations and the political "growth" industries they tend to create (new states, international organization, military-industrial complexes) correspond strikingly and almost without major exceptions to these "up" phases of the resource-price cycle. The only exception, as we look at table 5.5, seems to be the American Revolution, though the major impact of it made itself felt somewhat later, through the French Revolution. It will be noticed that the great periods of high demand for world order, and hence of political innovations, are also periods of major warfare and revolutionary upheaval.

2. The rise of leading sectors matches unexpectedly well the "down" periods of resource abundance and moderating prices. The industrial sec-

TABLE 5.5 **Alternating Waves of Innovation 1763–1980**

Political Innovations	Long Cycle Phases (Price trends)	Leading Industrial Sectors[a] (in maximum rate of expansion)
American Revolution	Deconcentration 1763–92 (stable)	Cotton textiles: Britain 1780s
Britain as world power French Revolution Vienna Congress Concert of Europe Latin American Independence	Global War 1792–1815 (up)	
	World Power 1815–48 (down)	Railroads: Britain 1830s
Revolutions of 1848 Italian and German unification Russia checked (Crimean War)	Delegitimation 1848–73 (up)	
	Deconcentration 1873–1913 (down)	Steel: Britain, France, Germany, U.S., 1870s Sulphuric acid: Britain, Germany, U.S. 1870s Electricity: U.S. 1880s Motor vehicles: Britain, France, Germany, U.S., 1900–10
U.S. as world power Russian and Chinese revolutions Nuclear weapons United Nations Indian Independence 1947	Global War 1914–46 (up)	Plastics: U.S. 1940–45
	World Power 1946–73 (stable)	Synthetics: U.S. 1950–55 Electronics, aerospace, travel, education, health: U.S. 1960s
SALT OPEC	Delegitimation 1973– (up)	

[a] Based on Rostow's *The World Economy*, pp. 379, 393, 400, 408, indicating the country (or countries) first in the expansion of that sector.

tors listed are those first showing the maximum rate of expansion in the decade shown, in the country (or countries) named for each sector. We have already noted that leading sectors may invariably be found to have risen first in the lead economies of the world powers: Cotton textiles, pig iron, and railroads were the harbingers of Britain's industrial Revolution; the bunching of industrial innovation in the 1873–1913 period still shows Britain's role to be strong in three out of four leading sectors of that period, but in one of these the role of leadership now has to be shared in steel, chemicals, and motors with two or three rivals. The structure of leading sectors thus exemplifies and corresponds to the parallel and ongoing change in global political structure of that time, best described as a process of "deconcentration" whereby the global economy too was becoming "multipolar." The U.S. rise to world power by 1945 is evidenced by U.S. leadership in a number of key industrial sectors and in particular in nuclear technology, computers, and air and space activities.[17]

3. The most important political upheavels, though, attend the periods of global war spaced out over a century apart and associated with the rise both of a world power and lead economy and a new international economic order. The world power, the solution arising out of these global wars, is in itself the embodiment of a major political innovation. The global wars form the major pulse of the world system, while the in-between "up" periods serve the function of mid-course correction. The political and economic fluctuations thus appear as movements of one system.

In sum, the predictions are confirmed by the evidence before us. Our analysis covers the period since the onset of the Industrial Revolution and applies to the entire "industrial" era of the modern world system. It does not cover the earlier "mercantile" era of about two and a half centuries since 1500, in part because comparable and satisfactory data is not now available.[18] The distinction between the mercantile and industrial eras of the modern world system, with a dividing point in the mid-eighteenth century, nevertheless remains convenient and possibly important. In the first period, the focus of innovative activity was in commerce, especially water-borne and oceanic; in the second, the locus of economic change shifted to industry, to its products and its raw materials, more often carried overland.[19]

Our model, moreover, gives us a single logic by which both the global political and global economic processes may be understood. In terms of Chase-Dunn's argument,[20] we have come out on the side of a unified conception and have offered a seemingly promising avenue for the explanation of the mutual interlocking of these processes.[21] By contrast with his analysis, however, we maintain the relative autonomy of politics and economics and do not regard the economy as the basic determinant.[22]

IMPLICATIONS FOR U.S. INTERNATIONAL POLICY

We hope that our analysis has shown that long cycles of world leadership provide a comprehensive framework for the consideration of the strategy of U.S. international economic policy. This framework combines on equal terms an empirically grounded theory of world politics with full attention to fluctuations of economic progress; its salient characteristics also include a determination to eschew abstract analyses in the neoclassical mode, including those customarily applied to state systems, and to anchor this investigation in a concrete framework of time and space bounded by the modern world system. If we are right in thinking so, then the consideration of international economic policy needs to be based not merely on economic theory but rather on politico-economic analysis of just this kind, for that alone is capable of handling in an explicit manner the interplay of world politics and world economics.

The following are some of the implications of this analysis for U.S. international policy:

1. The relevant experience is not just that of the United States, especially since 1945, but that of the earlier world powers and their "lead economies." That experience shows that world powers and lead economies have been the truly active elements of the modern world system and that world powers and lead economies have been invariably linked by a strong mutual bond: the Perroux linkages. While the world power gives form and shape to the international economic order, the lead economy gives substance to global economic relations. The evidence also demonstrates that the status of world power and of lead economy is impermanent and is subject to erosion.

2. Much attention was aroused in recent years over the decline in the size of the American economy as measured by GNP figures. In the world total the share of the U.S. fell from close to 50 percent in 1950 to 25 percent or less in the past decade. Our analysis suggests that the sheer size of the economy is not a reliable guide to the performance of world leadership. All previous world powers had sizable but not overwhelming economies. Given their limited population base, this could not have been otherwise. The extraordinary and unprecedented U.S. superiority in the years immediately following World War II could not be maintained because it derived from transitory, war-induced disruptions in both Europe and Asia.

3. The real question is, Will the United States remain a lead economy? Will it remain a zone of rapid investment, high innovation, growth of leading sectors? On that score the verdict is still open; if our analysis is correct, not before a time well into the next phase of the long cycle shall

we be able to say conclusively what other active zones have made their mark on the global economy and whether their impact is likely to be lasting, significant, and competitive. Of course, we can have our guesses. Will the information revolution, if that is to be the leading sector of the next few decades, remain centered in the United States? Or are there other fields about to be explored, in the United States or elsewhere?

4. If long-cycle analysis is valid, then the sources of experience for the decades of the 1980s and '90s are earlier mid-cycle phases of economic and political instability that we have called those of delegitimation. In the nineteenth century this was the period of revolutions and wars between 1848 and 1873; in the first British cycle, the time of wars between 1740 and 1763. If we accept this comparison, then by implication we are rejecting the "1914 analogy" (the argument that the present era bears resemblance to the pre-World War I period, one of imminence of global war[23]) that has recently gained some acceptance. We have even less use for the "Munich analogy" that has been influential for a number of years.

5. If the present phase is one of delegitimation, then its central characteristic is a crisis of legitimacy arising out of the waning of the leadership of the United States, now exposed to the blasts of rekindled nationalisms. This crisis of world order takes the form, as it has in times past, of, *inter alia*, a period of global scarcities. We have had earlier experience of them and may recognize them for what they are, crises of expectations and crises of confidence, hence tests of a political system unable to meet them and of a culture unable to restrain them. They are placing some limits on hopes of unbounded growth so current only a few years ago. But they need to be met principally as political and moral phenomena.

6. If our politico-economic model is valid, it points to the conclusion that this is the period in which strategic emphasis needs to be placed on political innovation. Periods of delegitimation have in the experience of past long cycles been periods of opportunity for successful and lasting political innovation. They were periods of mid-course correction, during which the ground was broken and the seeds were sown that predetermined the course of the subsequent struggles for world leadership and the path to global war. But the complexity of problems likely to arise in the coming decades stems also from the fact that we may now be approaching the end of the era of the modern world system (or the industrial segment of it) and entering a period of transformations in which the primary source of needed innovation is likely to be cultural. Momentous choices are ahead of us; may they at least be recognized for what they are.

NOTES

1. Substantially based on material presented in a paper read to the colloquium on "Les formes actuelles de la concurrence dans les echanges internationaux," Paris, 10–14 March 1980; and overlaps material appearing in The *Sage International Yearbook of Foreign Policy Studies*, vol. 6 (1981). Revised September 1980, August 1981.

2. For the theory of long cycles, see George Modelski, "The Long Cycle of Global Politics and the Nation-State," *Comparative Studies in Society and History* 20, no. 2 (April 1978): 214–35; and "The Theory of Long Cycles and U.S. Strategic Policy," in *American Security Policy and Policy-making*, ed. Robert Harkavy and Edward A. Kolodziej (Lexington, Mass.: Lexington Books, 1980), pp. 3–21; as viewed in the context of a structural analysis of the modern world system, see George Modelski, "World Politics and Sustainable Growth," in *Quest for a Sustainable Society*, ed. James C. Coomer (New York: Pergamon, 1981), pp. 145–63.

3. We are employing a conceptual framework based on the leading position in the modern world of certain *nation-states*. An alternative conception (Fernand Braudel, *Le Temps du Monde* [Paris: Armand Colin, 1979], p. 17 ff.) sees that world fashioned by a succession of "dominant capitalist cities": Venice, Antwerp, Genoa, Amsterdam, and London. It is hard to see how the role of such cities as Amsterdam or London can be seen in abstraction from the nation-states of which they formed a part, or that of Antwerp or Genoa in isolation from the Hapsburg political system.

4. See Modelski, "World Politics and Sustainable Growth."

5. "Outline of a Theory of the Dominant Economy," translated in *Transnational Corporations and World Order*, ed. G. Modelski (San Francisco: W. H. Freeman, 1979), pp. 135–54.

6. Ibid.; also Perroux, "Le progres economique," *Economies et Societes*, no. 21 (July–August 1967): 3–170.

7. F. Perroux, "L' economie des Etats-Unis: un 'Leadership' difficile," *Tiers Monde*, no. 370 (October–December 1963): 539–57.

8. Compare Talcott Parsons' use of "new lead society" for the United States in *The System of Modern Societies* (Englewood Cliffs, N.J.: Prentice-Hall, 1971), p. 86.

9. Perroux, "Outline of a Theory"; and Charles Kindleberger, "Systems of International Economic Organizations," in *Money and the Coming World Order*, ed. D. Calleo (New York: New York University Press, 1976), pp. 15–39.

10. As graphically depicted in Richard N. Gardner, *Sterling-Dollar Diplomacy: The Origins and the Prospects of our International Economic Order* (New York: McGraw-Hill, new ed., 1969).

11. A full bibliography of Kondratieff's writings may be found in George Garvy, "Kondratieff's Theory of Long Cycles," *Review of Economic Statistics* 25, no. 4 (November 1943): 203–20; cf. also the present author's discussion in the Appendix to "Explanations of the Long Cycle," presented to the meeting of the Peace Science Society (International) West, Stanford, Calif., February 1978.

12. In his *Business Cycles* (New York: McGraw-Hill, 1938), 2 vols.

13. W. W. Rostow, *The World Economy: History and Prospect* (Austin: University of Texas Press, 1978).

14. N. D. Kondratieff, "The Long Waves in Economic Life," *Review of Economic Statistics* 17, no. 6 (November 1935): 105–15.

15. A recent study of English and American price trends and their relationship to major wars since 1750 finds that it is "equally difficult to contend that price waves cause major wars or that major wars cause long price waves." W. R. Thompson and L. G. Zuk, "War, Inflation, and the Kondratieff Long Wave" (Florida State University, mimeo, 1981).

16. See *The World Economy*. We diverge from Rostow's account in the same way as we do from Kondratieff's periodization in that we regard the entire period from 1913 to 1945 as one long "up" phase, one basically of two world wars with a peace period in between, instead of a composite of three shorter trend periods.

17. For the political impact of new leading sectors, see James R. Kurth, "The Political Consequences of the Product Cycle: Industrial History and Political Outcomes," *International Organization* 33, no. 1 (Winter 1979): 1–35.

18. On the possibility of Kondratieffs in the preindustrial era, cf. Braudel, *Le Temps du Monde*, pp. 577, 64–65.

19. We leave open, at this point, the question of what might explain the transition from the mercantile to the industrial age. One possibility is that both these are phases of one strongly exponential process of growth that was set in motion at the creation of the modern world system and that could now be flattening out. Cf. Modelski, "World Politics and Sustainable Growth."

20. Christopher Chase-Dunn, "Interstate System and Capitalist World-Economy: One Logic or Two?" *International Studies Quarterly* 25, no. 1 (March 1981): 19–42.

21. In their study of the Kondratieff, Thompson & Zuk ("War, Inflation, and the Kondratieff") also find the hypothesis of a single underlying process attractive.

22. Some additional reinforcement of our conclusions is provided by recent work on analytical models of the long cycle. See G. Modelski and W. R. Thompson, "Testing Cobweb Models of the Long Cycle of World Leadership" (paper presented at the North American meeting of Peace Science Society [International], Philadelphia,, November 1981). A cobweb model predicts, for a production-exchange network characterized by substantial response lags, an alternation of periods of surplus (hence low prices) and shortfall (hence high prices). The availability of world order might be characterized by such response lags and consequent long-term swings; and there is evidence for suggesting that, in the period covered by our politico-economic analysis, phases of world order surplus alternated with those of shortage in much the same way and in the same time-frames as those of resource abundance and scarcity. It would, therefore, appear possible that periods of high prices generally are also those of world order shortfall (i.e., times when the political order is at a premium), and vice versa.

23. Miles Kahler, "Rumors of War: The 1914 Analogy," *Foreign Afairs* 58, no. 2 (Winter 1979–80): 374–96.

PART II

National Perspectives: Organization, Process, and Policy Content

6

Three Political Explanations for Crisis in the World Grain Market

Robert Paarlberg

During the past decade, the world grain market[1] has seemingly become more prone to rapid transformation, and simultaneously more prone to acute crisis. In 1972 the condition of that market was suddenly altered, from abundance to scarcity. In the two years that followed, grain prices tripled, food aid shipments were reduced, access to some markets was denied, many suffered while few prospered, and policy makers in rich and poor nations alike scrambled to adjust. Three years in a row of very good weather, between 1976 and 1978, then helped rebuild depleted grain stocks worldwide, but prices continued to fluctuate, up and down, by as much as 40 percent. Negotiations to create an international grain reserve collapsed early in 1979, just as bad weather was returning. Two poor world harvests, in 1979 and 1980, then brought carryover stocks all the way back down to earlier noted low levels. Simultaneously, dramatic shifts in trade occurred, as the world's most important grain exporting nation, the United States, sought to impose a grain embargo upon the world's most important grain-importing nation, the Soviet Union.

Some of this disruption in the world's grain markets may be attributed to factors unrelated to politics. In 1972, abnormally bad weather had caused a 3.7 percent reduction in worldwide per capita food production, the largest such decline in the last thirty years. Purely economic factors, such as growing demand for meat products, spurred by rising incomes throughout the world, played a role as well. The market changes noted since 1972 have been so discontinuous, however, as to suggest more than cumulative economic forces at work. Moreover, the return of very good weather in 1976–78 did not suffice to return the world grain market to its earlier condition of well-stocked security. Part of the continuing crisis in world grain markets since 1972 must be attributed to nonmarket forces, and to forces other than fluctuations in the weather. It will be argued here that political forces, broadly defined,[2] have long held sway over the shape and condition of the world grain market and that crisis and change in the world grain market of today is largely an artifact of politics.

Economists concede that recent changes in the world grain trade have been heavily determined by politics.[3] Bad weather reduced world harvests in 1972, but much of the price increase, the depletion of reserves, and the reduction in food aid that followed may be traced more directly to political decisions, some unforeseen, that were taken in reaction to the bad harvest. Taking a larger view, the structure of the market into which scarcity was suddenly introduced in 1972—the number of buyers and sellers, and the market share of each—was itself a product of politics, a product of concerted and continuous action, usually by national governments on behalf of powerful producer interests, to rig the market to an individual or collective advantage. Evidence for the underlying role that political intervention plays in the world market is found, most clearly, in those national and regional grain trade policies that distort world patterns of pricing and production. It is not uncommon, in this regard, to find national import restrictions that guarantee prices to inefficient producers at twice the level of import costs. Nor is it unusual to find surplus grain production dumped onto the world market through the use of export subsidies that often exceed the world price to which they are being added.[4] The decisive role of politics is also suggested by the prominence of national governments as buyers and sellers in the world grain market. Of the forty nations that account for three-fourths of world grain imports, twenty-four enforce state trading monopolies.[5] An alternative form of transnational political influence might be found in the apparent oligopoly power of the five private grain trading firms that handle more than half of total world exports.

We must do more than assert that crisis and change in the world grain market have a probable political cause. Since we have defined politics in the broadest sense possible, the range of possible causation, even within the realm of politics, remains impossibly broad. As a first step toward narrowing that range of possible causation, distinctions between the kinds of political actors that might shape the world grain market must be drawn, and the political logic behind their action must be described.

In the abstract, at least two different categories of political actors might emerge as influential in the process of shaping grain markets: nation-state and nonstate actors.[6] Of these two, nation-states must be further considered as to the logic behind their action. Introducing two different levels of analysis, nation-state action might be viewed as determined either at the unit level or the international system level.[7] Combining these actor distinctions and levels of analysis, three very different kinds of political explanation emerge. A *transnational* explanation would attribute crisis and change in the grain market to nonstate action. Emphasis would be placed upon the behavior of private grain trading firms. An *international* explanation would attribute the same result to state actions that are governed in turn by power relations within the international system. Crisis and change within world grain markets would be explained by the abscence of a hegemonic leader within that international system. Finally, a *national* political explanation would attribute crisis and change in the world grain market to state actions that are undertaken without reference to the international system. Emphasis would be placed upon the balance of political power and political interests within states rather than among states. What follows is a review of these three contending political explanations for crisis in the world grain market since 1972, and a critique of the value of each.

CRISIS IN THE WORLD GRAIN MARKET

Seldom, in peacetime, has the world grain market experienced such disruption as in the years since 1972. Below is a summary of changes occurring in 1972 and of instabilities experienced since 1972, both of which require explanation.

Throughout a remarkable twenty-year period prior to 1972, the international grain trading system was marked by stable growth at steadily falling real prices. Between 1955 and 1972, despite inflation, the world export price of wheat remained virtually unchanged, fluctuating by only 2 or 3 percent, around $60 per metric ton.[8] This steady and attractive price trend encouraged an ever-increasing utilization of the world market. Over the 1960–70 decade, world trade in grain grew by 56 percent, roughly twice the rate of growth of world production.[9] Growth in commercial sales during this era of stability was accompanied by growth in concessional sales as well. Throughout the 1950s and '60s, abundant food aid was available to those nations not prepared to pay market price. U.S. food aid shipments under PL 480 Title I, for example, increased from 8.2 million metric tons (MMT) in 1960 to 13.7 MMT by 1965, and remained at 5.8 MMT in 1970.[10]

This era of steady market expansion, stable and moderating prices, and the ready availability of concessional food aid came to an end in 1972. In that year alone, the volume of world grain exports increased by 27.5 percent, a one-year increase equal in quantity to the total increase registered over the previous ten years.[11] At the same time, average grain export prices nearly tripled, and food aid was sharply curtailed. Title I U.S. food aid shipments decreased from 5.8 MMT in 1970 to 4.6 MMT in 1972, to 2.5 MMT in 1973, and to a mere 1.3 MMT by 1974. After 1975, despite a three-year interlude of very good weather, the world grain market never recovered from the destabilization that occurred in 1972. Throughout the 1970s, average variation from trend in worldwide grain consumption remained twice the level of the previous decade. Over the 1974–80 period, world prices for wheat and corn first fell by as much as 30 percent, then rose by as much as 60 percent. By 1980, fears of insecurity returned, as world carryover stocks of grain were again projected at only 11 percent of utilization, the same low level that prevailed during the most serious crisis period, 1973–75.[12]

Political action, broadly defined, may be held responsible for much of the dramatic destabilization of world grain markets since 1972. As will be seen, however, some varieties of political action were far more directly responsible than others. Consider three very different political explanations for crisis in world grain markets, the evidence for each, and the deficiencies of each.

AN INTERNATIONAL POLITICAL EXPLANATION FOR CRISIS IN WORLD GRAIN MARKETS: EROSION OF U.S. HEGEMONY

To begin at the highest level of political analysis, it may be that power relations within the international system have introduced disruptions into the world grain market. The earlier period of secure and stable market growth was perhaps made possible by a concentration of international power in the hands of a hegemonic leader, the United States. The more recent period of insecurity and instability might be attributable to an erosion of that hegemony. At this systemic level of explanation, stable growth of the world's grain market is viewed as an international collective good,[13] preserved for all by the United States, at the peak of its power during the postwar era. The United States, accepting the burdens of global leadership, acquired and managed a large and expensive grain reserve, thereby stabilizing world prices while providing a constantly available source of concessional food aid. Meanwhile, the United States ensured reliability of world markets by placing no restriction upon commercial free world access to its very large grain supplies.

There is much to commend this emphasis upon a "leadership" role assumed by the United States in world grain markets prior to 1972. Large U.S. grain reserves did ensure price stability in the commercial market, as well as a steady flow of concessional sales. During the 1960s, when beginning stocks of wheat held by exporting nations were large (averaging 64 percent of annual total use), major fluctuations in production were accompanied by little or no fluctuation in world export prices. When these stocks were depleted (they had fallen to 47 percent of total use by 1972–73, and to only 28 percent of total use by 1973–74), normal fluctuations in world production were suddenly accompanied by very large fluctuations in price.[14] Prior to 1972, the United States had indeed carried the largest burden of holding and managing these critical surplus stocks of grain. In 1961, 65 percent of total world carryover grain stocks were held by the U.S. government.[15] Among exporting nations alone,[16] the United

States, together with Canada, held well over 90 percent of all surplus stocks of wheat and coarse grain during the 1960s.[17]

In food aid as well, the United States played by far the largest role. Of the $11 billion worth of food aid provided between 1965 and 1972, 80 percent came from the United States.[18] Finally, the U.S. refusal to place its commercial grain exports under any restriction (no export taxes, no government marketing board, no bilateral trade agreements giving one customer priority over another) did ensure that a very large "free supply" of grain would always be available on the world market, a further aid to price stability. This access guarantee encouraged inefficient grain producers to rely with greater confidence upon the world market as a source of imports, and thus to forego wasteful and expensive efforts to become self-sufficient in grain supplies.

According to the logic of international relations, it is argued that the United States had strong incentives, prior to 1972, to promote security and stability in the world grain market.[19] First, as a preponderant power within that market, as the largest single exporter, the United States knew that it would be the first to benefit from stable growth. Second, as a preponderant economic power beyond the grain trade, the United States stood to gain elsewhere, in its manufactured trade and in its investment relations, by the promotion of stable and secure trade expansion anywhere.[20] What is more, effective pursuit of hegemonic security objectives required the availability of food aid for shipment to free world client states in Asia, Africa, and Latin America. Likewise, among industrial states, effective leadership required forbearance from retaliation when faced with grain export competition from Canada or Australia, or with the heavily protectionist grain trading policies pursued by the EEC and Japan.

One characteristic of hegemonic leadership is the indulgence, on the part of the leader, of "free riding" policies by less powerful participants in the system. It is true that the United States, at times, did permit such an advantage to be taken by its less powerful junior partners. Smaller grain exporters, such as Canada, Australia, and Argentina, were seen at times promoting their grain exports through national marketing boards, pricing those exports advantageously in relation to the open market prices that prevailed in the United States, and also entering into bilateral agreements that stabilized their exports at the expense of U.S. trade. All the while, the United States shunned these same tactics, refusing to enter bilateral agreements or establish a state trading monopoly over its own much larger grain supplies, knowing that to do so would divide and perhaps close the market for all.[21] A still larger sacrifice was made to grain producers in the EEC. The United States permitted the EEC to subsidize its own much less efficient grain producers, to protect those producers from U.S. exports, and even to dump some of the resulting surplus production onto the world market in direct competition with U.S. grain. It is argued that the United States tolerated these elements of the European Common Agricultural Policy (CAP) in deference to a larger hegemonic interest in industrial trade and expansion, and cold-war security interests in European integration and prosperity. To this end, the United States even went so far as to encourage the entry of additional grain importing nations, such as Great Britain, into the EEC.

Just as U.S. hegemonic leadership is offered as one means to explain grain market stability prior to 1972, instability in the market since 1972 might be linked to changes in U.S. policy following a partial loss of hegemony in the international system. To the present day, of course, the United States remains the largest and most competitive exporter of grain, so in a very narrow sense it has lost none of its hegemonic power or incentive to promote the stable expansion of grain markets. But beyond the grain market, the American position in the world economy as a whole, and the power of the United States to pursue global security objectives, had both come under strain by 1972. It is this larger erosion of U.S. global hegemony that conceivably has weakened the ability and the inclination of the United States to continue to perform its vital market-stabilizing tasks. Perhaps grain market stability was still desirable, but it could no longer be maintained, by the United States alone, at acceptable cost to larger international interests. In a weakened condition overall, the United States was now tempted to seek a different sort of advantage from its continuing strength in the world grain market. Self-serving policies designed to maximize short-run gains for the United States replaced self-sacrificing policies geared to preserve long-run advantages for all.

International weakness along several critical dimensions required that the United States now pursue self-serving, short-run policies that eventually destabilized world grain markets. First, as the U.S. trade balance began to slip into deficit after 1970, foreign economic policy makers began to feel that they could no longer afford to sacrifice any short term grain sale opportunity, whatever the consequence for U.S. grain reserve levels, long-run price stability, or the continued availability of food aid to needy nations. A concurrent U.S. retreat from the burdens of free world alliance leadership reinforced this new attitude. Commercial grain exports could now be promoted, and food aid could be withdrawn, with less concern for the possible damage done to third world clients or industrial allies. Finally, due to its loss of strategic superiority in nuclear weapons, the United States could no longer afford to delay an accommodation with its cold-war rival, the Soviet Union. Thus, the United States found itself tempted to use large credit sales of grain to Russia as a means to improve the terms of this East-West accommodation, and also to gain Soviet assistance in its withdrawal from Vietnam.

At a systemic level of explanation, this might be why the United States abandoned its long-standing policy of market stabilization when the USSR entered the world market to buy grain in 1972. Instead of managing the market scarcities of that year by carefully releasing its valuable surplus stocks to established customers on equitable commercial terms, or to needy customers on concessional terms, the United States jolted the world market in 1972 by suddenly disposing of very large quantities of grain (selling no less than one-half its total carryover stocks of wheat, plus additional stocks of corn), on credit and under subsidy, to the USSR.[22]

According to this first mode of explanation, the fateful sale of U.S. grain stocks to Russia in 1972 was not just a colossal, inexplicable bureaucratic mistake. Instead, its logic is traced to profound patterns of change underway throughout the international system at the time. As Emma Rothschild observed,

> The reserves and food aid policies of the Nixon Administration can be seen, in retrospect, as part of a wider vision. U.S. policy, in the early 1970's, called for a retreat from the arduous costs of world power in economic policy as well as for policies more generally. And the U.S., albeit to its own profit, had borne a more than proportionate share of the costs of keeping world prices stable and paying for food aid to the poorest countries. The resolve of the U.S. government to dispose of its grain reserves was comparable, in this sense, to its resolve after August 1971 to limit the role of the dollar in the international monetary system.[23]

The liquidation of its grain reserves was not the only retreat from systemic leadership taken by the United States in 1972. Following the Soviet grain sale, the United States delayed until early in the next year the return of its idled cropland to full production. Indeed, wheat "set asides" were actually increased in July 1972, from 20 to 25 million acres, a decision that would delay the rebuilding of stocks during the 1973 crop year.[24] Nor was open access to the U.S. market any longer guaranteed. During the scramble for depleted stocks of food that followed the Russian sale of 1972, the United States requested on one occasion that its regular customers in Europe and Japan reduce their purchase of corn in the U.S. market by 10 percent;[25] and in 1973, soybean exports to all customers were briefly suspended. On two occasions, in 1974 and again in 1975, grain sales to the USSR were unilaterally suspended, and access to U.S. grain supplies became, more than ever before, a matter for political negotiation. Bilateral grain trade agreements were signed between the United States and the USSR, the EEC, Japan, Poland, Taiwan, Romania, and Israel. Rather than offering open access to its own domestic grain supplies, thereby stabilizing the world market, the United States thought more, now, about stabilizing its own export trade through use of bilateral agreements, which can have a tendency to destabilize all portions of the market not covered by such agreements.

This retreat from earlier habits of bearing leadership burdens in the world grain system was also sharply revealed in the diminished volume of

U.S. food aid shipments after 1972. By 1974, when the need for food aid was at an all-time high, U.S. shipments of Title I PL 480 commodities were at an all-time low—less than one-third the 1972 level. At the depth of the world food crisis, in November 1974, President Ford refused to provide assurances that food aid shipments would increase, despite a plea that he do so from the U.S. delegation to the World Food Conference in Rome.

This seeming U.S. reluctance to perform leadership tasks in the world grain market persists to the present day. U.S. grain reserves were rebuilt somewhat during the three years of very good weather (1976–78) that followed the deep crisis of the early 1970s, but only to the point that would provide some stability for the U.S. market alone. Having reached this point, with world stocks still very low in relation to use, the United States began to remove ever larger shares of its cropland from production rather than accumulate a larger surplus. Multilateral grain reserve negotiations collapsed in 1979, amid complaints from U.S. representatives that responsibility should be shared, and that the United States "will not be interested in any schemes in which the U.S. would end up making all of the effort." U.S. Secretary of Agriculture Bob Bergland then announced that the United States would use "whatever device needed to maintain our market share of world wheat trade. We are re-examining the possibility of export subsidies." In 1980, in addition to consumating yet another bilateral purchase and supply agreement (with China), the United States also entered into an unprecedented government-controlled marketing arrangement with Mexico.

Also in 1980, the United States set aside all reservations about using world grain markets to pursue diplomatic objectives. The 1980 partial embargo on grain exports to the Soviet Union (a use of U.S. "food power" to compensate for the growing sensation of U.S. weakness in other areas) politicized the world grain market as never before and threatened to slow the growth of trade and reduce the food efficiency and food security available to all who had earlier come to depend upon world food trade.

This seeming "retreat from leadership" did produce some of the short-term gains sought by U.S. policy makers. Sale of U.S. surplus stocks helped to double the volume of U.S. grain exports between 1971 and 1975. With the U.S. surplus gone, and with the rebuilding of that surplus delayed, export prices soared. As a result, annual U.S. export earnings from agriculture grew from $7.7 billion in 1971 to $21.3 billion in 1975.[26] A related step in the U.S. retreat from world leadership assisted in boosting these export earnings from agriculture: the dollar devaluations of 1971 and 1973, which made U.S. farm exports more attractive to foreign customers than ever before. Large grain sales to the USSR in 1972, and again in 1975, are also alleged to have made possible some short-term diplomatic gains including Soviet cooperation in the search for a cease-fire in Indochina and Soviet willingness to stand aside during

Secretary of State Kissinger's successful effort at shuttle diplomacy in the Middle East.[27]

These gains would be balanced, however, by the damage to U.S. interests that would surely follow from instabilities in the now "leaderless" world grain market. It was specifically damaging to the United States to witness some tendencies toward market closure that seemed to emerge following the loss of price stability and the termination of market access guarantees.[28] By 1976, it was noted that many wealthy food-importing countries had initiated policies designed to "reduce their dependence upon imported food, and specifically upon American grain."[29] The Japanese, for example, endorsed a plan to reduce the rate of growth of their very large feedstuff imports by almost 40 percent, to diversify imports of corn and soybeans away from the United States, and even to re-substitute rice for bread in school lunch diets.[30] In less developed regions as well, efforts to reduce reliance upon the world grain market were discussed in Mexico, Peru, Sri Lanka, and Malaysia, as well as in almost all OPEC countries.[31] These projects might not show results for some time. But in the end, without a hegemonic power such as the United States equipped and motivated to preserve stable patterns of market growth, a general retreat from food trade interdependence seemed likely. This would be a result damaging to the long-run interests of all, including the United States.

CRITIQUE OF INTERNATIONAL EXPLANATION

This international political explanation for crisis and instability in the world grain market is, in part, persuasive. It focuses attention, with much justification, upon the fateful U.S. decision to liquidate its surplus stocks of grain. In its emphasis upon the erosion of U.S. hegemony, and upon the reluctance of the Nixon administration, in the early 1970s, to continue to perform burdensome tasks of leadership in the world economy, it fits nicely with prevailing explanations for the almost concurrent destabilization of the international monetary system in 1971.

Only on second glance do the inadequacies of this mode of explanation emerge. The most serious of these is a misrepresentation of the purpose of U.S. grain policy prior to 1972. That policy was never closely tied to the pursuit of external objectives. The stabilization of the world grain market made possible by U.S. policy prior to 1972 was mostly an unintended effect of that policy. A large grain surplus was accumulated by the United States not for the purpose of promoting stability or security in the world market but to satisfy internal political demands for high and stable farm income.[32] The domestic farm price support programs that created this large surplus had been initiated in 1933, at a time when the United States exercised no leadership, and enjoyed no hegemony to speak of, in the international arena.

Not only were the external effects of the U.S. grain surplus unintended; the surplus itself was never desired. U.S. food aid shipments, which began on a regular basis in 1954, always had as their primary purpose the disposal of this surplus. Any accompanying increase in Third World food security or cold-war military security was usually judged a fortunate but secondary outcome. Nor were the secondary effects of surplus disposal through food aid always so positive. In some instances the continuous availability of U.S. food aid retarded the development of efficient food producers in poor countries, the result being less security in the world's food system.[33] These food aid shipments were of dubious value to alliance relations as well. During the 1950s and the '60s, the U.S. State Department received complaints about its unfair wheat trading practices from Canada, Argentina, New Zealand, Denmark, Mexico, Uruguay, Australia, Burma, Italy, and Peru.[34]

Dependency [margin handwritten note]

Beyond the question of motive, the "erosion of hegemony" explanation also misrepresents the timing of important changes in U.S. grain export policy. The domestic budgetary cost of carrying large surplus stocks of grain had inspired a conspicuous U.S. retreat from "responsible" policies of international grain trade stabilization long before any larger erosion of U.S. hegemony, and certainly before 1972. Surplus disposal through food aid began on a regular basis in the 1950s, while the United States was at the peak of its power. Programs to dispose of the surplus through expanded commercial exports were initiated in the early 1960s. In 1964 the United States began to set its wheat export subsidies as high as 30 percent of export value, as a means to enlarge its share of commercial markets at the expense of smaller exporters such as Canada. This aggressive commercial export drive, undertaken in the peak years of U.S. hegemony, boosted the U.S. share of exports to important markets such as Japan, where Canada had previously outsold the United States by 2 to 1.[35] Far from allowing Canada to take a "free ride" on U.S. leadership during this period, the United States used export subsidies to push its surplus onto the market at the expense of Canada, which could not afford such expensive export promotion policies. Indeed, it was Canada that assumed a larger "leadership" role at times. Canada held grain stocks to support the price floor established by the International Wheat Agreement of 1967, for example, even after the United States had undercut that price, in July 1969, in efforts to further promote its own exports.[36]

Nor was the United States so obligingly tolerant of the grain trading policies of its European allies during this early period of supposed "leadership." Throughout the Kennedy Round of trade negotiations, completed in 1967, the United States pushed hard on the Europeans for a lowering of CAP protectionist barriers, and also for "burden sharing" in the shipment of food aid to poor countries. When the Europeans refused to grant such concessions, the Americans did not respond by carrying a larger share of the burden itself. Instead, the United States intensified its commercial export drive and began to withdraw an even-larger share of its own cropland from production, to further reduce the size and expense of its grain reserves. The time required to bring idled cropland back into full production—a year or more—made these U.S. policies only a second-best means to guarantee market stability in the event of a global production shortfall. The best means—holding adequate stocks—had in fact been abandoned as the policy of the United States long before 1972. Total U.S. carryover stocks of grain, which represented about 70 percent of annual U.S. utilization in 1960–61, had been cut all the way back to 25 percent by 1970–71. The crisis years 1972–75 did push these stocks even lower, but the U.S. leadership role in holding stocks had clearly been abandoned some time before the perceived erosion of U.S. hegemony in 1972.[37]

As further evidence against the systemic view, it deserves mention that the United States never did take a timely lead in promoting the kind of open grain trading system that should have seemed attractive, given its unchallenged hegemonic status after World War II. Despite its comparative advantage in agriculture, the U.S. placed itself in the vanguard of a postwar trade policy movement toward agricultural protection.[38] It was at the initiative of the United States, in the early 1950s, that the member nations of the GATT deliberately excluded agriculture from international negotiations to liberalize trade.[39] Instead of making early leadership efforts to open up the world grain market, in hopes of gaining most from the stable growth that would result, the United States continued to pursue domestic farm price support policies which priced U.S. grain out of the world market. Only in the 1960s, when the budgetary cost of these farm policies grew intolerable, and only when the dwindling U.S. farm population left these expensive policies more open to political attack at home, did the United States make a determined trade expansion effort abroad.[40]

The sudden release of remaining surplus grain stocks in 1972 does conform, on the U.S. side, to an international "power erosion" view of grain market destabilization. But the behavior of the USSR, the initiator of these very large purchases, cannot be so easily tied to the logic of international power relations. In previous years, when faced with bad grain harvests at home, the Soviet Union had decided to forego heavy dependence upon imports. The shift in Soviet policy that led to the very large purchases of 1972, the decision to import large quantities of grain in lieu of cutting back on livestock herds at home, conforms to no obvious international power imperative.

Finally, it must be noted that the logic of international political action would have failed to predict the continued growth of world trade in grain since the market became "leaderless" in 1972. At the beginning of the 1970s, less than 10 percent of world grain production entered international trade. Instead of slowing down in the aftermath of the 1972 destabilization of world markets, international trade in grain continued to accelerate. By 1980, 17 percent of world grain production was entering world trade.[41] Importing nations that might have been expected to turn away from a "leaderless" world market have instead permitted the cost and the volume of their annual grain imports to continue to grow. Countless grain-importing nations have recently become even more dependent upon the world market, notwithstanding the new instabilities of that market and the new unpredictability of access to that market. Despite a significant erosion of U.S. military and economic power, despite the diminished inclination of the United States to guarantee stable growth in the world grain market, despite the demonstrated willingness of the United States to pursue self-serving grain trade policies in search of its own short-run economic advantage, and now despite the use, by the United States, of food export controls as a "diplomatic weapon," the earlier trend toward increasing national participation in the world's grain market has not yet been reversed. The closure of the world grain market that might have been expected to follow from the erosion of U.S. hegemonic power has not yet taken place.

Having noted at some length these shortcomings of an international political explanation for crisis in world grain markets, it might be helpful to turn to an entirely different mode of explanation, one that rejects the dominant role of international power relations. The discussion, until now, has ignored the prominent role which nonstate actors, specifically the five largest multinational grain trading firms, continue to play in shaping the international grain market. Perhaps a superior explanation for recent crises in the grain market can be found by turning to this second realm, the realm of "transnational" political action.

A TRANSNATIONAL POLITICAL EXPLANATION FOR DESTABILIZATION OF THE WORLD GRAIN MARKET: ABUSE (AND LOSS) OF OLIGOPOLY CONTROL

A second explanation for the destabilization of the world grain market pays little or no attention to changing distributions of power, or to the waning of U.S. power, within the international state system. This second explanation concurs in the belief that concentrations of power influence trade, but here the most interesting power concentration takes the form of an oligopoly of nonstate actors, which functions apart from, and at times in defiance of, the power of nation-states. The structure of the world grain market, viewed from this second perspective, is shaped by the transnational private sector, by those who actually handle most of the world's grain transactions. Preeminent among these nonstate actors are five very large privately owned multinational grain trading firms—Cargill, Continental, Bunge, Louis-Dreyfus, and Andre.

The prominent role that these five private companies play within the world grain trade has been widely noted.[42] Together they handle 85 percent of all grain exported from the United States, a quantity equal to about one-half of the total world exports.[43] The export business they do beyond the United States, about which less is known, adds still more to their formidable position in the trade. These five firms dominate not only the U.S. grain export business but the grain trade of the Common Market as well (Cargill, in some years, has been the leading exporter of wheat from France), the Canadian barley trade, the South African maize trade, and the Argentine wheat trade.[44] The Big Five are genuinely multinational in character. Bunge, for example, has been located at various times in Holland and Argentina, and is at present operated, under the continuing ownership of the Born and Hirsh families, from Brazil and Spain.[45] According to one highly critical account of the behavior of these firms, "what 'multinational' really means is that these conglomerates cannot be policed by any one individual nation. Their billion-dollar holdings ... are too farflung across too many international borders to ever be held in check."[46]

One particularly noteworthy feature of these large multinational grain trading firms is the tradition of private ownership. To this day, the Big Five are owned and managed by just seven European and American families.[47] Private ownership permits greater secrecy than would ordinarily be tolerated in such large international trading operations, and lends much mystery to the behavior of these companies. While conducting an investigation of these trading firms, Senator Frank Church (D-Id.) complained that "no one really knows how they operate, what their profits are, what they pay in taxes, and what effect they have on our foreign policy—or much of anything else about them."[48]

We shall see that it is easy to exaggerate the oligopoly control over the world grain market—or the power over U.S. foreign policy—that these five grain trading firms enjoy. Yet it will be appropriate, in view of the recognized significance of transnational political action, to consider briefly how the destabilization of world grain markets might be attributable to the autonomous behavior of these grain trade multinationals. After all, the destabilization of the postwar international oil market has been attributed, in part, to a loss of oligopoly control on the part of seven major international petroleum firms.[49] The passage from stability to instability within the postwar grain trade might also be attributable to changing transnational power relations.

At the least, the services performed by these private grain trading firms did contribute to stable market growth prior to 1972, as they moved grain about the world at decreasing cost and with enormous efficiency, encouraging customers to rely more heavily than they might have otherwise upon the international grain trade. More difficult to understand is the manner in which these nonstate actors might have contributed to instability in the market after 1972. Most speculation in this regard has focused on the visible role played by these firms in the first large sale of U.S. grain to the Soviet Union.

It was the private grain trade, after all, that actually sold one-half of the entire U.S. wheat reserve to Soviet purchasing agents in 1972. This 1972 sale proved to be several times larger than government officials were expecting at the time they reached their export credit agreement with the Russians in early July.[50] The U.S. government did not know how much grain was being sold to the Russians until it was too late to do anything about it.[51] This 1972 Soviet grain sale also brought abundant profits to some within the private grain trade, in part because of the willingness of the U.S. Department of Agriculture to continue to pay the companies an unnecessary export subsidy, which grew automatically to match the widening gap between the low purchase price originally offered to the Russians and the much higher prices within the United States, which were one immediate result of the sale. Later on, higher export prices alone were enough to guarantee record breaking company profits, as high as 53 cents per bushel on some non-Russian sales by 1973. The apparent power of the companies to form the market in their own interest was also seen in two subsequent grain sales to the USSR, in 1974 and 1975. In October 1974 Continental and Cook Industries (a newcomer to the trade) surprised consumer interests and government officials with an unexpected sale of 3.2 MMT of wheat and corn to the Russians, a large amount in that very tight crop year. In a struggle to regain control from these private companies, the U.S. government temporarily suspended both of these export contracts and imposed a requirement for "prior approval" on any such large sales in the future. Following the relaxation of this requirement, however, in July 1975 the private trade went forward with yet another 10 MMT sale to Russia, again quite suddenly, within less than a week's time. Fearing the return of very high prices and renewed market instability, the U.S. government responded this time with a two-month embargo on further sales to the Soviets.

One impression that can emerge from these events is that of beleaguered government officials battling against private industry to gain control over U.S. grain exports—and not always winning. The ability of the private grain trade to operate beyond the control of the government, and to sell off U.S. grain reserves in hopes of stimulating higher prices, might be offered as a transnational explanation for instabilities noted in the world grain market since 1972.

Such an argument might require one additional refinement. Since it is seldom the intention of an effective oligopoly to introduce instability into its own operating environment (or to invite closer government regulation), the motive for these most disruptive private sales to the Soviet Union remains somewhat unaccounted for. At best, it might be argued that a momentary weakening of the grain trade oligopoly in the 1970s had something to do with this uncharacteristic behavior. Just as the ability of the seven major international oil companies to continue to stabilize world oil prices was impaired by the entry of independents into Middle East production, so was the oligopoly control of the Big Five grain companies impaired, perhaps, by the entry of an aggressive new competitor, Cook Industries, into the trade with Russia. Cook was indeed responsible for one of the imprudent sales of grain to Russia in 1974, at a time when the long-run interests of the Big Five might have dictated export restraint.

CRITIQUE OF TRANSNATIONAL EXPLANATION

In fact, any such transnational explanation for market instability can be confidently rejected. A closer look at the grain trade multinationals reveals their long-standing *lack* of control over the shape or condition of the world market. Unlike the major international oil companies, the private grain trading firms have never enjoyed control over production and transport of their product. They do not own the farms that produce the grain; they do not own the grain on the farms, and they do not control the dealings of the Baltic Exchange, in London, through which most shipping agreements for grain cargoes are completed.[52] It is not within the power of these large private firms to determine the availability, price, or destination of the grain they export. Their function is that of a middleman, bridging a rather narrow gap between producers and consumers, making profits on a narrow margin by arranging for the most efficient movement of grain from one to the other.

This middleman role does require that they become both buyers and sellers of grain. But at any given moment they will own only a small fraction of total world supply, and the price at which they buy and sell remains beyond their control. Within the bounds laid down by nation-state policies, international sales are priced in open markets in the United States, London, Hamburg, and Rotterdam.[53] The remainder takes the form of public tender, private tender, and negotiated sales, and many of these trades are effectively priced in relation to competitive and quasi-public futures markets, where oligopoly control over price again remains beyond reach.[54] The many smaller firms that compete with the Big Five for sales (over fifty separate firms, plus farm co-ops, are engaged in the U.S. grain export business alone) add yet another competitive dimension to the market. The inability of the Big Five to control the entry of these competitors into the market is adequately demonstrated by the dramatic rise of Cook Industries, from a mere trader of cotton in the 1960s to the third-largest grain trading firm in the world by 1973, and a major participant, as previously noted, in sales to the USSR. The five major companies also compete with great energy against one another. Indeed, in 1972 it was this competition among the Big Five that left them vulnerable to the purchasing tactics of the Soviet Union and robbed them of antici-pated profits. Because of a lack of communication among the companies, Russian purchasing agents were able to momentarily hide the total volume of their take, much to the disadvantage of some private com-panies. According to General Accounting Office (GAO) estimates, three of the six companies dealing with the Russians in 1972 actually sustained losses on the sale, of .9 to 1.9 cents per bushel. Cargill claimed to have lost more than $600,000 in the deal, by promising to sell grain to the Rus-sians that had not yet been acquired, not realizing how fast the price the company would have to pay for that grain was going to rise. [55]

While they do not control the market, perhaps these transnational actors nonetheless contribute to instability in that market, by remaining vulnerable to the disruptive purchasing tactics of the Soviet Union. If so, however, the dominant role of national action (Soviet action, in this case) is only reaffirmed.

Nor should the eager role of the U.S. government in encouraging large private grain sales to the Soviet Union in 1972 be overlooked. In June 1971, more than a year before the sale, the Nixon administration had gone out of its way to terminate the need for these private companies to seek Department of Commerce permission before making grain sales to communist countries. It was under explicit direction from national security adviser Henry Kissinger, early in 1972, that the Agriculture De-parment took the lead in negotiating an extension of Commodity Credit Corporation (CCC) credits to the USSR, to make larger U.S. food sales possible.[56] Moreover, it was the Nixon administration that refused Rus-sian requests for a direct government-to-government sale and insisted that purchases be made through private companies.[57] When those sales then proved larger than originally planned, steps were taken, as noted, to place tighter restrictions on company behavior, even to the point of canceling export contracts in 1974 and placing an embargo on further sales in 1975, to limit U.S. vulnerability to a repeat of the "grain robbery" of 1972. In 1980, when the Carter administration decided to suspend grain exports to the Soviet Union for reasons of foreign policy (acting under authority provided in the 1979 Export Administration Act), validated ex-port licenses were actually denied for the export of about 14 million tons of grain that had already been sold to the Soviets by private firms. During the first six months of the embargo, the big grain export companies even accepted an "informal agreement" with the U.S. Department of Agricul-ture, to restrict overseas sales of *non*-U.S. grain to the Soviet Union. Overall, the private companies find themselves functioning, more often than not, at the sufferance of national governments (more often, of late, the U.S. government), rather than in defiance of national governments. It is back to the policies of these national governments that we must now turn.

A NATIONAL POLITICAL EXPLANATION FOR CRISIS IN THE WORLD GRAIN MARKET: THE COMBINED EXTERNAL EFFECTS OF MANY SEPARATE NATIONAL GRAIN POLICIES

A rejection of the transnational explanation for the destabilization of world grain markets requires that we return to the recognized importance of nation-state action. Consider the possibility that the character of the world market is determined not at the "system" level, not according to the logic of international relations, but at the "unit" level, at the level of the nation-state itself, according to the separate logic of each national political system. Consider that the shape and the condition of the world grain market has no systemic logic of its own at the world level. At any one time, the state of the world market may reflect little more than the combined external effect of many separately determined national grain policies, each undertaken according to a separate logic at the "unit" level, with little regard for external conditions or for external consequences.

This "national" political explanation is favored, either implicitly or explicitly, in much of the traditional literature on world grain markets.[58] It has long been fashionable to stress the "residual" function of the world market in grains.[59] The principal markets have long been separate national and regional grain markets, most of which are heavily insulated from one another by a host of man-made barriers to trade—tariffs, levies, import quotas, export taxes, and currency restrictions. Despite its recent growth, the "world market" consists of a still-small relative volume of trade among these many national markets, and still performs a largely residual function. For most nations, the world grain market has usually been seen as the place into which an unwanted domestic surplus may be dumped, or from which a marginal national need may be filled. Unlike the world oil market, it is not the principal market through which most needs are satisfied. More than half of the world's oil production enters international trade every year, while less than one-fifth of the world's grain is ever traded among nations.

Since the world grain market is still so much a residual of many separate national grain markets, perhaps it is to be expected that its condition and its shape will have no systemic logic. Stability or instability in the world grain market will depend upon the independent behavior of many separate national markets, which is to say, upon the independent grain policies of many separate nation-states. To understand those policies, it becomes necessary to look at political actions and relations within states rather than at actions or relations among states.[60] The events of 1972 are a case in point.

The destabilization of the world grain market in 1972 may be viewed as the unintended result of separate but concurrent national political actions, principally those taken by the United States and the Soviet Union. In the United States, the Nixon administration decided to proceed with the liquidation of expensive stocks of grain and to delay the return of idle cropland to full production, primarily to reduce costs to the U.S. Treasury and increase farm prices in an election year. In the Soviet Union, the party leadership decided to persevere, at all cost, in an ambitious plan to expand livestock herds, hoping to appease long-suppressed consumer demands for an improved diet. These two national political actions were of separate origin. In combination, they ensured that the world grain market would suffer through a period of serious instability and insecurity following the bad harvests of 1972.

A third subsystemic source of instability in the world grain market has been food price policies pursued by the nations of Europe and Japan. The EEC sought to continue to stabilize internal farm and food prices during the period of scarcities that followed 1972, by reducing its variable levy on wheat to zero and taxing exports, thereby reducing the volume of such exports and shifting a heavier burden of adjustment onto the already unstable residual "world" market. During this same period, Japan's Food Agency also took steps to protect its consumers at home from high prices, subsidizing imports by selling to domestic millers at a loss. By one estimate, domestic price stability schemes such as these reduced the amount of wheat available to the world market by over 19 MMT in 1971–74, an amount roughly equal to the Soviet purchases of 1972.[61]

The origin of the U.S. decision to liquidate its expensive surplus stocks of grain can be found in national political trends that had developed well before 1972. As Bruce L. Gardner has said of U.S. farm policy, "the purpose is to take from those who have less political clout and to give to those who have more."[62] Price support policies, which stimulated so much surplus production, met this political test in 1933, when 25 percent of the U.S. population still lived on farms. By the 1960s, with the farm population down to less than 10 percent, and with legislatures at last reapportioned to reduce the overrepresentation of rural districts, the growing cost of U.S. farm subsidies (over $3 billion a year in the mid-1960s) no longer made political sense. Hence the adoption of a less costly farm income support policy, the aggressive promotion of commercial exports, beginning in the 1960s, and culminating in the Russian grain sale of 1972.

International trade balance and payments concerns, together with an early diplomatic enthusiasm for detente, doubtless played a role in the U.S. decision to sell so much grain to the Soviet Union in 1972. But the haste with which these stocks were sold, and the marked reluctance to return U.S. cropland to full production so soon thereafter, also reflect "unit-level" domestic political calculations. During 1967–71, real prices of wheat and corn received by U.S. farmers had fallen to the lowest levels recorded since the 1930s.[63] Although diminished in overall strength, farm state and agribusiness interests, championed by Secretary of Agriculture Earl L. Butz, were still positioned, in an election year, to demand remedial price actions from the government. The combination of policies pursued in 1972—aggressive export promotion plus continued acreage diversion—was calculated to produce short-term increases in farm income without adding to the federal farm budget.[64] Only after the 1972 election victory (and only after the discovery that domestic food prices were rising too quickly) did it become the policy of the government to increase wheat acreage and to restrict further sales to the Soviet Union. Domestic politics continued to dominate, however. Labor and consumer groups, rather than producers, were now the object of concern. It was a fear of consumer backlash at home, rather than a quest for diplomatic advantage or "food power" abroad, that led to the interruption of U.S. soybean exports in 1973, as well as to restrictions on further sales of grain to the Soviet Union in 1974 and 1975.

Much less can be known about the Soviet decision to begin to import very large quantities of grain in 1972. Years before, Soviet efforts to increase livestock herds had been constrained by a reluctance to become dependent on grain from abroad. In May 1957, when Nikita Khrushchev first called for an increase in Soviet per capita meat consumption, eventually to equal the U.S. level, his hope had been to reach this goal through expanded feed grain production at home. Only when it became clear, following two serious harvest setbacks in the 1960s, that Soviet agriculture would not be capable of providing the steady supply of animal feed needed to sustain this effort were provisions tentatively made to import larger quantities of grain from abroad. The Soviet Union communicated its desire to begin buying corn from the United States on a continuing basis as early as 1969.[65] This Soviet decision to expand meat production even at the cost of importing feed grain on a regular basis was no doubt reinforced by the example of the 1970 Christmas food price riots in Poland. Polish dockworkers, protesting a government decision to increase the retail price of food, seized the shipyards in Szezecin and burned party headquarters in Gdansk, forcing not only a return to lower prices but the replacement of party leader Gomulka. It is significant that in the following year, the Soviet Union imported 8.3 MMT of grain from abroad, even though it had recently enjoyed two very good grain harvests in a row at home.

The first very large Soviet grain purchase, in 1972, thus reflects much more than the happenstance timing of détente, the availability of commercial credit from the United States, or other such international motivations. The requirement for feed grain within the USSR had been building steadily, in response to an internal political commitment to increase per capita meat consumption. As Leonid Brezhnev explained to U.S. Secretary of Agriculture Butz in Moscow in April 1972: "The Soviet Government [has] publicized its intention of increasing the protein component in the people's diet by 25 percent, and the goal [can] not be met with domestic production." Butz, perceiving a partial solution to his own domestic political problems, responded with an assurance that Brezhnev would be "absolutely safe in building up the livestock population upon a grain supply from [the U.S.]."[66]

The domestic origins of Soviet grain trade policy are also visible in the exact timing of the 1972 purchase. For two months, in April and May, the Russians refused U.S. offers of grain sold on standard credit terms, insisting instead upon an even more generous concessional rate of interest. Grain sales were discussed with Nixon at the Moscow Summit in late May, but Soviet officials continued to refuse U.S. terms of credit, and no agreement was reached (one of the very few topics on which agreement was not reached at that Moscow Summit). Then, in late June, quite suddenly, within a week of reviewing their own monthly crop reports, the Soviets changed their mind, sent a purchasing team to Washington to accept the previously rejected U.S. credit offer, and made their first round of very large grain purchases. The timing suggests preoccupation with internal requirements more than with international concerns such as access to U.S. credit, foreign policy developments, the condition of the world market, or the behavior of the multinational firms.

The predominance of "subsystemic" national political action may also help to account for the absence of any significant closure of the world grain market since 1972. Recall that national dependence on the world market has continued to grow. From a subsystemic perspective, this needs be no surprise. If political relations within nations remain unaltered, their external behavior, including their volume of grain purchases, will remain unaltered as well, whatever the imprudence of those purchases.

In the Soviet Union, where the Brezhnev leadership remained in place and remained motivated by the need to improve diets, food imports continued to increase, despite a very large drain on foreign exchange (about 15 percent of total nonoil hard currency imports in recent years), and despite new uncertainties over access to U.S. grain supplies. In 1980, despite external experience with a troublesome U.S. grain embargo, internal needs motivated the Soviet Union to import more grain (more than 31 million tons) than in any previous year in its history. Also, in Japan, where projects to reduce the rate of growth of grain imports were widely discussed in 1975 and 1976, grain imports nonetheless continued to grow. The Japanese political system has been slow to reduce its dependence upon feed grain imports, in part because of consumer resistance to higher food prices, and in part because Japanese agricultural policy remains captive to the interests of rice producers, who continue to lay claim to the largest share of the agricultural budget, despite an unmanageable rice surplus.

Political coalitions within the European Community have been equally unaffected by international grain market disruptions. These coalitions remain biased, as ever, toward high and stable producer prices. Despite the inefficiencies and the enormous public expense, and despite the destabilizing external effects, European farmers continue to receive protection from the world market. The result is not to be interpreted as a drive toward greater self-sufficiency motivated by external market disruptions. European grain policies were in place a decade before 1972, indicating that national decisions that reduce dependence upon the world market may be just as unrelated to external conditions as those that, in other nations, have led to deeper dependence.[67]

Also among many poor grain-importing nations, internal politics once again provides a key to understanding continuities in external policies since 1972.[68] Within many of these nations, opportunities for development abound within the food sector; and the rising cost of food imports since 1972 might therefore have been expected to trigger a long overdue redirection of national investment toward food production for local consumption. Yet the use of scarce development funds for this purpose continues to meet resistance, as it runs counter to the interests of powerful landowning rural elites (who may profit more from growing nonfood cash crops, or food crops for export), and urban dwellers (who prefer low food prices in the short run and who pursue industrial development projects dependent upon the foreign exchange earnings that cash crop agriculture sometimes provides). This maldistribution of internal political power continues to bias many LDC development strategies away from local food production, leading relentlessly to deeper dependence upon an unstable, and ever less dependable, world grain market.

Adopting these unit-level explanations, note that prospects for future world grain market growth become unhinged from prospects for market access or price stability. Nations responding to short-term domestic political demands are fully capable of pursuing "irrational" international grain trade strategies, such as deeper dependence upon an undependable market or progressive withdrawal from a stable and reliable trading system. Some national responses will be more important than others in this regard. Market stability in the future will depend most of all upon the national politics of the United States (the largest exporter and a source of stability in the past). If, in times of short supply, consumer pressures in the United States grow strong enough to overwhelm the interests of producers, then U.S. exports will be restricted, exacerbating shortages abroad and destabilizing the world market. Of simultaneous importance will be separate political developments within literally scores of potential grain-importing nations. If the configuration of political forces within these nations continues to discourage abundant local food production, reliance upon imports will grow and the world grain market will continue to grow, to the advantage of some importers if world market stability can be ensured, but more likely to their disadvantage, if instabilities and crisis persist.

CRITIQUE OF NATIONAL EXPLANATION

These unit-level explanations for crisis in the world grain market provide the most persuasive means to understand the past. They may apply with much less force to developments in the near future. The logic of national political action has produced, for some, a much deeper dependence upon world grain markets. This deeper dependence may now feed back into the national political system, eroding the heretofore separate logic of national action.

Since 1972 the world grain market has grown into something more than a "residual" market. This is certainly the case from the perspective of the United States, which now exports into that market one-third of its annual production of corn and about two-thirds of its annual production of wheat. Whatever the reason for the original surge in U.S. grain exports in 1972, the continued pursuit of U.S. trade balance objectives now requires that they continue. Annual export earnings from grain, which totaled $17 billion in 1980, have become ever more critical to preserving U.S. strength in the world economy as a whole. The longer this remains so, the more likely that political perspectives in the United States toward grain exports will be "internationalized." The stable growth of an open export market will then become a dominant foreign policy objective, one that is less likely to be neglected for internal political reasons alone. Alternatively, U.S. grain export policy might become tied to external imperatives of a diplomatic rather than an economic nature. If U.S. foreign policy leaders, sensing their weakness in traditional forms of competition, should seek to rely, ever more often, upon their "food weapon," then the result might well be destabilizing for the world grain market, and the total volume of exports might eventually be diminished. In either case, U.S. grain export policy would no longer be driven by an isolated logic of internal U.S. politics.

As with the United States, so it is also with the internationalization of food policy perspectives in some poor food-deficit nations. Internal political imperatives that have long encouraged reliance upon grain imports may soon yield to a variety of counterpoised external constraints. High or unstable world prices, the possible denial of access to commercial and concessional grain sales in times of short supply, or perhaps inadequate foreign exchange earnings, are international barriers that may soon stand in the way of the continued growth of grain imports. Many poor food-deficit countries have, until now, given in to national political pressures to postpone investment in local food production. They may not be able to resist the international incentive to make such investments in the future.

For a few, external considerations may continue to play a small role in policy choices which govern participation in the world grain market. The EEC, for example, is wealthy enough to continue to insulate itself from that market, spending whatever may be required to provide producers with high prices (in times of a world surplus) and consumers with stable prices (in times of a world shortage). Likewise, most OPEC nations can afford to pursue national development strategies that are both neglectful of the food sector at home and indifferent toward the security or stability of the grain market abroad. The grain needs of these nations are small enough, and their purchasing power is great enough, to allow them to shift all adjustment burdens away from their own societies. Barring a more effective Western grain embargo, even the Soviet Union might have some capacity, in the years ahead, to continue to pursue a domestically determined "import led" dietary improvement policy, one that pays little regard to external market conditions. Compared to the $20 billion or more which the Soviet Union spends every year on its own internal agricultural subsidies, simply to hold down retail food prices, the marginal cost of its feed grain imports to permit increased meat production might seem rather small. The Soviet Union is in its own way a wealthy nation, wealthy enough to "afford" even the inefficient agricultural policies that its political leadership seems to prefer.

Ironically, then, it is primarily the richest and the poorest—the United States and the non-OPEC developing nations—who are most likely to find themselves in the future less capable of building grain policy around the comfortable and familiar requirements of national politics alone. These are the nations that will be most drawn into an internationalization of their grain trade policies. The United States, to protect its place in the world economy, may be required to continue to export grain in large quantities, tolerating and absorbing fluctuations in external demand, along with the resulting income instabilities suffered by domestic producers and the food price complaints of domestic consumers. The nonoil developing countries, to protect their foreign policy position, and to protect themselves from the diplomatic risk of excessive grain-import dependence, may be required to purchase less grain from abroad than they might if domestic political pressures alone were to continue to determine policy.

For both rich and poor, this transition from national to international policy calculations will be slow and painful. Nor is there any guarantee that international perspectives, once achieved, will permit cooperation. The international needs of the United States to increase exports, and the international needs of some food-deficit poor nations to reduce imports, may be at times in conflict with each other.

CONCLUSION

The political logic of the world grain market seems in an awkward phase of transition. The structure and condition of that market, until now, have been largely a byproduct of separate and separately determined national policy actions. Stability and growth were encouraged before 1972 through a fortunate coincidence of national farm and food policies, pursued in the United States and elsewhere, that placed little strain on the world market. A coincidence of national decisions to solve domestic farm and food problems by heavier reliance upon the world market, culminating in 1972, then brought an end to this era of stability. These several years of heavy use were accompanied by crises and instabilities that may now, at last, have begun to alter the residual quality of the world grain market. Some important participants can no longer afford to pursue national grain policies that pay little heed to external market conditions. In part because of the way in which domestic food policies transformed the world market in 1972, the primacy of domestic food policy has been challenged.

Dependence upon the world market has now grown large enough, for some, to begin to produce grain trade policies predicated upon larger calculations of world market conditions, or of external diplomatic relations. For the United States, efforts to influence world market conditions toward stability and growth might now be made, for the first time quite consciously, in hopes that the United States will be the largest direct beneficiary of stable growth. It must only be hoped that U.S. power, in the grain market and beyond, has not eroded so far as to discourage or to defeat these leadership efforts. Poor food-deficit countries, if they sense the likelihood of continuing crisis in the world market, may now begin to search for ways to hedge against the costs and risks of still deeper participation in such a market.

This is an unstable situation. An important international market has emerged just at a moment when some importers cannot afford deeper participation in such a market, while the dominant exporter, the United States, has fewer international means to ensure the stability and security of that market. What the logic of national politics hath wrought, the international system, which lacks a confident hegemonic leader, now must seek to manage.

NOTES

1. Grains occupy over two-thirds of the world's harvested cropland. They provide over one-half of the world's food energy supply when consumed directly and much of the remainder when consumed in the form of animal products. Grains constitute one-third of the value of world food trade.

2. Political forces may be described as those that guide transactions in the absence of a competitive price system. In the extreme, as Nye and Keohane

observe, any departure from perfect competition always introduces such political factors into an analysis. See Robert O. Keohane and Joseph S. Nye, Jr., *Power and Interdependence* (Boston: Little, Brown, 1977), p. 39. This very broad definition of political action has been selected to permit consideration of a political explanation for grain market crisis based upon the oligopoly behavior of five large "transnational" actors, the private grain trading firms.

3. See Panos Konandreas and Hernan Hertado, "Analysis of Trade Flows in the International Wheat Market," *Canadian Journal of Agricultural Economics* 26 (3), 1978, pp. 11–12.

4. See D. Gale Johnson, *World Agriculture in Disarray* (London: Macmillan, 1973), p. 23. Also, Harold B. Malmgren, *International Economic Peacekeeping in Phase II* (Rev. ed.; New York: Quadrangle Books, 1972), p. 26.

5. Gary L. Seevers, "Food Markets and Their Regulation," in *The Global Political Economy of Food*, ed. Raymond F. Hopkins and Donald J. Puchala (Madison: University of Wisconsin Press, 1978), p. 160.

6. It might be suggested that supranational actors (such as international civil servants) are also capable of shaping the world grain market. By one count there are at least 89 international governmental bodies with food related missions. Claims made for the influence of supranational actors are, in the author's view, exaggerated.

7. An extended and recent discussion of systemic and unit level (or "reductionist") theories of international politics is found in Kenneth N. Waltz, *Theory of International Politics* (Reading, Mass.: Addison-Wesley, 1979).

8. Hopkins and Puchala, *The Global Political Economy of Food*, pp. 13–14.

9. "The World Food Situation and Prospects to 1985," Foreign Agricultural Economic Report No. 98, Economic Research Service, U.S. Department of Agriculture, Washington, D.C., 1974, p. 22.

10. Lester R. Brown, *By Bread Alone* (New York: Praeger, 1974), p. 65.

11. "The World Food Situation and Prospects to 1985."

12. U.S. Department of Agriculture, Foreign Agricultural Circular FG-32-80, 13 November 1980.

13. Mancur Olson, Jr., *The Logic of Collective Action* (Cambridge, Mass.: Harvard University Press, 1965).

14. Hopkins and Puchala, *The Global Political Economy of Food*.

15. "The World Food Situation and Prospects to 1985," p. 45. These data exclude the USSR, PRC, and East Europe.

16. Stocks available in exporting countries are a better measure of world food security than total working stocks world wide. See Hopkins and Puchala, *The Global Political Economy of Food*.

17. Philip H. Trezise, *Rebuilding Grain Reserves* (Washington, D.C.: Brookings Institution, 1976), p. 2.

18. "The World Food Situation and Prospects to 1985."

19. Emma Rothschild has argued, for example, that "the security of the world food economy has required immense expense, immense political effort. And this effort, in the 1950's and 1960's, was almost entirely American. The two supports of the system were the grain reserves owned by the U.S. government, and the U.S. policy of exporting food on favorable credit terms, as a part of its foreign aid program. The U.S. government used its reserves to keep prices stable, and to maintain a secure supply of grain for export. Foreign customers came to depend

upon U.S. food in a market where prices were stable and exports subsidized."
See "Food Politics," *Foreign Affairs*, 54, (2), p. 289.

20. See Robert O. Keohane and Joseph S. Nye, Jr., "World Politics and the International Economic System," in *The Future of the International Economic Order*, ed. C. Fred Bergsten (Lexington: Lexington Books, 1973), p. 132.

21. Rothschild, "Food Politics."

22. I. M. Destler, "United States Food Policy 1972–76," in Hopkins and Puchala, *The Global Political Economy of Food*, p. 46.

23. Rothschild, "Food Politics," p. 290.

24. Destler, "U.S. Food Policy," p. 47.

25. Robert Paarlberg, "Shifting and Sharing Adjustment Burdens," in Hopkins and Puchala, *The Global Political Economy of Food*, p. 91.

26. Dan Morgan, *Merchants of Grain* (New York: Viking Press, 1979), p. 12.

27. Marshall Goldman, "Will the Soviet Union be an Autarky in 1984?" *International Security* (4), 1979, pp. 31–32.

28. For one recent discussion of how and why market closure so often follows the erosion of hegemonic power, see Peter J. Katzenstein, ed., *Between Power and Plenty* (Madison: University of Wisconsin Press, 1978), p. 9.

29. Rothschild, "Food Politics," p. 292.

30. Once before, in the 1930's, Japan had retreated from the world grain trade in response to market disruption, increasing its own home production of wheat by 60 percent, to reach self-sufficiency. See Morgan, *Merchants of Grain*, p. 77.

31. Rothschild, "Food Politics," p. 293.

32. See Trezise, *Rebuilding Grain Reserves*, p. 2: "Neither the U.S. nor Canada had accumulated these holdings as a precaution against poor crops at home or anywhere. Rather, stocks acquisition had been dictated by the need to hold undesired surplusses off the market in order to sustain farm prices. In effect, these sizeable reserves were the unintended result of national price support policies during a period when North American crop yields were advancing at a rapid pace." Luther G. Tweeten describes the stabilizing influence of this propitious accumulation and release of U.S. buffer stocks in the past as "largely a matter of blind luck." See "Agriculture Policy: A Review of Legislation, Programs, and Policy, in *Food and Agricultural Policy* (Washington, D.C.: American Enterprise Institute, 1977), p. 56.

33. See L. Dudley and R. J. Sandilands, "The Side Effects of Foreign Aid: The Case of P.L. 480 Wheat and Colombia," *Economic Development and Cultural Change* (1), 1975, pp. 325–36.

34. Morgan, *Merchants of Grain*, p. 10.

35. Ibid., pp. 104–5.

36. Henry R. Nau, "The Diplomacy of World Food," in Hopkins and Puchala, *The Global Political Economy of Food*, p. 217.

37. 'Food and Agriculture Policy Options," U.S. Congress, Congressional Budget Office Issue Paper, Washington, D.C., 1977, p. 59.

38. William Diebold, Jr., *The United States and the Industrial World* (New York: Praeger, 1972), p. 259.

39. Nau, "Diplomacy of World Food," p. 202.

40. Diebold, *US. and Industrial World*, p. 259.

41. U.S. Department of Agriculture, Foreign Agricultural Circular, FG-32-80, 13 November 1980.

42. See *Multinational Corporations and United States Foreign Policy—International Grain Companies, Hearings Before the Senate Subcommittee on Multinational Corporations*, 18, 23, and 24, June 1976.

43. Seevers, "Food Markets," p. 164.

44. Morgan, *Merchants of Grain*, p. 6.

45. Ibid., p. 7.

46. Stephen Diamond and Stephen Armbruster, "Against the American Grain," *New Times*, 12 December 1975, p. 25.

47. Morgan, *Merchants of Grain*, p. 7.

48. Ibid., p. ix.

49. See Raymond Vernon, "An Interpretation," *Daedalus* (4), 1975, pp. 3–7.

50. Destler, "U.S. Food Policy," p. 46.

51. See Morgan, *Merchants of Grain*, p. 149, for recent evidence that the U.S. Department of Agriculture knew more about the volume of these sales sooner than the date originally admitted in public.

52. Seevers, "Food Markets," p. 165.

53. Ibid., p. 162.

54. Ibid., p. 164.

55. Robert L. Paarlberg, "The Soviet Burden on the World Food System," *Food Policy* (5), 1976, p. 393.

56. Morgan, *Merchants of Grain*, p. 145.

57. Diamond and Armbruster, "Against American Grain, p. 27.

58. See, for example, D. Gale Johnson, *World Agriculture*, p. 20: "The trade measures that each country adopts are an adjunct of its domestic farm policies. In most cases, a specific trade restrictive or interfering device has been adopted, not for its particular direct benefits, but because it is a device that will make it possible for a domestic measure to function." Also, Malmgren, *Economic Peacekeeping*, p. 119: "The problems in agricultural trade are primarily symptoms of domestic agricultural policies. It is the interaction of the various national farm policies which has led to the enormous trade distortions and highly protectionist policies which can be seen in many countries, developed and developing alike."

59. See the "World Food Problem," p. 185: "Most developed countries view their domestic markets for food and fiber as a preserve for their domestic producers and engage in international trade in farm products only as a residual source of supplies or as an outlet for surpluses."

60. The need to pay greater heed to domestic political explanations for change in the world economy is explicitly recognized in Keohane and Nye, *Power and Interdependence*, p. 224. See also Katzenstein, *Power and Plenty*.

61. See Dale Hathaway, "The Relationship Between Trade and World Food Security," in *International Food Policy Issues, A Proceedings*, Foreign Agriculture Economic Report No. 143 (Washington, D.C.: U.S. Department of Agriculture, 1978), p. 56.

62. *Food and Agriculture Policy*, p. 64.

63. "The World Food Situation and Prospects to 1985," p. 24.

64. Destler, "U.S. Food Policy," p. 45.

65. Morgan, *Merchants of Grain*, p. 142.

66. Robert Paarlberg, "Lessons of the Grain Embargo," *Foreign Affairs* (Fall 1980).

67. These European grain policies are not likely to change as a result of external pressure. See Diebold, *U.S. and Industrial World*, p. 278.

68. See Nau, "Diplomacy of World Food," p. 222. See also Norman K. Nicholson, and John D. Esseks, "The Politics of Food Scarcities in Developing Countries," in Hopkins and Puchala, *The Global Political Economy of Food*, pp. 127–30.

7

Approaches to the International Economic Policy-Making Process

Stephen D. Cohen

International economic policy is a diverse phenomenon, and the process by which it is made is also a diverse phenomenon. Like the surfer's search for the perfect wave, the student's search for a single model of decision making is unfulfilled and unending. This assertion by no means suggests that the procedures of policy making are not an important field of inquiry. Procedure is substance; a full understanding of the nature and quality of policy presupposes an appreciation of the spectrum of policy making procedures from haphazard to meticulous, from argumentative to pro forma. After placing the issue of international economic policy making in its context, this chapter will examine the impact of organization and process on the end product—policy substance—by using case studies to document the applicability of different models of decision making. It will try to examine a sufficiently broad base of international economic policy actions to avoid the all too common fallacy of drawing conclusions from a limited number of decisions.

DEFINITIONS AND ACTORS

Before examining the policy making process, it is necessary first to define that which is being made: international economic policy. The latter is a very general umbrella term that probably should be used in the plural form ("policies") instead of the singular. A number of distinct actions are being taken in a number of different, albeit interrelated policy sectors: trade, monetary, finance, development, energy, investment, science and technology, and so forth. The components of "international economic policy" can be disaggregated into a multitude of parts, each possessing as many unique characteristics as similarities.

In the aggregate, international economic policy encompasses the means by which the government influences and controls how the private sector and certain government programs interact with the economies of other countries. It is viewed by some as being the economic dimension of foreign policy, while others view it as the external dimension of domestic economic policy. It is both. International economic policy can be viewed as an intersection where domestic economic, international economic, domestic political, and external political concerns meet. The need to reconcile politics and economics and domestic and internal policies makes the international economic policy-making process a distinctive phenomenon.

When international economic policy is disaggregated, a number of different governmental actions combine to produce a series of equally different kinds of policies to be used in meeting the exigencies of international economic relations. The heterogeneity of policy can be demonstrated by various techniques of disaggregation. First, policy can be separated according to issue sectors: trade, finance, development, investment, energy, and so on. Policy can also be broadly divided between enunciation of broad principles (e.g., support of floating exchange rates and opposition to generalized debt relief), participation in multilateral pursuits of global objectives (e.g., contributions to the World Bank and engaging in efforts to liberalize barriers to international trade flows), and finally, determinations of how to administer a program in a specific case (e.g., provision of import relief in an escape clause case or prohibition through the export control program of a computer export to the Soviet Union).

On a different plane, international economic policy can be viewed as consisting of (1) initiatives (e.g., the Kennedy Round of tariff negotiations); (2) defensive reactions (e.g., imposing dumping duties on foreign-made goods sold in the United States at less than fair value); (3) incremental policy, that is, efforts to clarify existing international economic issues (e.g., exchange-rate management). Policy includes a hierarchy of problems ranging from those deemed vital to domestic, international, and bureaucratic interests down to those that are so technical or narrowly focused that the issue at hand will not rise beyond the working level. Policy proposals may be designed to provide incremental financial benefits to nationals or to foreigners (export promotion and grants to poor countries, for example), while some policy proposals are designed to redistribute benefits from overseas to the domestic market (import restrictions to protect domestic production). There is also the policy of "economic denial" to pursue broader objectives (e.g., limiting petroleum imports or restricting grain exports on national security grounds). Some international economic policy issues focus U.S. government attention exclusively on domestic interests (e.g., the reorganization of the policy-making process or the tax rates for U.S. citizens working abroad). Other policy issues focus attention on international negotiations with other governments (e.g., international monetary reform).

The fact that international economic relations embraces the two principal objectives of the modern nation-state—national security and economic prosperity—make it a very important phenomenon both to the "national interest" and to a broad number of bureaucratic actors. The sheer volume of these actors across two branches of the U.S. government is without parallel in any other country. In the executive branch, half of the cabinet departments—State, Treasury, Commerce, Agriculture, Energy, and Labor—are active and regular participants. Within the Executive Office of the President, the U.S. Trade Representative, the Council of Economic Advisers, the Office of Management and Budget, and the National Security Council are important participants. A number of agencies and commissions also play significant parts in the international economic policy-making process, including the Federal Reserve Board, the International Trade Commission, the Export-Import Bank, and the International Development Cooperation Agency.

In the legislative branch, a significant majority of members of Congress have either a political interest or intellectual commitment to at least one phase of U.S. international economic policy. At least seven sets of congressional committees are significant to this policy: the agriculture, appropriations, banking, commerce, energy, finance/ways and means, and foreign relations committees in each House, as well as the Joint Economic Committee.

Traditional foreign policy models have relevance for the international economic policy-making process. But no single model that focuses on the State-Defense-NSC triangle can have a broad applicability in this area. The active participation or nonparticipation of certain bureaucratic actors can and does skew the process by which international economic policy is made towards domestic priorities and away from international concerns.

THE NEED FOR A MULTIPLE THEORY OF POLICY MAKING

The principal obstacle to a unified theory of U.S. international economic policy making is the diversity, fluidity, and unpredictability of exactly how such policies will be formulated and implemented and by whom. The inherent strength of the domestic U.S. economy and its strength relative to other economies are key variables in determining exactly which of many possible procedures is to be utilized. During the 1950s and early 60s, when the United States still enjoyed postwar economic and political hegemony, the constellation of premises, priorities, perceptions, and personalities were substantially different from the late 1970s and '80s, when the U.S. economy was and is suffering from stagflation, soaring energy costs, intense foreign competition in a wide range of goods, and anxiety over the exchange-rate value of the American dollar.

The only constant in terms of U.S. international economic policy since 1945 is the effort to promote maximum worldwide growth and prosperity by minimizing governmental obstacles to the free international flow of goods, services, and capital. At the same time, such goals were to be pursued with a minimum of disruption to domestic business and labor conditions. The U.S. "national interest" in international economic relations is definable, but only in broad terms. The routes to this destination are often not clearly marked, and the need for short-term compromises frequently necessitates detours in the form of compromise. Different perspectives within the bureaucracies, concentrating as they do on different aspects of U.S. economic relations with the rest of world, have different ideas about which path or which detour should be taken at any given time. In other words, the competition is severe for the role of chief pathfinder for U.S. international economic policy.

The irregular casts of decision makers and the heterogeneity of the issues involved in the entire gamut of U.S. international economic relations preclude construction of a universally applicable model of policy making. Since bureaucratic actors and the nature of the official actions required will vary from issue to issue, it is difficult to determine the existence of a significant number of uniform principles. On a very general and abstract level, one consistent rule can be anticipated: Policy makers are sincerely trying to resolve at least three simultaneous concerns. The latter consist of each decision-maker's sense of urgency of action, individual perceptions of what priorities would best serve the long-term national interests, and individual assessments of short-term constraints on flexibility of action.

Ultimately, a consensus, or *modus vivendi*, will be reached. Different techniques will be used in accomplishing this task. The success of the effort in serving the national interest will be measured against the value system of the observer. Each policy maker and each outside observer will define appropriate policy moves by assigning weights, or priorities, to each of the four elements of international economic policy: domestic and foreign political concerns, as well as internal and external economic policy management objectives. This "value weighting" process is done in different ways, but it is the principal constant in the making of U.S. international economic policy.

To argue that the U.S. decision-making process in the international economic area is too irregular to be the subject of a single model of action is not necessarily a criticism of either officials or existing procedures. The large size of the U.S. government and the increasing array of international economic issues do not lend themselves to predictable consistency. Proponents of a one-model approach would appear to be guilty of either an insufficient disaggregation of the term "policy" or of utilizing too narrow and selective a set of supporting case studies to demonstrate purportedly universal truths.

The case-study approach to explaining how the system functions has severe limitations in constructing any overall understanding or pattern. Some of these limitations would be obviated if literally dozens of separate decisions and operations were to be examined on a comprehensive basis and then meticulously cross-referenced according to very specific criteria. Even so, a relatively brief time frame would need to be chosen in order to examine a system reflecting similar presidential styles and prevailing global realities. A random sample of ten to fifteen events is likely to produce interesting and illustrative anecdotes, but could not be extrapolated on any scientific basis to produce a systematic diagnosis. A carefully pre-selected sample of decisions, however, could be employed to support arbitrarily any number of hypotheses.

Recurring patterns in decision making do exist. However, they are far from being sufficiently significant statistically to lead to categorical theories or assertions. For example, the eleven case studies in international economic policy decision making written for the Commission on the Organization of the Government for the Conduct of Foreign Policy (and published in Volume 2 in the *Appendices* to its report) were vivid and expensive evidence of the fallacy of trying to capture the essence of universal truths about the organizational system from a small random sample. Collectively the case studies provide no means to either diagnose the system or predict future actions.

The heart of the matter is that key U.S. international economic policy decisions and actions have been made on a highly idiosyncratic basis. Some were quickly devised in crisis situations; others grew by inertia. Furthermore, the dynamics of decision making in one sector, in one year, are not necessarily representative of those in other sectors, or even in the same sector in different years.

All the major models utilized in the foreign policy decision-making process can be shown, both in pure form and in variations, to be applicable in international economic relations. At this time, it does not seem possible to predict *a priori* exactly which model will be relevant for any given problem or issue. Nor is the interrelationship among these models fully explainable. The policy-making procedures that follow are an exercise in diversity.

MODES OF EXECUTIVE BRANCH POLICY MAKING

This section draws on several models of policy making that have been advanced to explain the governmental decision-making process in matters involving national security affairs and economic policy. After briefly explaining the rationale of each of these models, I will provide examples of their applicability to specific policy formulation efforts. It is a strength of the American system that it is flexible enough to provide a number of procedures to make international policy depending upon the prevailing circumstances. It might also be suggested that it is a weakness when the method of policy making materializes on an inconsistent, catch-as-catch-can basis. The final determination is in the eyes of the beholder (i.e., whether or not he approves of the resulting policy substance). Persistent policy and a consistent policy-making process is a mixed blessing if one is in disagreement with the contents and impact of that policy.

Presidential Fiat

Decisions under the presidential fiat model reflect the direct intervention and clear dictation of the President. The latter's personality, his operating style, and the attitude of his senior advisers represent in this case the critical determinants of decision making. In theory, all U.S. international economic policy could be made by such a highly centralized mode in the White House. In practice, very few such decisions have been made this way. The primary reason is that presidents only infrequently have elevated foreign economic relations to sufficiently high levels as to warrant their active and continuing leadership. In this model, the White House participates and dominates from the early formulation of policy through the effort to achieve the objectives selected. Such continuity differentiates this model from instances when the president is drawn into an issue merely to ratify a bureaucratic consensus or to arbitrate at the last minute a dispute among the line departments.

Ironically, the stamp of presidential pressure is relatively seldom found in trade policy. Although the bureaucracy can handle all routine issues, trade is, in dollar terms, the most important component of international economic policy and the sector having most direct impact on domestic and foreign industry, jobs, and consumers' pocketbooks. The main exception to this rule was President Nixon's demand in 1969 that Japan and other textile-exporting countries "voluntarily" restrict their shipments of man-made textile fibers to the U.S. market. The economics of the issue were all but entirely subordinated to the political imperative of fulfilling a campaign pledge to obtain political support, not redress actual economic dislocations. For almost three years, the clarity and emphasis of the U.S. position were perfectly clear. However, the absence of flexibility and input by a foreign-policy point of view caused a costly and unjustified trauma in U.S.–Japanese relations completely out of proportion to either the degree of import penetration or the benefits eventually obtained. Ironically, the results of the eventual export restraints agreement were soon dissipated as Japan began losing its competitiveness in international textile trade. From beginning to end, U.S. policy never wavered. It attained its objective, even if it never made sense in economic terms.

Presidents have participated actively in the international economic policy formulation process in selected crises associated with the chronic

U.S. balance-of-payments deficits. The classic example was President Nixon's 1971 decision to terminate dollar-gold convertibility and to impose a 10 percent import surcharge as part of the overall new economic policy. This drastic, abrupt shift in economic policy was constructed by the President and a handful of senior advisers during a single fateful August weekend at Camp David. The parallels with the textile dispute are striking. U.S. policy was formulated quickly and enunciated at the highest level. Objectives were then pursued ruthlessly and unequivocally by the President's men with relatively little regard for foreign political sensitivites or foreign policy considerations. Once again, the United States extracted maximum concessions from other countries while yielding relatively little. This country successfully attained its international economic objectives, but at a foreign policy cost. Offsetting the responsiveness of the bureaucracy to presidential direction was the obvious drawback of not having an effective senior-level mechanism to analyze and integrate the political and economic dimensions of an international issue.

Shared Images and Perceptions

Many international economic policies of the United States are routinely handled by a bureaucracy hampered by no real differences of opinion. In most cases, U.S. policy concerning international investment issues smoothly emanates from several shared assumptions. The dominant one is that the market mechanism should be allowed to function: a liberal investment system should exist side by side with a liberal trading system. No agency wishes to drastically alter the tax treatment of overseas corporate income (the tax deferral and tax credit) on a punitive basis, as advocated by the AFL-CIO in the Burke-Hartke bill. No agency had problems with U.S. participation in the OECD exercise to produce a voluntary code of conduct for multinational enterprises. And no agency has opted for any shift in the essentially open-door policy that exists in this country for foreign direct investors.

An example of the shared-perceptions model joining with bureaucratic politics occurred in early 1976 on the international business question of U.S. corporations' response to Arab boycott demands. Fearful of disrupting foreign policy and overseas U.S. business ventures, the international economic policy leaders—State, Treasury, and Commerce—opted for a very low government profile. The Justice Department's lonely determination to enforce the letter of U.S. law found itself completely isolated in one of its infrequent ventures into international economic policy.

The lack of any major dissension and the absence of any priority departmental interests in most international investment issues have resulted in a very loose, decentralized decision-making apparatus. This lack of bureaucratic fervor was responsible for the White House's Council on International Economic Policy being given significant coordination responsibilities in the past and for the virtual absence today of a formalized pattern of jurisdiction or decision making in the international investment sector.

Another example of shared perceptions has occurred repeatedly in the attempted formulation by the U.S. government of the broad outlines of an international energy policy. With the exception of the explosive State-Treasury feud in 1975 on the concept of a guaranteed floor price for oil, no continuing, serious differences of opinion have become public. The State, Treasury, and Energy Departments, and the concerned White House offices, have not disagreed on the need for certain basic policies: reduced dependence on oil imports, reduced vulnerability to future embargo threats through stockpiling and international sharing arrangements, increased cooperation by oil consumers to develop alternative energy sources and conservation techniques, and the need to develop a permanent multilateral dialogue between oil-producing and oil-consuming countries. Nor was there any disagreement on the fact that the high price of oil was at the root of energy-induced problems; that OPEC was imposing a political, nonmarket price for oil on the world; that divisiveness in OPEC should be encouraged; that international financial recycling measures could, and should, be put into effect; and that special financial facilities should be established in the IMF to provide extra balance-of-payments financing for oil-importing countries.

A final example of shared perceptions involved the identical economic analyses and policy recommendations emanating from the State and Treasury Departments in response to the LDCs' demands for generalized debt relief. Unlike the ideological split that initially characterized the U.S. response to the Integrated Commodity Program, this aspect of the North-South economic dialogue never became a contentious issue or bureaucratic battle. Both departments since 1976 have steadfastly maintained that there was no universal debt crisis. Hence a generalized, or across the board, writeoff of the LDCs' external development loans was deemed unjustified, political pressures from the Group of 77 notwithstanding. Both departments agreed that debt relief (like creation of international commodity agreements) should be handled on a case-by-case basis. Countries facing a debt crunch that suggested an impending default on repayment obligations should continue to be dealt with individually in the so-called Paris Club.

Generalized debt relief, it was agreed, would not reflect individual financial needs; rather, it would benefit only a few big debtor countries that accounted for a disproportionate share of the LDCs' bilateral external debt arising from official development loans. Both departments were fearful of Congressional anger at the "back door" (or nonappropriated) foreign aid implications of debt foregiveness, and they worried about the precedent that would be set by allowing debtors to void their contractual commitment to repay lenders. Finally, State and Treasury agreed that the poorer LDCs have an aid problem, not a debt problem. The more appropriate policy response to this situation was judged to be an enhancement of new aid commitments to the poorest LDCs, not a writeoff of their relatively small outstanding external debts.

Multiple-Advocacy Model

Decisions taken under the multiple-advocacy model involve the forceful management of the competitive bureaucratic viewpoints by a dispassionate, neutral adherent to a presidential perspective. Power brokering is removed from representatives of line departments. Normally a White House official, the coordination manager has the responsibility to ensure an equitable distribution of power, information, staff resources, and access to the President among the participating bureaucratic actors. Ideally, the President participates from the beginning of the debate.[1] Advocacy from the Congress and interested groups in the private sector may also be included in this form of policy-making process.

The closest example of what might be posited as potentially the ideal means of decision making was the interagency deliberations in 1972–73 that produced a proposal for major trade legislation. The latter was submitted to Congress in April 1973 and eventually became the Trade Act of 1974. The process by which the trade bill was drafted reflected two principal realities. First, U.S. trade policy, then in the period subsequent to that of the new economic policy, was at a major historical crossroads. Intellectually, the questions of where and how to proceed legislatively were exceedingly complex. Even the basic question of the wisdom of submitting a comprehensive trade bill to the Hill had to be thrashed out. Second, the number of bureaucratic entities in 1972 with an overall or specific interest in major trade legislation was enormous. More than a dozen departments and agencies regularly participated in the interagency drafting sessions. Others attended occasionally. About twenty-five persons reportedly attended a typical meeting.

The so-called Trade Legislative Committee, the interagency group that handled the statute- drafting chore, was established formally in the Council on International Economic Policy (CIEP) machinery by George Shultz's acting in his informal capacity as "economic czar" and in his formal capacity as head of the Cabinet-level Council on Economic Policy and a body senior to the CIEP. The Committee was chaired by the deputy executive director of the CIEP and reported to the cabinet-level Executive Committee of the CIEP. This committee was headed by Shultz by virtue of his also being chairman of the CIEP.

The starting-off point for the interagency discussions was provided by a nonbureaucratic source: the report submitted in 1971 by the President's Commission on International Trade and Investment Policy. It had been formed in 1971 by President Nixon to study independently and exhaustively all the options open to the United States on all international commercial issues during the 1970s. The dozens of specific policy recommendations contained in the report were methodically sifted by the trade legislative group as its initial exercise in debating the issues.

By late 1972, work began in earnest to put the language of the bill in final form. This effort also was under the overall supervision of Shultz, the President's man. Although he was the Treasury secretary, Shultz's personal traits and style permitted him to play the role of the neutral custodian of the presidential perspective. His demeanor in this exercise was usually soft-spoken, at times enigmatic, and always pointed in the direction of building a consensus. His firm commitment to producing the best possible trade bill was reflected in his occasional opposition to Treasury positions.

Differences in goals and viewpoints abounded in the continuing interagency deliberations. State and the Office of the Special Representative for Trade Negotiations shared a preference for a very liberal bill with a maximum of negotiating authority. The Treasury and Commerce Departments were anxious to protect and promote the balance of payments and the business sector, respectively. The Agriculture Department was anxious to rectify what was presumed to be an insufficient agricultural liberalization package produced in the Kennedy Round. All these viewpoints were valid inputs in a major governmental debate on trade strategy. Although these disagreements slowed down the drafting process, they forced an exacting and thorough debate on the issues and eventually produced a bill with broad support in the administration.

The reason that the bureaucratic-politics model is not an accurate description of the work of the Trade Legislative Committee is based not only on the means of supervision but on the means of making final decisions as well. When an immediate consensus was not forthcoming on a relatively minor issue, the committee's chairman, who was the deputy executive director of the CIEP, would make a ruling, in effect on behalf of the President. Substantive disagreements and appeals immediately would be sent up to the CIEP's Executive Committee for a decision. If no consensus developed there, the President's economic chief, Shultz, personally would make the final decision or request a presidential decision.

A second example of the multiple-advocacy model involved an issue of a far more narrow scope but one that is a classic representation of an international economic policy dilemma: Economic interests, political virtue and the national interest were tinged with soft nuances, not clear truths. In late 1978, President Carter ordered the drafting of a formal policy statement on the export of hazardous substances whose use had been banned for safety or environmental reasons within the United States, but whose use was legal overseas. Only in the final days of his Presidency, in mid-January 1981, was President Carter able to sign the long-awaited Executive Order.

The two-and-one-half-year effort and five written drafts that preceded this signing were reflective in part of the inevitable difficulty of achieving consensus among more than twenty-two bureaucratic actors that constituted the task force assembled to draft the document. Eleven cabinet departments were regularly represented (only the Department of Housing and Urban Development and the Department of Education were absent). Regular participants also included the Consumer Product Safety Commission, the Environmental Protection Agency, the Export-Import Bank, the Agency for International Development, the Office of Management and Budget, the U.S. Special Trade Representative, the Regulatory Council, the Overseas Private Investment Corporation, the Nuclear Regulatory Commission, and ACTION. The twenty-second participant consisted of multiple representatives from the Executive Office of the President. Cochairing the task force was a member of the President's Council on Environmental Equality and the President's Consumer Affairs Adviser. At various times, the Office of Domestic Policy, the Council of Economic Advisers, and the Office of Science and Technology (all in the Executive Office of the President) participated in the deliberations.

The policy-making process moved beyond a brokering of the numerous sentiments of the executive branch. Six sets of public hearings were held by the interagency task force with invited representatives of interested industries and consumer groups. Comments were also received when a draft report was published in the *Federal Register* in August 1980. In addition, task force members periodically testified to congressional hearings that were independently considering revisions in various statutes affecting exports of the various hazardous substances: drugs, chemicals, pesticides, nuclear materials, and so forth.

The Bureaucratic Politics Model

International economic policy is one of the prime examples of the bureaucratic politics model of decision making. At the roots of the model is the broad contention that the executive branch of the U.S. government does not think and act in a monolithic manner. This contention rests on two intermediate premises. First, there are relatively few instances when the best policy option to promote the national interest, be it in international economic policy or national security policy, is unequivocably, unambiguously clear. Second, different bureaucratic actors have different missions, and each is concerned with a different phase of the totality of the country's involvement in international economic relations. Each agency has been created to advance and defend certain perspectives and priorities. The State Department is in business to worry about U.S. relations with other countries and the political milieu in general. The Treasury Department is paid to be concerned with the U.S. economy. The Commerce, Agriculture, and Labor Departments have as their "constituents" the industrial, agricultural, and labor sectors respectively. Political appointees and career officials in those and in the many other bureaucratic agencies have a sincere belief that their viewpoints and needs are valid and that their influence in the policy-making process should be maximized.

The bureaucratic politics model therefore downplays the notion of the executive branch as a unified, rational actor. Instead it suggests that in most instances policy formulation can best be understood as the outcome of bargaining among participants in various parts of the bureaucracy, each with a unique set of perceptions, priorities, and missions. To the extent that their policy prescriptions differ, the pursuit of consensus tends to become more of a pragmatic search for a mutually acceptable course of conduct than an idealistic pursuit of optimal policy.

The initial response by the United States to the less developed countries' (LDCs) economic demands that are collectively known as "the new international economic order" was a classic case of bureaucratic politics at work. Predictably, the Treasury Department assumed an orthodox free market approach, decrying suggestions that government intervention and budgetary funds be used to rig the international economic system to favor the LDCs. Sensitive to the political implications of an angry group of nations capable of disrupting the international order, the State Department is anxious to develop a serious dialogue wherever and whenever possible. With regard to some of the more extreme LDC proposals (e.g., indexing of commodity prices according to the price trends of industrial goods), there never has been a major State-Treasury dispute. The search for a common bureaucratic meeting ground was successful on a number of the aid proposals floated because of common perceptions. In general, U.S. policy has emphasized the use of official and private capital flows in lieu of price-fixing proposals. No U.S. agency prefers to emphasize antimarket forces to foster the development process.

An unusual number of organizational strains and innovations are associated with this new, complex discussion of how to alter the North-South status quo. They include the inherent difficulties of constructing a policy where a minimum number of precedents exist, where the technical questions associated with some of the proposals are very complex, where a clear mix of economic and political factors exist, where jurisdictional lines are blurred, where differences of opinion between departments escalate into a public, no-holds-barred rivalry, and where no arbitration mechanism is readily available to hammer out a harmonized policy.

From the official birth of the new-international-economic-order concept in the spring of 1974 at the Sixth Special Session of the United Nations General Assembly until May 1975, the United States has assumed a hostile attitude, opposing the general view that structural changes were necessary to reduce the international economic system's alleged bias against the poor countries. The session produced a document entitled

"Declaration on the Establishment of a New International Economic Order"; a subsequent document approved by the General Assembly, entitled the "Chapter of Economic Rights and Duties of States," contained a long shopping list of demands to redress the imbalance of world economic wealth. International commodity agreements to raise and fix commodity prices, unilateral reductions in industrial country barriers to exports of LDCs, elimination of all restraints on the expropriation of foreign direct investments including the requirement of full and prompt compensation, a general debt moratorium, transfer of technology on easier terms, and a generally increased voice for LDCs in international economic organizations—these were among the demands written in harsh, uncompromising terms.

Initial U.S. policy was negative for a number of reasons—the United States was still a leader of and a firm believer in a market-oriented international economy. In addition, the initial LDC rhetoric was extreme and uncompromising. There was a widely held, lingering hope that the OPEC would disintegrate, and thus a hard line—not appeasement—was necessary to prevent further cartels from being formed. In addition, the United States had a relatively minor dependence on developing countries for critical raw materials, exclusive of oil. This country is able, therefore, to risk more antipathy by the developing countries than could the far more resource-dependent Europeans and Japanese.

A major turning point in the heretofore unified U.S. position took place in the wake of the failure of the April 1975 preparatory meeting that was to set the stage for an international conference between producers and consumers of energy. The talks collapsed when an irreconcilable split developed between industrial and developing countries on the question whether the agenda for the energy conference should be broadened to include discussion of other raw materials and the rest of the South's economic demands. Plans for an international energy conference between producers and consumers were postponed indefinitely; in short, a dead end had been reached. The time had come for an initiative. It would shortly be Kissinger who took it.

Separate studies by the State and Treasury Departments of the international-commodity-agreement issue had begun in 1974 but were merged into an interagency task force on international commodity agreements in February 1975. This group in turn reported to two other review groups, the EPB (Economic Policy Board) and the NSC, the former having a spiritual and intellectual affinity with Treasury, the latter with State. Thus, while a more efficient cooperative effort resulted, neither State nor Treasury yielded any control over the options-exploration process. Some consensus emerged, nonetheless. The principal conclusion reached by the task force was that the United States should be prepared to discuss commodity price and supply arrangements on an individual basis and should avoid a single grand approach to commodity arrangements.[2]

In late April, Secretary of State Kissinger was reviewing the text of a speech concerning food policy, which he was scheduled to deliver on May 13 in Kansas City, Missouri. He thought the speech both boring and unresponsive to the existing issues. He thereupon ordered his staff to include language proclaiming a new U.S. flexibility on the North-South dialogue. By the time the rewritten text had been approved within State, there was time only for a perfunctory, eleventh-hour clearance at the top levels of the Treasury Department. Despite the fact that technically there was an approval by Treasury, the last-minute, hasty clearance process permitted no opportunity for any real input by other departments. And so Kissinger announced that the United States was prepared to discuss "new arrangements in individual commodities on a case-by-case basis as circumstances warrant." He also stated that this country was anxious to attend a new preparatory meeting for a North-South dialogue. His talk began an unprecedented process of forcing U.S. new-international-economic-order policy by speechmaking. A major policy decision had been forged by Kissinger's last-minute command to his senior staff, to allow him to enunciate publicly a new U.S. posture on commodities. Interagency deliberations had at best been perfunctory.

A close analysis of Kissinger's speech would reveal a carefully hedged, least-common-denominator approach, which committed this country to very little in the way of specifics. Nevertheless, the speech triggered a savage bureaucratic counterattack at Treasury. The latter, whose legal jurisdiction in the issue of international commodity agreements is somewhat unclear, issued the first of what would be many broadsides against State, suggesting that U.S. policy had not really changed in this case. In a late May 1975 White House meeting, Treasury Secretary William Simon attempted to impress upon the President that nothing Kissinger had said or would say would bind this country to anything specific. Assistant Treasury Secretary Gerald Parsky told a press interviewer shortly afterwards that "no decision has been made to make a change in the basic thrust of this country's policy in the commodities area, which is to maintain to the maximum extent the free functioning of the marketplace." What Kissinger said is settled U.S. policy; what it means is not yet settled policy, an official of the special trade representative's office was quoted as saying.[3]

The very subtle shift in attitude and the nonshift in actual policy notwithstanding, the commodity-cartel question assumed a life far out of proportion to its actual merits and importance. It became a symbol of the larger and oversimplified ideological question as to the need to occasionally circumvent the market mechanism with negotiated price fixing as a means of assuaging the economic demands of the poorer countries.

The approach of the UN Seventh Special Session, in September 1975, meant another speech and the opportunity for another U.S. initiative.

Not wishing to repeat the coordination fiasco associated with the May speech, the State Department initiated an *ad hoc* series of consultations, primarily with the Treasury and Agriculture Departments. Once it was decided to have Secretary Kissinger's speech include a major series of resource-transfer proposals, each one was negotiated and cleared at all levels of the other agencies. An August meeting at the cabinet level went over each of the proposals for which technical agreement had been reached at the working level. In a few cases, the President had to resolve basic points on which no consensus could be reached. In each case he took the side of Kissinger against opposition from one or more top officials, their opposition largely stemming from budgetary concerns. Contact was also maintained with interested members of Congress who generally encouraged a responsive U.S. approach.

The Kissinger speech delivered to the United Nations on September 1, 1975, contained more than forty proposals, some old, some new, some borrowed, and some misconstrued. They emphasized new or expanded financing facilities in the IMF and the World Bank. The scope and positivism of the U.S. program caused the speech to be extremely favorably received by everyone. The U.S. bureaucracy, too, was happy. The executive branch had agreed to support a number of new financial facilities to transfer resources to LDCs, to demand guaranteed access of supply, as well as to oppose some of the South's more extreme economic proposals, such as indexing of commodity prices according to the price trends of industrial goods. After a concerted effort at interagency coordination, only one major difference remained in the wide range of aid policies.

Only the vexatious question of commodity agreements was not laid to rest by the second great policy-by-speech initiative. The policy-by-speech syndrome took another turn when Assistant Treasury Secretary Parsky told a San Francisco audience in January 1976 that "there appears to be a growing willingness to sacrifice economic principles for the sake of political gains. If, for political reasons, we agree now . . . with demands for a new economic system, it will be impossible to justify on economic grounds our desire to preserve our system later." He also announced that the United States would not sign the then pending international cocoa agreement.

None of this speech had been cleared with a horrified State Department. The latter had been hoping to push positively for a revision of the cocoa agreement's proposed language, not opt for a public declaration of opposition. Parsky's equivocal written clarification of U.S. commodity-agreements policy to the press on the next day did nothing to clarify U.S. policy. Despite the statement's reiteration of the principle of case-by-case approach for commodity agreements, he allegedly told the assembled reporters verbally that U.S. policy in principle opposed the concept of such agreements. The degree to which the relevant officials in the State and Treasury Departments pursued bureaucratic politics exacerbated a unique characteristic of the American way of disagreeing: a propensity to air the disagreement in public, for all to see.

And so the U.S. government's posture toward a major element of the new international economic order festered on an open-ended basis for more than a year. The Treasury assumed the role of protector of the market mechanism, while the State Department argued for a pragmatic posture to allow price stabilization discussions (as opposed to commitment) on any commodity. In the meantime, an interagency Commodities Policy Coordinating Committee, reporting to both the EPB and the NSC, formed to continue intragovernmental discussions on this subject.

Another example of pure bureaucratic politics involves the question of export promotion. Among the many basic questions involved here are these: Is it necessary and proper for the government to provide support services to help the private sector increase its sales and profits? If so, are present techniques cost effective and efficient? And finally, how much priority should be placed on export promotion per se? The ensuing policy debate was, and is, one of those rare occasions when neither the State nor Treasury Department is involved as a primary actor; neither department has any mission or constituency directly involved.

A further example of a relatively pure application of the bureaucratic politics model occurred when the Ford administration reached its decision in April 1976 as to what would be its reaction to the ITC's (International Trade Commission) recommendation that the U.S. footwear industry be granted relief from import competition. Rather than invoke the escape clause to impose higher tariffs or quotas, President Ford accepted the narrow (one-vote) majority recommendation of his cabinet-level Trade Policy Committee that funds for adjustment assistance be made available to the industry. In addition to the predictable votes of the foreign-trade-related departments who are members of the committee (State on the liberal side, and Commerce and Labor on the protectionist side), the Department of Defense's vote was exactly the one that conformed to its interests and mission. Two of the major shoe-exporting countries to this market are Spain and Italy. Since the former is the site of important military bases and the latter is a NATO ally facing serious economic difficulties and an increasingly powerful Communist party, and since domestic suppliers of footwear to the American military were secure from foreign competition, the Defense Department also is prone to see its mission and values enhanced by the liberal trade approach. A minimum of trade barriers increases competition, while a protectionist policy is an anathema to the enforcers of anti-trust laws.

This exercise also provided a valuable insight into the limits of the bureaucratic politics model and the need for inside information to comprehend all the twists and turns of bureaucratic behavior. The Office of the U.S. Trade Representative (USTR) is charged with negotiating the worldwide reduction of trade barriers; as such, fears of retaliation and hostile trading partners must weigh heavily in the spirit of its bureaucratic "essence." Nevertheless, the USTR vote was cast with the protectionist side in this footwear escape clause.

The USTR's behavior in this case is best predicted and explained by the inside knowledge of that agency's marketing efforts in the public sector to assure Congressional passage of the Trade Act of 1974. During the course of this effort, USTR officials emphasized to representatives of import sensitive industries that the bill, if passed, would provide them with easier access to governmental import relief programs. In fact, the "sales pitch" went further. The USTR promised that after the bill became law, it would not play an active role in denying relief to petitioning industries that had been declared qualified for it under the more flexible language. When USTR voted with the protectionist bureaucratic actors in the 1976 footwear case, it may have been acting contrary to its immediate bureaucratic mission. But it was keeping its word, extended in conjunction with the pursuit of a larger interest: passage of major new trade legislation. In other instances, the USTR office has demonstrated its institutional affinity for congressional sensitivities by favoring the negotiation of voluntary export restraint agreements in cases where a politically sensitive industry has been adversely affected by import competition.

Another example of the applicability of the bureaucratic politics model occurred when opposite sides squared off in the spring of 1980 concerning the restoration of the Trigger Price Mechanism for steel. A *quid pro quo* had been struck between the United States Steel Corporation and the two leaders of administrative trade policy: the Office of the USTR and the Commerce Department. The former agreed that it would withhold on its threat to file numerous antidumping petitions alleging a number of European steel producers with selling steel at less than fair value in the U.S. market. In return, the administration would adopt a more sympathetic posture toward the U.S. steel industry's economic problems. This posture would center on an increase in the price level at which the recently suspended Trigger Price Mechanism would, in effect, establish minimum prices for steel imports.

The domestic economic perspectives of the chairman of the President's Council of Economic Advisers (CEA) and the secretary of the Treasury were not pitted against the foreign trade and domestic political concerns that generated the proposed imported steel arrangement. The CEA chairman and Treasury secretary successfully convinced President Carter that the deal should not be invoked because it would have unacceptably bad inflationary consequences. But the deal became unstuck only temporarily. In the fall of 1980, essentially the same deal was agreed upon. As events unfolded over the summer, it had become clear that the administration would probably be confronted with the need to make a final decision on the merits of the steel dumping petitions just days before the fall elections. Rather than make a critical decision on trade policy at such a hectic time, the administration apparently decided to defuse the situation with an immediate negotiated settlement with the domestic steel industry.

A final demonstration of the bureaucratic politics model occurred early in the Reagan administration, as it deliberated the merits of possible import restrictions on automobile imports from Japan. The Departments of Commerce, Transportation, and Labor took a domestic perspective and argued on behalf of the importance of giving the ailing domestic industry breathing space from foreign-import competition. On the other side, the Departments of State and Treasury, the Council of Economic Advisers, and the Office of Management and Budget adhered to the liberal trade perspective. They argued that import restrictions would be inflationary, would contradict the new administration's emphasis on reducing governmental regulation of the economy, would not assist in gasoline conservation efforts, and in general would not be an effective means of addressing the domestic industry's problems.

The complexity of the automobile import issue as it had unfolded by the early spring of 1981 also provided evidence to demonstrate the over-simplication that results in attempting to explain the international economic policy-making process as operating strictly within the confines of bureaucratic politics (i.e., the search for compromise between different bureaucratic viewpoints).

In the first place, it was clear that President Reagan ultimately would be called on to make the final decision, presumably either deciding among several policy options or ratifying a consensus recommendation. Second, the Congress since 1980 had been exerting considerable pressure to place ceilings on Japanese automobile imports. Resolutions and legislation had been introduced, and at least four committees had held hearings to examine the effect on the U.S. automobile industry of import competition. In sum, the clear signals emanating from Congress that the auto industry needed help could not be ignored in the executive branch's policy-making exercises.

Two relatively unique factors were also relevant to the policy-making process. The first was the active lobbying in Washington (including a visit to the White House) of eight Republican governors from states whose economies are tightly linked to the production of automobiles and the production of materials and components for that industry (steel, rubber, glass, and so forth). Second, signals from Tokyo had become clear by March 1981 that the Japanese government was fully prepared in principle to negotiate an orderly marketing agreement prior to the then impending official visit to Washington of Japanese Prime Minister Zenko Suzuki. The Japanese, in effect, were indicating that they awaited the official application of arm-twisting pressures by the Reagan administration as the prelude to a voluntary export restraint agreement.[4] One thing that was not unique was the prolific use of leaks to reporters and columnists that provided a public insight into the contending sides of the auto issue within the Reagan administration.

Single-Agency Domination

Shared jurisdiction among bureaucratic entities is a dominant, but not universal, norm in international economic policy making. When specialized expertise is involved, it may be that only one department or agency matters. The most important example of single-agency control is the Treasury Department's dominance of U.S. international monetary policy. The latter includes the balance of payments, exchange-rate adjustments, use of monetary reserves, voting in the IMF, and the monetary role of gold. These issues are exceedingly arcane in nature. They are also divorced from domestic politics and public concern, inasmuch as they do not effect the public in a direct or measurable manner. Outside of Treasury, only the State Department and the CEA in the administration have even a limited interest and expertise. Only the Federal Reserve Board, which formally is independent of the executive branch, shares with Treasury a major interest, expertise, and, through the Federal Reserve Bank of New York, operational responsibilities. In the public sector, a select handful of academics and Wall Street types maintain an active interest and sought-after opinions.

The normal pattern of international monetary policy decision making is for proposals and positions to be developed within Treasury by its relatively large complement of financial economists, all of whom report to the undersecretary for monetary affairs. The main vehicle for interagency consultation is the International Monetary Group, which achieved prominence as the Volcker Group when Paul Volcker was the Treasury's undersecretary for monetary affairs in the early 1970s. In terms of efficiency and effectiveness, it has proven to be one of the best of all coordinating groups in international economic policy. It has several factors working in its favor: For example, it is a small, tight group of technicians with similar analytical approaches, all of whom acknowledge and respect Treasury's dominance. The group has also successfully prevented the relatively conservative posture of the Federal Reserve Board (part of the central bankers' mentality syndrome) from charting the course of U.S. international monetary policy.

Extraordinary monetary developments such as the dollar devaluations have required presidential involvement. Important initiatives, such as the 1972 endorsement of flexible exchange rates, required consultation with cabinet-level economic officials. But on a day-to-day basis, the Treasury position is cleared neatly by the subcabinet International Monetary Group and thereupon becomes U.S. policy. Certain technical decisions on exchange-rate flexibility during the Rambouillet meeting in November 1975 were relegated to the finance ministries of just two countries, France and the United States. With only a few points preventing final agreement on a monetary reform package, the finance ministers of the other countries participating in the economic summit charged the financial officials of those two countries to reconcile the few remaining differences. The feeling was that whatever final language was agreed upon by the two delegations, it would be one that all of them could live with. Indeed, so much in command of the monetary reform exercise were the finance ministers that they were in a position to select a two-nation subcommittee to reach a final understanding affecting the whole world.

There are numerous other cases where specialized or noncontroversial issues are dealt with by a single department or agency. For example, interagency clearance is little more than a limited, pro forma courtesy in such matters as the bilateral taxation treaties negotiated by the Treasury Department, and the routine GATT business attended to by the Office of the U.S. Trade Representative.

The Personality Factor

Strong personalities being in the right place at the right time can force decisions and short-circuit the established operational decision-making organization. When the cult of personality successfully intervenes, all bets are off. Personalities can and do substitute for established organizational patterns.

Illustrative of this model was the intervention by senior officials who, operating on their own, encouraged President Nixon to order a shift in U.S. policy on exchange-rate realignment in late 1971. In the aftermath of the new economic policy, foreign exchange rates were floating in response to free market forces. This was a highly unsettling experience to the financial authorities of almost every other free world country. John Connally, then secretary of the Treasury, personally dominated U.S. international economic policy during the latter third of 1971 as the result of his extraordinary relationship with the President and his hard-driving personality. His strategy was to press hard on other industrial countries to revalue their currencies and reduce their barriers to U.S. exports, all the while refusing to be specific on the administration's terms for a negotiated settlement on exchange rates. The United States was relatively insulated from the prolonged international monetary chaos, and Connally was playing his strong hand for all it was worth.

Had the State Department enjoyed strong leadership and influence with the President at this time, a classic confrontation of bureaucratic politics would have developed. Economic initiatives were causing political problems of great concern to foreign policy priorities. As weeks stretched into months, the economic strains were increasingly likely to spill over into the political-national security sectors. The timing was particularly inopportune for creating disarray in the Atlantic alliance, since presidential summit meetings with China and the Soviet Union loomed on the horizon.

A very informal alliance to alter U.S. policy began to develop between Kissinger, in his role as the President's national security adviser, and Arthur Burns, chairman of the independent Federal Reserve Board. Peterson, head of the CIEP, and Robert Hormats, Kissinger's assistant for economic affairs, played supportive roles by raising questions within the White House noting that the U.S. demands on the Europeans and Japanese were unreasonable, unattainable, and damaging to overall U.S. foreign policy objectives. The immediate problem was tactical: The sheer force of Secretary Connally's personality and his close relationship with the President suggested the folly of a frontal attack that would force the president to choose between sides. In addition, the State Department as an institution was not in the picture to lend support.

Both Kissinger and Burns made informal, personal presentations to the President concerning the dangers of prolonging agreement on a monetary settlement. The former emphasized the political ramifications, while Burns reportedly emphasized the growing dangers of foreign retaliation, a move that could lead to global economic chaos.

> By mid-November (1971) the voices of Kissinger, Burns and the President's own friends on Wall Street began to make an impression on Mr. Nixon. They tried to convince him that to continue to follow the Connally policy could have disastrous consequences, that the United States could no longer keep the world on tenterhooks and had to make it clear that it was ready to devalue the dollar in terms of gold and agree to a new set of exchange rates. The President listened and gradually... decided to end the waiting game.[5]

Technically, the presidential model of decision making was operational. But it was bent by the force of two senior personalities.

Other Methods of Executive Branch Decision Making

Not all means of organizational decision making in U.S. international economic policy conform to one or even a combination of the modes described above. Other decisions and positions spring from the idiosyncratic and unique factors operating in specific areas. Any typology of decision-making techniques in U.S. international economic relations must be open ended to some extent. The very imprecision of the system precludes a narrow approach. A sample of the prominent examples of extraordinary policy formulation follows.

On some occasions, the pursuit of excellence on a given policy issue must be subordinated to larger or more important objectives. The linkage factor is inherent in international economic relations, the crossroads of internal and external political and economic considerations. The net economic cost-effectiveness of restricting grain exports to the USSR was judged incidental in 1980 to the national security imperative of imposing financial (if not dietary) costs on the Soviets for their actions in Afghanistan. Another example of linkage occurred in senior-level discussions of the Carter administration on its posture on a sugar program. The then secretary of the Treasury, Michael Blumenthal, had made a presentation that emphasized (for anti-inflation reasons) a sugar support price that was a fraction of a cent below the minimum level being demanded by interested congressional leaders. With import duties linked to the support price, Robert Strauss, at that time the U.S. Trade Representative, had an important stake in these deliberations. When Mr. Blumenthal was finished, Mr. Strauss rebutted his colleague's proposal with an opinion that an excellent sugar program had just been outlined. However, he declared that "we are running a government, not a sugar program." He went on to argue that the administration would not be able to get approval for major legislation from the Senate Foreign Affairs (then chaired by Senator Frank Church of Idaho) or the Senate Finance Committee (then chaired by Senator Russell Long of Louisiana) if the proposed price support level was not increased to accomodate congressional representatives from those states producing sugar products.[6]

A second set of policies and decisions can be looked at in terms of organizational shortcomings brought about by the failure of the system to foresee and quickly react to unforeseen and unsettling events. One example of this phenomenon was the federal government's being caught flat-footed by the massive Soviet grain purchases in 1972. The belated realization of the magnitude of Soviet buying, it is generally agreed, increased domestic prices because of resulting reserve shortages, and wasted millions of tax dollars in unnecessary wheat subsidies. In its haste to unload what were then major grain surpluses, the Agriculture Department ignored reports by its own attaché in Moscow (and perhaps forecasts by the CIA as well) concerning the major shortfall in the Russian harvest. Because it did not collect data on the magnitude of the sales contracts handled by private grain exporters, the U.S. government had no way of foreseeing the depletion on reserves or the strain on transportation facilities. Nor was there any mechanism to guarantee that wheat subsidies were terminated as soon as it became obvious that only the United States had exportable quantities of wheat in 1975 and therefore was fully capable of establishing the world price. "At virtually every step ... the grain sales were ineptly managed," concluded the Senate's Permanent Subcommittee on Investigations.[7]

A systematic reporting system was instituted, requiring that all U.S. grain trading companies promptly notify the Agriculture Department of all major export orders received. Using this data and keeping lines of communication open with the appropriate offices in the Soviet government, the Agriculture Department has increased its ability to forecast the size of harvests in and demand for U.S. agricultural commodities by the Soviet Union and other key importing countries. The changed situation was demonstrated by the meticulous management of grain exports to the Russians by an inflation-conscious Ford administration in 1974 and 1975. An informal set of export controls in 1974, and a temporary suspension of grain sales to the Soviets announced in August 1975, invoked the wrath of a farm bloc desirous of unfettered sales and higher prices.

Whereas the wheat deal demonstrated shortcomings of single-department organization, the soybean export embargo in 1973 demonstrated the limits of *ad hoc* interagency organizational arrangements designed to meet an unforeseen shift in U.S. trade policy. Branding the United States as an undependable supplier in foreign eyes, the embargo made suspect U.S. claims that foreign agricultural trade barriers were an unnecessary but important detriment to U.S. exports.

The soybean decision was mainly the result of a limited soybean crop to begin with, a growing foreign demand, and President Nixon's food price freeze imposed on June 13, 1973. Exports were not subject to these price controls, and the government immediately established a reporting system for exporters of agricultural commodities. Everyone realized that soybeans were the most likely candidate for export restrictions because of the tight supply situation.

The monitoring facility in retrospect amounted to a self-fulfilling prophecy. Private soybean export contracts soared in anticipation of formal export controls. An Interagency Task Force on Food Exports Controls, chaired by the CIEP, was established by the more senior Council on Economic Policy at the working level on June 16, to study the situation and the government's options. The group's initial interpretation of the soybean supply and demand situation suggested an imminent exhaustion of that commodity, and they recommended to the White House that export controls be adopted. They were imposed on June 27.

The key to the recommendation for export controls was the *ad hoc* task force's inability to interpret accurately the data on export contracts collected for the export monitoring system by the Commerce Department. Despite soaring prices, a physical shortage of soybeans was never really a serious threat. Unfortunately, the interagency group lacked the expertise to recognize the immense padding of reported export contracts written as a hedge against later controls. The tremendous volume of double counting inherent in the contract totals was not appreciated at that time because only experts could have disregarded what in fact were a large number of "phantom" contracts. The actual amount of export contracts on the books as of June 13, 1973, later proved to have been almost double the amount of export business actually conducted.

A case study of the soybean decision written for the Murphy Commission noted that many of the government officials later interviewed insisted that if a more accurate and better researched set of data had been available in mid-1973, the decision would not have been made as it was. The study concluded that even without the export controls, foreign buyers would have received the same amounts of soybeans that they received under the export control system. "Therefore, the American consumer was left with the same amount of soybeans that he would have had without an export control system. The decision . . . hardly achieved any of the U.S. objectives for an export control system."[8] In the main, the decision reflected government ignorance of commercial operations.

The U.S. government's efforts to accumulate a strategic Petroleum Reserve reflect the dynamics of bureaucratic politics, as well as the dynamics of administrative ineptitude. The objective of stockpiling the equivalent of a 90-day supply of oil imports has not been achieved. After some five years of effort, the equivalent of about 16 days of imports was in the Reserve in late 1980; the approximately 90 million barrels stored at that time was less than 10 percent of the established target. This shortfall reflects the impact of several factors, principally (1) the successful effort by OMB (Office of Management and Budget) to restrain governmental oil purchases as a means of achieving its priority goal of reducing federal spending; (2) the calculated effort not to increase demand for oil after prices began to surge in 1979; (3) the controversial respect shown since 1979 for Saudi Arabia's admonitions that the United States restrain purchases for the Strategic Petroleum Reserve, and (4) technical problems. Prior to 1980, however, the amount of oil in the Reserve was academic. The Department of Energy had not yet put into place the pumps necessary to draw oil out of its underground storage caverns should it be needed.

Finally, some decisions are made through an organizational plan that is especially devised because of the extraordinary nature of the policy being developed or pursued. For example, the multiphased negotiating apparatus established to secure the Japanese voluntary textile export restraints demanded by President Nixon was unique and occasionally bizarre. Negotiations were pursued through front channels, secret back channels, and quasi-legal public-congressional channels. Secretary of Commerce Maurice Stans, who failed at the first crack at negotiations, eventually was replaced by presidential aide Peter Flanigan. He in turn was succeeded by special ambassador David Kennedy. Intermingled with these official negotiations were discussions involving Kissinger on the back channel, and unofficial talks with the Japanese by Congressman Wilbur Mills (then chairman of the Ways and Means Committee) and by business leader and presidential friend Donald Kendall. Noticeably absent among the plethora of active U.S. government officials were representatives of the State and Treasury Departments and the President's special representative for trade negotiations.

An earlier effort at voluntary export restraints, this one involving steel, was quietly and quickly conducted on harmonious terms with the European and Japanese industries in 1968. Antitrust and other legal considerations dictated that the restraints appear to spring unilaterally from the respective national steel industries. The State Department acted as a quiet intermediary and provided its good offices to bring together the foreign companies offering to participate in an unofficial arrangement and the domestic steel industry. The need for restraints stemmed from the latter's pressuring Congress for import protection on national security grounds. The State Department's role was low keyed, but not enough to prevent the officials involved from being named as defendants in a suit filed by a consumer group in 1971 against senior State Department officials, as well as individual U.S., Japanese, and European steel companies. The suit charged them with conspiring to restrain trade in violation of U.S. antitrust laws and with circumventing the established escape-clause procedures of the Trade Expansion Act used to determine if import injury in fact existed. "Law-abiding" bureaucrats are not likely to opt for this procedure in the future.

The Congress and the Executive-Legislative Mode of Policy Making

It is only a slight exaggeration to argue that two different governmental entities are responsible for the formulation and implementation of U.S. international economic policy: the executive branch and the legislative branch. The degree to which the overall U.S. government is based on the concept of a separation of powers is as unique as the variable blend of economics and foreign policy considerations that comprises international economic policy. This organizational situation—sometimes characterized as separate institutions sharing broad powers—has created a uniquely complex partnership between the legislative and executive branches in the conduct of U.S. external economic relations. The resultant dynamics of this interactive relationship is an important variable in the policy-making process.

A simple conclusion results: No model of U.S. international economic policy making that examines only intra-executive branch dynamics is adequate. In no other form of government does the legislative branch have the power, the capabilities, and the inclination to affect the formulation and administration of external economic policies above and beyond the executive branch's preferences. The reason for this is simple. The American Constitution clearly delegates more authority over this country's foreign commerce and finance to the Congress than to the President.[9]

There are three principal operational variants of the executive-legislative mode of decision making in international economic policy. The first is represented by unilateral measures imposed on the administration by legislative initiative. Examples of this variant include the New Direction guidelines for the bilateral foreign aid program imposed in 1973 by statute and the 1978 legislative provision authorizing the United States to in effect convert some of its old bilateral development loans into grants in connection with the LDCs' debt relief demands. In both cases, the administration was not responsible for creating the congressional initiative, but was responsive and favorably disposed to it. In other cases, a congressional initiative can be forced on an unwilling, unappreciative administration. In some of these cases, it appears as if the latter might have underestimated Congress's ability to act in the face of presidential opposition. The 1980 legislation banning President Carter's imposition of a special duty on imported petroleum demonstrates this potential clash of wills. The limitations imposed on the President's extension of nondiscriminatory (MFN) tariff treatment to communist bloc countries by the Jackson-Vanik Amendment to the Trade Act of 1974 also exemplifies this adversary form of executive-legislative dynamics in international economic policy.

The second variant of this model involves a friendly joint effort to develop new policy through legislation. The drafting of major legislation in 1962, 1974, and 1979 exemplifies positive, give-and-take consensus formation. The process by which the Congress considered and then modified the Trade Reform Act, as submitted in 1973 by the Nixon administration, reflected harmonious congressional-executive working relations at their best. Despite the latent protectionist attitudes on Capitol Hill and despite the emerging Watergate-induced sentiment against any new extensions of power to the President, the resulting Trade Act of 1974 bestowed an ample amount of authority on the Chief Executive to negotiate reductions in trade barriers and contained a minimal amount of overtly restrictive provisions.

At the conclusion of the Tokyo Round of multilateral trade negotiations in 1979, additional legislation was needed to provide formal approval of executive branch agreements involving the liberalization of nontariff barriers to trade. The Trade Agreements Act of 1979, which subsequently emerged, had been drafted by what was effectively a cooperative effort by the administration, the Senate Finance Committee, and the House Ways and Means Committee. When the final statutory proposal was formally submitted to the Congress, the latter had already been approved unofficially. Not surprisingly, the bill overwhelmingly passed the House and Senate in the summer of 1979 by votes of 395 to 7 and 90 to 4, respectively.

The third variant consists of actions undertaken by the executive branch in anticipation of possible congressional action. This process is most frequently illustrated in import policy. Congress has given itself the ability to force the executive branch to accept the recommendations of the International Trade Commission (ITC) for import restrictions where import-induced injury has been found in an escape-clause petition. Perhaps the best example of the sensitivities to congressional intentions was demonstrated by the cabinet-level Trade Policy Committee during its formulation of the presidential response in March 1976 to the ITC's recommendation that through the escape clause, import quotas should be imposed for five years to relieve injury alleged to have been suffered by the domestic specialty steel industry. The resulting decision to opt for a voluntary export restraint very clearly reflected the increased role stipulated for the Congress in escape-clause cases. Normal bureaucratic politics would have dictated a united stand (exclusive perhaps of Commerce and Labor) against the quota recommendation. At best, dubious economic analysis was used to demonstrate import-induced injury suffered by the U.S. specialty steel industry at a time that major trade liberalization negotiations were in progress in Geneva. Shared bureaucratic interests and attitudes had to be subordinated to the fact that the Trade Act of 1974 stipulates that Congress can override a presidential rejection of a majority ITC escape-clause recommendation by a simple majority of members voting in both houses. There were in fact indications that such an override would have resulted if the bureaucracy's (State's and Treasury's) instinct for a liberal trade approach had been chosen. The administration's course, therefore, was molded by the practical need to respect the private sector's ability to convince elected representatives in Washington of the domestic political need for import protection. Congressional influence had offset the normal guideline that a State-Treasury consensus presupposes the making of U.S. policy.

CONCLUSIONS

The implications of the empirical evidence is that multiple modes of decision making exist, and that any one of them might be operational in a given international economic policy-making exercise according to prevailing circumstances. Since those circumstances also fail to lend themselves to observable patterns of repetition, then a theory whose task is to explain and predict U.S. international economic policy making must respect the inevitability of diversity. On the whole, there is always the need to reconcile the four core elements of policy: internal and external economic and political objectives. Sometimes those objectives conflict, sometimes they are compatible.

NOTES

1. Alexander George, "The Case for Multiple Advocacy in Making Foreign Policy," *American Political Science Review*, September 1972, p. 751 ff.
2. "U.S. Takes First Hesitant Steps Toward Shift in Commodities Policy," *National Journal*, 21 June 1975, p. 915.
3. Ibid., pp. 915–16.
4. A major factor encouraging this willingness was presumed to stem from a

form of bureaucratic imperialism. Japan's Ministry of International Trade and Industry had long been frustrated in its efforts to influence the Japanese automobile industry. The leverage over it that would accrue to the ministry from administering a voluntary export restraint agreement must have looked quite attractive to it.

5. Harry Brandon, *The Retreat of American Power* (New York: Delta, 1973), p. 236.

6. Not for attribution interview with former U.S. trade policy official, January 1981.

7. U.S. Senate Committee on Government Operations, *Russian Grain Transactions* 93rd Congress, July 1974, p. 55.

8. Griffenhagen Kroeger, Inc., "Cases on a Decade of United States Foreign Economic Policy: 1965–74," vol. 1 (mimeographed, November 1974), pp. 62, 64.

9. For additional detail on Congress's authority, operations, and actions in the realm of international economic policy, see chapter 6 in the second edition of my book, *The Making of United States International Economic Policy* (New York: Praeger, forthcoming in 1982).

8

Organizing International Economic Policy Making

Roger B. Porter

U.S. international economic policy, once a subject of interest to a relatively small number of businessmen, academicians, and government officials, now commands broad public attention. The media is filled with reports on the strength of the dollar in international markets, the actions of OPEC, and the difficulties of declining domestic industries confronted by severe foreign competition. The links between America's economic fortunes and events abroad have multiplied dramatically.

Several developments illuminate why international economic policy has become a more widely discussed topic. The end of the cheap energy era sent the cost of U.S. net oil imports from slightly over $1 billion in 1970 to $72 billion ten years later. While inflation, as measured by the Producer Price Index, rose 124 percent during the decade of the 1970s, net exports of agricultural and other raw materials grew ninety-fold from $300 million to $27 billion. Over the same period, net manufactured goods exports rose from $4 billion to $26 billion. During 1980, exports represented nearly 20 percent of all goods produced in the United States. At the same time, the nation imported more than 50 percent of its needs for nine of the thirteen key industrial raw materials. In short, the U.S. economy has become increasingly dependent on foreign markets and on foreign products.

Not only are the domestic and international economies increasingly interrelated but the relative economic power of the United States has waned. The preeminence of the dollar in international markets is now challenged and its strength relative to other currencies has eroded substantially over the last decade. Dependence on foreign sources of oil and slow U.S. productivity growth have damaged U.S. trade competitiveness. U.S. firms must increasingly compete with state-controlled or supported enterprises. Moreover, as national economies have grown more interrelated, diplomats and those in the national security community show heightened interest in using economic means to achieve foreign policy objectives.

ORGANIZATIONAL CHALLENGES

While the perceived importance of international economic policy is now much greater, the fundamental organizational challenges that underlay the Dodge Report on "Organization for the Development and Coordination of Foreign Economic Policy" in 1954 have altered little in nearly three decades.[1] The first is the interrelatedness of the substantive problems that a government is expected to address. As Joseph Dodge put the problem: There is a need for "the orderly development of foreign economic policy and programs in support of foreign policy objectives and in relation to domestic economic policy."[2]

Major foreign economic problems touch many concerns—important bilateral relationships between the United States and other governments, overall foreign policy objectives, the health of the domestic economy, the strength of particular economic sectors, and the competitive relationships among domestic and international firms. Indeed, issue interrelatedness is especially evident at the intersection of domestic and international concerns. How the President and his administration organize to make decisions—compartmentally or comprehensively—will influence how much integration occurs between individual policy decisions and how much of that integration the President must do himself.

The fragmented structure of the executive branch presents a second major organizational challenge. Authority and resources within the executive branch are divided into bits and pieces, encouraging bureaucratic jockeying for jurisdiction over issues and making consensus building more difficult. Moreover, this fragmentation has grown in recent decades: officials are organized into more layers in the upper reaches of departments and divided into more specialized divisions—with more staff—in each layer.

For the President, the interrelatedness of issues and the fragmented structure of executive departments and offices make organizing foreign economic policy both difficult and important—difficult in that pulling the strands of policy together is a complicated task at best; important in that he wants the parts to bear some relationship to the whole since he is uniquely accountable for the comprehensiveness and coherence of his administration's policies.

FOREIGN ECONOMIC POLICY ADVICE TO THE PRESIDENT: INSTITUTIONAL ARRANGEMENTS

Organizing foreign economic policy advice for the President during the past three decades has varied widely reflecting the decision-making styles of the President and his leading administration officials.

The Eisenhower administration, attracted to orderly, systematic, formal interagency processes, established the Council on Foreign Economic Policy (CFEP) with a mandate "to assure the effective coordination of foreign economic matters of concern to the several departments and agencies of the Executive Branch." Its creation grew out of Eisenhower's preference for focused responsibility and his aversion to *ad hoc* arrangements for forging policy. He observed:

> I am impressed with the fact that at present, the Executive Branch lacks an orderly way of identifying and reconciling conflicting points of view and interests in the development of long-range international economic objectives. . . . This is also true in arriving at solutions to individual foreign economic problems in a way that reflects our best overall national interest.
>
> Some of these problems have been handled by the State Department, some by one or more of my immediate assistants, some by cabinet committees, some by the National Advisory Council, and in a few cases, by the National Security Council or by the Cabinet. Despite the best efforts, the handling of such problems on an ad hoc basis has not always produced the timely or decisive action required by the seriousness or urgency of the problem encountered.[3]

The Council was formally created by a presidential letter on December 11, 1954. Chaired by a special assistant to the President for foreign economic policy (Joseph M. Dodge until July 1956 and then Clarence B. Randall), its members included the secretaries of State, Treasury, Commerce, Agriculture and the director of the Foreign Operations Administration.[4] There were also three *ex officio* members, the President's administrative assistant for economic affairs (later special assistant for economic affairs), his special assistant for national security affairs, and a member of the Council of Economic Advisers. Representatives from other departments and agencies were invited to participate in meetings of the Council when issues concerning them were under consideration.

The Council on Foreign Economic Policy operated formally with agendas, issue papers, and minutes, holding 110 meetings in the little over six years it existed. It was served by a small staff of three professional and four clerical employees in addition to the chairman. The CFEP shared responsibility with another senior interagency economic body, the Advisory Board on Economic Growth and Stability (ABEGS), which had principal responsibility for coordinating domestic economic policy, and with several more narrowly focused groups such as the Trade Policy Committee and the President's Special Committee on Financial Policies for Postattack Operations.

Like much else in the Eisenhower administration, the search for consensus dominated the CFEP's approach to issues. As its chairman, Clarence Randall, described its operation:

In advance of a meeting, an agenda is circulated, usually supported by a brief position paper from the proponent agency.

Quite often, to bring the thinking of the various departments into as sharp focus as possible before the meeting, I designate an interagency working group to prepare a position paper.

Our meetings last precisely one hour. I operate them on precision timing in order that the important officers who attend may safely make other engagements.

Almost invariably a lively and healthy discussion takes place, and every phase of the question is brought out. My function is to chair the conference, and to make sure that everyone has a chance to be heard.

Just before the close of the meeting, I announce the consensus as I see it from the discussion, and this becomes policy at that point, subject to one very important exception. I have, of course, no authority, and it would be wrong for me to possess authority. The decision must rest upon good will and mutual acceptance. While any Cabinet officer or agency head may appeal to the President, this course of action has been taken in only one instance.[5]

This operating approach could be called collegial multiple advocacy. A variety of viewpoints were presented and heard, but the participants understood that the purpose of the discussions was to reach consensus rather than define options for the President. Its chairman assumed two roles: As honest broker, he guaranteed due process to interested departments and agencies; as magistrate, he announced decisions or policy. Apparently the Council itself never met with the President and eventually its meetings were attended primarily by senior and mid-level subcabinet officials. It coordinated reasonably well a broad range of routine issues for a President who had limited interest in foreign economic policy.

John F. Kennedy, who disliked highly structured processes, not only quickly dismantled the National Security Council apparatus but also abolished ABEGS and the Council on Foreign Economic Policy. Instead he encouraged less formal arrangements and created several new committees in 1961 to deal with specific economic problems.

Most of these dealt with primarily domestic issues: an *ad hoc* committee on housing credit, a White House committee on small business, an advisory committee on labor-management policy, and "new machinery for interagency cooperation in formulating fiscal estimates and policies," later referred to as the *"troika"* consisting of the chairman of the Council of Economic Advisers, the secretary of the Treasury, and the director of the Budget Bureau. An Interdepartmental Committee of Under Secretaries on Foreign Economic Policy and informal arrangements under the direction of Carl Kaysen, deputy special assistant to the President for national security affairs, handled most foreign economic policy issues other than monetary affairs.

In June 1962 President Kennedy asked Douglas Dillon, his secretary of the Treasury, to chair a Cabinet Committee on Balance of Payments, both "to consider broad policy questions and to keep a sharp eye on our overseas expenditures." The committee originally included the secretaries of Treasury, Defense, and Commerce, the undersecretary of State, the administrator of AID, the director of the Bureau of the Budget, the chairman of the Council of Economic Advisers, and a member of the senior White House staff, initially Carl Kaysen.[6] Since the President wanted the committee to operate informally, he issued no Executive Order or other formal document to create it. The committee reported to the President, usually two or three times a year, on the U.S. balance of payments and the gold situation.

Soon after becoming President, Lyndon Johnson established the Long-Run International Payments Committee (LRIPC), which prepared the U.S. position papers for the Group of Ten discussions on the international monetary system. In 1965, a group of high-level subcabinet officials from the Treasury and State Departments, the CEA, the Federal Reserve Board, and the White House Staff began meeting regularly to discuss reforms of the international monetary system. The group, chaired by Frederick Demming, undersecretary of the Treasury for monetary affairs, was known as the Demming Group and was soon acknowledged as one of the most effective small interagency groups in Washington.

While the CFEP had served as a focal point for foreign economic policy issues in the Eisenhower administration, the National Security Council became the central locus of coordination during the Kennedy and Johnson years. Shaping the work of the various interagency groups dealing with major foreign economic policy questions was a deputy assistant to the President for national security affairs, first Carl Kaysen, and later Francis Bator. Kaysen, then Bator, operated with an immediate staff of two professionals and became the key White House staffer on such issues as the balance of payments, trade negotiations, foreign aid, and international monetary problems. Both leveraged their own modest-sized staff by drawing on specialists in the Bureau of the Budget, the Council of Economic Advisers, the Office of the Special Trade Representative, and the Departments of Treasury and State. Both soon developed independent access to the President and worked directly with cabinet officers on many foreign economic issues.

At the end of the Johnson administration, the NSC's dominant role on foreign economic policy questions waned; the title of deputy was abolished with Bator's departure, and the job was divided between two officials. One dealt with foreign aid, the other with trade and monetary affairs. Other White House officials, the assistant secretary of state for economic affairs, and the STR played stronger roles.[7]

Richard Nixon brought to the White House a preference for formal interagency mechanisms and for increased staff capabilities at the center. He enlarged the National Security Council staff and expanded the committee structure that supported it. He also created an Urban Affairs Council, a Rural Affairs Council, and a Cabinet Committee on Economic Policy (established by Executive Order on January 24, 1969), chaired by himself and including the vice-president; the secretaries of the Treasury, Agriculture, Commerce, Labor, Housing and Urban Development; the counselors to the President (Arthur F. Burns and Daniel P. Moynihan); the director of the Budget Bureau; the deputy undersecretary of state for economic affairs; and the chairman of the CEA. These committees were designed to be the principal mechanisms for shaping administration policy. Curiously, no entity was established early in his administration to specifically address international economic policy issues. No deputy assistant to the President for national security affairs was appointed to handle foreign economic policy problems at the NSC. Indeed, Henry Kissinger, the national security adviser, had only a marginal interest in most foreign economic policy issues.

In August 1970 the President's Advisory Council on Executive Organization (the Ash Council) offered the President its recommendations on organizing foreign economic affairs, observing: "Little that we have studied to date impresses us of the need for change as much as the Federal Government's organization in this area."[8] Its recommended solution to the "proliferation of involved units and coordinating bodies, now totaling more than sixty," was twofold: transform the Office of the Special Representative for Trade Negotiations (STR) into an Office of International Economic Policy, and establish a cabinet-level Council on International Economic Policy "to work with and guide the Office in the performance of its functions."

As in the case of the Domestic Council staff, established in July 1970 along the lines proposed by the Ash Council, the emphasis was on strengthening staff capabilities within the Executive Office of the President. A strong centralized staff would help bring order and coherence to the fragmented structure of authority. Nixon adopted most of the recommended approach creating yet another cabinet-level council, the Council on International Economic Policy (CIEP); appointing an assistant to the President for international economic policy (Peter Peterson); and, rather than transforming STR, establishing one more entity in the Executive Office of the President, the CIEP staff.

Ironically, even though Nixon approved these major structural innovations, his interest in the phalanx of White House councils and committees was waning and he met with them less and less frequently. His appointment of John Connally in December 1970 as secretary of the Treasury marked a new phase in Nixon economic policy making. Nixon wanted a czar to whom he could delegate most economic policy decisions.

In Connally he found the czar he wanted and soon publicly designated Connally as the administration's chief spokesman on economic policy matters.

In the Spring of 1972, George Shultz, formerly secretary of Labor and director of the Office of Management and Budget, succeeded Connally. Shultz held the same title as Connally, but by temperament Shultz was more collegial in his approach.

In January 1973, in addition to his Treasury portfolio, Shultz was simultaneously appointed assistant to the President for economic affairs and chairman of a cabinet-level Council on Economic Policy (CEP) designed to coordinate all economic policy decision making. At the same time, Shultz quietly replaced Nixon as chairman of CIEP. While formal meetings of both CEP and CIEP were infrequent, Shultz personally set up an interagency process that involved most senior administration officials in issues that affected their interests. However, the CIEP staff never acquired the same power as Kissinger's NSC staff or Ehrlichman's Domestic Council staff, partly because CIEP did not have their responsibility for managing a regular flow of issues for the President.[9]

As Shultz prepared to leave government in the spring of 1974, William Simon, Shultz's deputy at Treasury and the energy czar, and Roy Ash, director of the Office of Management and Budget, were both anxious to succeed him as the administration's leading economic figure. Rather than choose between them, Nixon selected Kenneth Rush, deputy secretary of State, as his counselor for Economic Affairs and made him chairman of the major interagency economic committees including CEP and CIEP.

Within weeks, Nixon had resigned and Gerald Ford had replaced the Nixon machinery with a new Economic Policy Board designed to coordinate both foreign and domestic economic policy. It was chaired by Secretary of the Treasury Simon, but managed by an Assistant to the President for Economic Affairs, L. William Seidman. The Ford EPB was very different from its predecessors. Rather than relying on a large centralized staff, the EPB operated with a relatively small staff, involving departments and agencies as the primary sources of information, analysis, and alternatives in developing policy.[10]

Two and a half years later, Jimmy Carter abolished the Economic Policy Board, allowed the statute authorizing CIEP to expire, and created an Economic Policy Group (EPG), initially cochaired by the secretary of the Treasury and the chairman of the CEA. While the EPG existed throughout the Carter administration, its influence at the White House and with the President waxed and waned. Frequently, it struggled unsuccessfully with the Domestic Policy Staff for control of major economic issues. Most international economic policy issues were coordinated through Henry Owen, who managed preparations for the annual international economic summit conferences. Owen and his small staff were technically part of the larger National Security Council staff and worked closely with their counterparts at State and Treasury.

This brief overview of foreign economic policy-making arrangements in the last six administrations reveals several characteristics.

First, there has been no continuous foreign economic policy staff comparable to the National Security Council staff. The small CFEP staff in the Eisenhower years and the larger CIEP staff in the Nixon and Ford administrations never established the permanent institutional bases of the NSC, the CEA, and OMB. While the CEA has always had some interest in international economic issues, its primary concerns have focused on macroeconomic policy and sectoral issues. Likewise, no cabinet-level interdepartmental council on foreign economic policy has survived the transition between administrations.

Second, most administrations have created separate cabinet-level committees or councils to deal with foreign and domestic economic policy issues.

Third, while many administrations have established an interagency council with broad responsibility for developing foreign economic policy, virtually every administration has also created a number of cabinet committees to deal with specific issues.

These committees have generally operated with little overall direction or direct access to the President. Most have quickly become in effect sub-cabinet-level committees with cabinet officers not attending the meetings. In contrast, Ford's Economic Policy Board met 520 times at the cabinet level in two and a quarter years (an average of almost five meetings a week), had direct access to the President, and was involved in making virtually all his economic policy decisions.

Fourth, in the place of genuinely effective formal structures, most administrations have evolved a set of informal relationships among the leading officials. In surveying foreign economic policy-making patterns over the past thirty years, one finds that interagency committees and groups have played a major role in organizing advice to the President on specific issues but that most Presidents have generally not relied principally on general purpose, formal entities. Most frequently, Presidents have relied on a trusted adviser or group of advisers, settling many issues bilaterally with the interested parties.

Fifth, Presidents have generally not relied heavily on White House foreign economic policy assistants to organize advice and coordinate decision making as they have for national security affairs (Robert Cutler, McGeorge Bundy, Walt Rostow, Henry Kissinger, Brent Scowcroft, and Zbigniew Brzezinski) or domestic affairs (Theodore Sorensen, Joseph Califano, John Ehrlichman, Kenneth Cole, James Cannon, and Stuart Eizenstat).

Foreign economic policy is becoming increasingly complex at a time when more departments and agencies have both the interest and capability of influencing it. *Ad hoc* committees and personal arrangements are becoming less satisfactory, particularly for those concerned with developing a coherent and integrated administration program.

ORGANIZATIONAL ALTERNATIVES

This brief historical overview provides a context in which to consider the organizational challenge of developing coherent policy in an environment of interrelated issues and fragmented authority. A central burden of the Presidency is the integration of policy. There are at least four broad alternative ways of achieving such coordination and integration.

One alternative is consolidating functions in a super department. Students of federal organization frequently criticize executive departments and agencies for being too closely tied to particular constituencies and special interests. Superdepartments with comprehensive interests would, they argue, resist the pleas of special interests. In 1964, the President's Task Force on Government Organization recommended creating a single Department of Labor and Commerce. In 1967, the Heineman Task Force Report made a similar proposal. In 1970, the Ash Council recommended that "four major executive departments which handle highly interdependent economic matters: Commerce, Labor, Agriculture, and Transportation" be combined into a Department of Economic Affairs. Richard Nixon in his State of the Union Address on January 22, 1971, proposed a sweeping executive branch reorganization calling for four new superdepartments to join the four "inner cabinet" departments (State, Defense, Treasury, and Justice).[11]

More recently, the last decade has produced repeated suggestions for creating a new Department of International Trade and Industry, which would combine the trade and commercial functions of the Department of Commerce with the trade policy development and negotiating functions of the Office of the U.S. Trade Representative and the quasi-judicial functions of the International Trade Commission. The inspiration for much of the interest in such proposals is the success of Japan's Ministry of International Trade and Industry (MITI). Admittedly, many of these proposals would leave untouched the international monetary functions currently lodged in the Department of the Treasury and the international energy responsibilities of the Department of Energy.

Proponents of the unified department concept point to several potential advantages. To the extent senior department officials effectively control the department's activities, policy integration would be aided since those "who deal with common or closely related problems would work together in the same organizational framework." The department "would be given a mission broad enough so that it could set comprehensive policy directions and resolve internally the policy conflicts which are most likely to arise."[12] As the Ash Council pointed out: "The present organizational structure encourages fragmentation when comprehensive responses to social and economic problems are needed. Problems are defined to fit within the limits of organizational authority, resulting in piecemeal approaches to their solutions by separate departments and agencies."

Second, a superdepartment would help the President provide overall direction to foreign economic policy development. When responsibility for realizing basic objectives is clearly focused in a specific governmental unit, that department can be held accountable for achieving them.

Finally, a large, comprehensive department could ease the President's decision-making burden. "Decisionmaking responsibility is often shifted to the Executive Office of the President because no official at the departmental level has the authority to decide the issues."[13] Thus, it may help in pushing some problems away from the President. As one seasoned Executive Office veteran remarked: "Our difficulty is that we clutch tightly to us every problem that appears on the horizon."

While there are several potential advantages—authority to resolve problems short of the President, enhanced accountability, a greater likelihood of comprehensive rather than piecemeal approaches to policy problems, and easing the decision-making burden on the President—the concept of an international economic superdepartment has several limitations.

Many who press for larger and more comprehensive executive departments do so in the belief that consolidation will undermine narrow departmental perspectives. Yet there is reason to question whether aggregating responsibilities within larger entities will produce the desired effect. Few would argue that the size and scope of the Department of Defense or the Department of Health, Education, and Welfare eliminated, or even significantly reduced, the power of special interests and specific constituencies. Aggregating functions into larger departments may transfer the resolution of certain disputes and the weighing of certain tradeoffs from the White House to the office of the departmental secretary, but there is no guarantee that narrow interests will not remain or that the President's interests will prevail in those decisions made at the departmental level. From the President's vantage point, even large, consolidated departments will have a different outlook, perspective, and constituency than his own. Moreover, as the complexity of problems grows, it is increasingly difficult to concentrate authority in one place without the entity soon looking like the entire executive branch.

A second alternative for the President is either designating one cabinet official as a supersecretary for economic affairs or effectively delegating responsibility for economic policy decisions to a czar.

John Connally, as Treasury secretary, had a public and private mandate from the President that extended well beyond his Treasury portfolio and from which he dominated foreign and domestic economic policy decision making. According to Connally:

Most of the meetings that I had with the President were one-on-one. In the economic field, he made it clear that I was his chief economic adviser. Throughout my entire time there, it was a situation in which he clearly delegated the authority to me. I kept in constant contact with George Shultz, with Paul McCracken, with Arthur [Burns]. When we had all these meetings in Rome and London and Washington on the international monetary currency exchange rates, we were the only people who had any authority to do anything. There wasn't a finance minister in the room in any of those meetings, in my judgment, that could commit to anything. But the President had clearly said to me, "Just go ahead and do what you think you have to do." He just gave me almost unlimited authority and delegation of authority. Of course, I kept him fully informed all the way along.[14]

The "czar" approach has many of the same potential advantages as the superdepartment—resolving disputes short of the President, concentrating responsibility and hence accountability, and clarifying the public perception of who speaks for the administration. Moreover, this approach may be congenial to a President with limited interest in foreign economic policy questions who prefers to delegate to *an* individual.

But this approach also has problems. Just as it is difficult to effectively consolidate power under a superdepartment, it is perhaps even more difficult to concentrate power in a czar. Bits and pieces of economic policy responsibility are scattered throughout the federal government because they are linked to other important governmental responsibilities. Decentralized operating responsibility is a fact of governmental life and a formidable challenge to concentrating authority in any one set of hands. Moreover, the success of the czar approach depends heavily on the individual selected. He must not only enjoy the President's confidence but must be perceived by other department and agency heads, external groups, the press, and the Congress as having the clout and the powers of persuasion to truly be first among equals.

Thus far we have identified several difficulties with the superdepartment and supersecretary approaches. But a capacity for central oversight is badly needed. There is a need to raise issues to the presidential level when the President's personal decision is desirable and it is necessary that he receive the views of his senior advisers with responsibilities relevant to the issue.

A third alternative organizational approach is a centralized White House staff similar to the Nixon-Kissinger NSC or the Nixon-Ehrlichman Domestic Council staffs. A staff of perhaps forty or fifty professionals could not only manage the flow of day-to-day communication between economic departments and the President but could pull the strands of a policy problem together and assess relevant information and alternatives.

As Alexander George has pointed out, a centralized management approach sees the President as a "unitary rational decision maker, shielded from raw disagreements over policy."[15] This approach gives primary responsibility to the President's Executive Office and immediate staff; emphasizes careful, systematic examination of policy questions; and puts the process in the hands of individuals familiar with the President and his views. Executive branch departments and agencies might have substantial input on particular issues but generally would play a distinctly secondary role because centralized management is designed to overcome what is viewed as departmental parochialism and inertia.

While such a staff can increase the President's control over the policy-making process, raise issues for his attention that might not otherwise reach the White House, and increase his control of the timing and announcement of a new policy or initiative, a large centralized management staff also involves substantial costs and risks for the President. If he relies primarily on his immediate staff for information and advice, the morale and initiative in departments and agencies will inevitably suffer. Moreover, "objectivity" may be an illusion if the staff ends up mirroring and reinforcing what it perceives as the President's preferences. It cannot mobilize the same resources nor reflect the range of concerns that exist in departments and agencies. Furthermore, implementing many issues depends on the cooperation of departments and agencies that will withhold it if they feel alienated. Thus, centralized management widens the gulf between policy formulation and implementation, and separates the President from his own executive branch.

A fourth alternative would be a cabinet-level council of the administration's leading economic policy officials who would regularly advise the President on a broad range of economic policy issues. It could either have responsibility for both foreign and domestic economic policy or the President could create separate councils for foreign and domestic economic policy. In either case, a core group of officials would have collective responsibility for advising the President. Whatever the size of the "core group," its deliberations would include representatives from all departments and agencies that had a legitimate interest in an issue under discussion. A small professional staff based in the White House would coordinate the council's work. In the role of honest brokers, they would attempt to mobilize the resources of departments and agencies rather than transcend them. If successful, the council would engage the executive branch's best expertise and, by providing a regular forum for interagency discussion, help departmental officials see their responsibilities in a broader setting. Such an approach combines multiple advocacy (exposing the President to competing arguments made by the advocates themselves rather than having viewpoints filtered through a staff) and collegiality (a continuity among advisers who share responsibility with the President for policy development over a broad area).

There are many limitations on such a system in practice. Disparities in the advocates' resources, talents, and abilities can distort the process. As Theodore Sorensen has observed: "The most formidable debater is not necessarily the most informed, and the most reticent may sometimes be the wisest."[16] Moreover, there is no guarantee the advocates will represent *all* viable alternatives rather than lowest-common-denominator recommendations. Group norms stifling creativity and reflecting a single ideology may emerge with time. Such a system can consume enormous amounts of time, risk leaks on sensitive issues, force a large number of decisions to the top, and weaken the ability of senior executives to "deliver" on commitments to their constituencies and to the Congress.

No structure can consistently transcend the limitations of its individual actors. But many of the collegial experiments in providing policy advice to the President have been underminded by structural deficiencies. Several organizational guidelines can help minimize the potential limitations of such a system in practice.

1. Unquestionably, the council or committee's effectiveness depends on its presidential authority. Departments and agencies must perceive it as the President's vehicle. If he consistently permits private appeals from individual officials, departments will not take the process seriously. Thus, such a system depends heavily on the President's commitment to it.

2. Equally important, an honest broker or process manager should control the council's operations. Senior department and agency officials must see him as interested in due process, free from competing responsibilities, intelligent enough to be considered a peer, and trusted by the President. By temperament, he should find satisfaction in pulling the strands of a problem together into a balanced presentation rather than drive the process toward a particular outcome, using advocacy as an instrument of brokerage rather than undertake brokerage because he is told to do so. Not least, he should have what the Brownlow Committee called "a passion for anonymity."

3. The council's staff should be small and consist of generalists. A large staff can exercise greater quality control; but invariably such staffs become specialized, tend to ignore departments and agencies—which naturally view them as competitors—and are tempted to circumvent the process themselves.

4. Such a council should meet regularly at the cabinet level. Its power will depend on the capacity of its members to speak authoritatively for their department or agency.

If given responsibility for advising the President over a broad policy area, the council could help ensure that a comprehensive approach is taken, that the President is not left to integrate interrelated issues on his own, and that senior departmental officials are exposed to a context that transcends their own departmental responsibilities.

Multiple advocacy is a difficult system to operate. Its success depends on consistent presidential resistance to end-runs. Furthermore, it requires the "right" people to manage it. The other participants must view them as fair and evenhanded in coordinating policy development. The necessary combination of skills that an honest broker needs are not frequently found in those most closely associated with presidential candidates. Powerful personal factors and political forces often guide a President-elect in selecting his immediate staff, and that staff has a decisive influence on organizing the pattern of advice he receives. In short, such a system depends on the President recognizing its value, appointing individuals with the requisite abilities and temperament as the managers of his policy-development process, and then demonstrating his commitment by not allowing individual officials to circumvent the system.

FOREIGN AND DOMESTIC ECONOMIC POLICY FORMULATION: COMBINED OR SEPARATE?

For most of the past thirty years, different processes have existed for considering foreign and domestic economic policy issues. Parallel cabinet-level committees have often existed—the Council on Foreign Economic Policy and ABEGS, the Council on International Economic Policy (CIEP) and the Cabinet Committee on Economic Policy; and the most continuous informal arrangements—the Troika and the Quadriad—have concentrated almost exclusively on domestic economic policy questions. Not until the Nixon Council on Economic Policy under George Shultz and the Ford Economic Policy Board have foreign and domestic economic policy questions been considered regularly by a single entity.

The Council on Foreign Economic Policy and the Council on International Economic Policy were created because those responsible were convinced that international economic policy questions merit high-level attention but were being neglected by the current machinery. While Carl Kaysen and Francis Bator were with the National Security Council during the 1960s, they effectively coordinated a host of foreign economic policy questions. But they were trained economists who were given the mandate to do so by their superiors, Bundy and Rostow, and Presidents Kennedy and Johnson. Under the Kissinger and Scowcroft National Security Councils there was less interest in economic policy questions and on Kissinger's part a reluctance to delegate. Moreover, CIEP never acquired the clout to fill the gap adequately. When CIEP was abolished, international economic policy coordination was once again partially returned to the NSC by its assignment to Henry Owen whose role resembled the Kaysen-Bator model.

Yet the attraction for reestablishing a formal entity to advise the

President on foreign economic policy questions remains strong. There are two principal arguments against establishing a separate channel to advise the President on foreign economic policy making. First, it is increasingly difficult to separate foreign policy, domestic economic, or foreign economic problems. The distinctions have blurred with the growing complexity of considerations and interests that presidents must weigh. Second, experiments with such channels suggest that they have not succeeded in consistently engaging the President's interest and attention, largely because they have not been tied to a regular presidential work flow.

However, deciding against a separate channel still leaves open the question of whether foreign economic policy issues, to the extent they can be identified, should be tied to the national security or economic policy machinery. An excellent discussion of the arguments in support of both positions is found in I. M. Destler's *Making Foreign Economic Policy*.[17] Destler argues, and I concur, that the substance and politics of current foreign economic issues "encourage the conclusion that it is more realistic to build their coordination around economic policy officials and institutions." Most foreign economic policy issues are more closely related to domestic economic policy than to foreign policy. Moreover, senior foreign policy officials have generally been able to effectively influence economic policy-making processes more easily than economic officials have been able to penetrate foreign-policy-making processes.

Presidents are inclined to devote their time and energies to those areas where they have the greatest interest and where they feel they have the greatest opportunity to influence events. Most Presidents have spent a disproportionate amount of time on foreign policy matters, partly because of fewer domestic and congressional constraints but also because the machinery for making national security policy has been relatively well developed. The National Security Council apparatus, for all its limitations, has generally produced good issue papers and options memoranda for the President.

Consistently engaging presidential interest in shaping the major foreign and domestic economic policies his administration will pursue requires machinery that can effectively identify alternatives and generate quality analysis across a wide range of issues. The intertwining of foreign and domestic economic policy interests make it more crucial than ever that the President have the benefit of a structure that will enhance the prospects for developing coherent policies to address the economic problems facing the nation.

NOTES

1. The Dodge Report was a special study commissioned by President Eisenhower in August 1954 in cooperation with the President's Advisory Committee on Government Organization chaired by Nelson Rockefeller. Joseph M.

Dodge, having returned to private life after serving as Eisenhower's first budget director, undertook the study at the personal request of the President, completing his report in just over three months.

2. Joseph M. Dodge, *Report to the President on the Development and Coordination of Foreign Economic Policy, November 22, 1954* (Dwight D. Eisenhower Library, CFEP Office Series, Box 2, History CFEP [1]).

3. Letter from Dwight D. Eisenhower to Nelson A. Rockefeller and Rowland R. Hughes, 12 July 1954 (Dwight D. Eisenhower Library).

4. The Foreign Operations Administration preceded the International Cooperation Administration, which was thereafter represented by the Department of State.

5. Clarence B. Randall, *Position Paper with Respect to the Council on Foreign Economic Policy, Prepared for the Incoming Administration, November 16, 1960* (Dwight D. Eisenhower Library, CFEP Office Series, Box 4, Transition Material).

6. The Cabinet Committee on Balance of Payments was later expanded in the spring of 1963 to include the special representative for trade negotiations, in the fall of 1965 to include the secretary of Agriculture, and in November 1967 to include the secretary of Transportation. Henry H. Fowler, *Memorandum for the President on the Addition of the Secretary of Transportation to Cabinet Committee on Balance of Payments, November 3, 1967* (Lyndon B. Johnson Library).

7. For example, the key decision changing U.S. policy on trade preferences for developing countries was made through a White House assistant rather than the NSC staff. See President's Advisory Council on Executive Organization, "Organization for Foreign Economic Affairs," 17 August 1970, Appendix C, *Some Previous Attempts to Coordinate Foreign Economic Policy*, pp. 269–71.

8. President's Advisory Council on Executive Organization, Memorandum for the President, "Organization of Foreign Economic Affairs," 17 August 1970.

9. During this period there were three CIEP executive directors: Peter Peterson, Peter Flanigan, and William Eberle.

10. Roger B. Porter, *Presidential Decision Making: The Economic Policy Board* (New York: Cambridge University Press, 1980), describes and evaluates the EPB as an example of multiple adovcacy.

11. *See Papers Relating to the President's Departmental Reorganization Program* (GPO, March 1971).

12. President's Message, 25 March 1971, Ibid., p. 11.

13. Ibid., p. 235.

14. Interview.

15. Alexander L. George, "The Case for Multiple Advocacy in Foreign Policy Making," *American Political Science Review* 66 (September 1972): 752.

16. Theodore Sorensen, *Decision Making in the White House* (New York: Columbia University Press, 1963), p. 62.

17. (Washington: Brookings Institution, 1980).

9

Process and Policy in U.S. Commodities: The Impact of the Liberal Economic Paradigm

Karen Mingst

The burgeoning discussion of commodity policy has resulted in a plethora of books and articles. Some studies have focused on international commodity negotiations (Mikdashi, 1976: Hveem, 1978) and implications for the creation of the New International Economic Order (Rothstein, 1979); others have been commodity specific (Fisher, 1972; Choucri with Ferraro, 1976); a third group has analyzed commodity policies of specific state-actors (Krasner, 1973; Krasner, 1978; Cohen, 1977; Destler, 1980). Conspicuously absent from this literature is any examination of the basic paradigm for U.S. commodity policy and an assessment of how policy influences and in turn is influenced by that paradigm. This chapter seeks to assess the relationship between paradigm and policy by examining two levels of analysis. At the systemic level, what are the parameters of the policy debate? What are the incentives and constraints imposed on decision makers? At the subsystemic micro level, what is the operative policy process given the systemic paradigm? What is the relative importance of different modes of decision making on actual commodity policies? What are the linkages between policy process and policy substance? In other words, do the systemic and subsystemic levels make any difference for the substance of policy? Having explored these questions, we propose a taxonomy of present and future commodity policy, based on the two levels of analysis and an assessment of specific commodity characteristics. Commodity policy is classified as reactive, regulatory, confounding, or anticipatory. The prevalence of certain types of commodity policies is explained on the basis of these factors.

THE SYSTEMIC PARADIGM: LIBERAL ECONOMICS

Policies are circumscribed by systemic considerations. The basic thesis is that U.S. commodity policy is derived from a historic tradition, a tradition that provides the foundation for participation in a social world. As Kisiel (1970:156) explains,

> ... to belong to a tradition means to inherit a network of presuppositions which serve as the precedents that provide the anticipations of meaning that guide our understanding of anything whatsoever.

Thus, policy makers inherit a historic structure of shared understandings. These understandings provide both the parameters from which policy discussions begin and the basis for continuing communication. Discussion is directed toward certain forms of thought; action is mobilized.

The structure of shared understandings that form the tradition for U.S. commodity policy center on the desirability of a domestic liberal economic system, one in which market forces determine the supply-and-demand balance, largely unfettered by government. Under this system, there are commitments both to the elimination of barriers to the movement of goods and services and to control of this movement by private enterprise. Brown (1974:30–31) explains the nexus in a succinct fashion:

> The essence of the classical view of the economy is that it is a market economy. There are many markets, for goods and for factors, and many entrants to each market, none of them big enough to influence the price or rate of exchange by entering or holding back. Employers in a capitalist market system are essentially traders like their mercantile predecessors. . . .

These arrangements are readily extended to the international arena:

> The classical vision of an economy where there is perfect competition reaches its apogee in the Theory of Free Trade. A static condition is assumed without movements of capital or of labor *between* countries, but with complete factor adaptability to ensure full employment *inside* each country. Then movements of relative prices equalize the values of imports and exports, and the pursuit of individual profit leads each country (as it does each individual in the home market) to specialize in producing those goods and services in which it has the greatest comparative advantage. This result is "an equilibrium position in which competition leads to the maximum *utility* in the world as a whole being produced from given resources" (Robinson, 1962:62).

Foreign economic policy has become an extension of these domestic understandings and ideology; negotiations and goals at the international level reflect its constraints. Andrews (1975:524) explains,

...we could say that the rules suggest a pattern of prescribed or proscribed behavior, resembling a canon of appropriateness or *social paradigm*. Metaphorically, we might speak of the way in which a society maintains its conception of itself, and of the attributions and role which it forces upon the governmental actors. In doing so, the outer boundaries of both international choices and "non-decisions" are set and legitimated. Rather than determining a specific choice, the rules tend to narrow the range of possibility to a realm in which state policies appear "pre-shrunk" or pre-interpreted. By helping to structure the policymakers' hierarchy of preferences and values, these norms and expectations will in turn come to structure their presuppositions about the international setting—foreshortening the range of perception, desired objectives, and alternative paths of action. Agendas are shaped, universes are delimited, and actors are provided with a rough explanatory framework within which their own international actions can be understood.

Thus, the domestic liberal economic paradigm becomes the dominant understanding through which commodity policy is screened.

Policy makers are cognizant of the strength and impact of the paradigm. Gerald L. Parsky (1976:110), former assistant secretary for international affairs in the Department of the Treasury, states the position unequivocally:

It is our firm conviction that the market mechanism is on the whole the most efficient method of assuring that supply and demand of commodities are kept in balance in a dynamic world. Although markets do not always operate efficiently, the appropriate remedy is to strengthen their functioning, not intervene, or further impede market operations.

His colleague Julius Katz (1976:34), former deputy assistant secretary for economic and business affairs, Department of State, amplifies the argument:

...I should note that in our examination of individual commodity problems, we proceed on the fundamental premise of our economic policy, that of seeking an open world economy that permits market forces to operate with minimum restrictions on the flow of goods, services, capital, and technology across international boundaries.

The free market paradigm is logically consistent with a conception of economic development held by many policy makers. As Parsky (1976:107–8) argues, economic development is largely a function of internal economic change: LDCs must create a suitable domestic climate for investment by emphasizing the private sector. Although the free market may be imperfect, no other system will stimulate growth. This view of economic development leads policy makers to reject categorically demands made by LDCs for managed commodity markets on economic development grounds.

This liberal economic paradigm is a long-standing tradition. The tradition has survived intact despite numerous challenges in international commodity negotiations since the mid-1950s. Although stability of the paradigm has been the prominent characteristic, we do not suggest absence of variations. Andrews (1976:527) comments,

> Behavior may fit into predicted patterns of causal regularity . . . actors may do what we expect "of" them by following their articulated goals along the lines of domestic conventions, or by substantiating our account of the international aims of a state as a choice of means toward a more inclusive domestic end. Unexpectedness will come in two varieties. State behavior may diverge from (and become an exception to) causal laws or behavior, or state actors may deviate from normative or customary rules of conduct and engage in socially unintelligible actions.

These unexpected variations will be confined to the margins of the paradigm.

That a systemic-level paradigm forms the basis of commodity policy is acknowledged by Rothstein (1979) in *Global Bargaining: UNCTAD and the Quest for a New International Order*. Rothstein supports the argument that ideological tradition is an important limiting parameter to the policy debate. These ideologies become polarized in the international setting and thus mask incremental differences. In discussing why the United States permitted the issue of the Integrated Program for Commodities to build to a crisis, Rothstein (1979:139) argues,

> But the difficulty was compounded in this case by the dominance of an unsophisticated and frequently hypocritical ideology at the top levels of the administration. This tended to turn discussions of the IPC into metaphysical confrontations between competing faiths. In some cases, ideology masked (or buttressed) personal hostility toward the developing countries (and especially their leaders), a hostility exacerbated by the resentments generated by the oil crisis . . . and by the inflammatory and frequently absurd rhetoric dominant in the UN system.

Where Rothstein's observations differ from my own is the relative importance of the "hypocritical ideology" at the top levels of administration. Rothstein tends to dismiss this upper echelon and focuses on bureaucratic politics at the lower administrative levels. The thesis of this chapter is that no major decisions will be taken that fundamentally contradict the basic tenets of the paradigm; the incremental decisions leading to commodity policies all are confined within the parameters of the paradigm. Other factors, including organizational, bureaucratic, and personal politics are inconsequential at the systemic level. When confronted with choices whose outcomes would alter or essentially modify the parameters of the paradigm, policy makers are constrained.

DECISION MAKING WITHIN THE LIBERAL ECONOMIC PARADIGM

Decision makers are confronted with marginal choices. Why and how these choices are made and courses of policy pursued can be explained on the basis of a variety of decision modes (see Stephen D. Cohen's essay in this volume). These modes are a valuable analytical tool for micro-level analysis. Yet in each case, our critique of the mode affirms the primacy of the systemic paradigm.

Individual-Level Decision Making

Two of the modes of policy-making focus on the individual decision maker: the presidential fiat mode and the personality mode. In the former case, the direct intervention of the President determines policy. He sets the tone for the policy, communicates that position, and relies heavily on the prestige of his office to ensure compatible outcomes. Only when an issue of overriding national importance is at stake does the President intervene directly in commodity policy.

Two examples confirm the dramatic circumstances of presidential intervention. In March 1961, President John Kennedy announced that the United States was ready to cooperate in serious case-by-case examination of commodity markets. Frequent and rapid changes in commodity prices seriously injured the economies of many Latin Americcan countries. Following the Castro takeover in Cuba and his subsequent announcement of communist-Soviet affiliation, this phenomenon acquired new political significance. With presidential initiative, a Latin American Task Force was established to examine the problem of coffee oversupply and its relationship to political instability in Latin America. On recommendation of the task force, the President announced U.S. readiness to make a commitment to join a yet undefined coffee agreement (Fisher, 1972). A commodity program emanating from the President himself, supporting sagging coffee prices vital to Latin American economies, represented an affirmative economic step in guaranteeing political allegiance (Mingst, 1974).

The 1980 decision not to sell American wheat to the Soviet Union in response to the Soviet invasion of Afghanistan is another example of commodity policy by presidential fiat. This dramatic Soviet action precipitated the economic policy response. Evidently the decision to impose the wheat embargo was taken primarily by President Carter. Even major economic advisers were not consulted in advance of the decision. In both cases, commodity policy was used as an instrument to achieve broader political objectives.

In the personality mode of decision making, the presence of strong individuals with established convictions about the course of action forces a policy decision. Aside from those cases when the dominance of the President is exhibited by virtue of his office, there are few cases in commodity issues where personality alone is the dominant factor. Some evidence suggests that Secretary of State Kissinger attempted to use his forceful personality in public posturing (Cohen, this volume: 159–60) for concessions to the New International Economic Order without clearance from other agencies or lower-level State Department bureaucrats. However, the example is suspect, since Kissinger had exhibited little interest in commodity affairs and his forays, although widely publicized, resulted in no substantive policy change.

Both modes focus on the individual decision maker: An individual perceives a problem and acts upon it. The basic criticism of this approach is that the individual is viewed in relative isolation from the social sources of his belief or ideological constructs. If one accepts the suppositions that policy is derived from a historic tradition and that the continuity of the tradition is inherent in everyone, then individuals will reflect the dominant paradigm. In neither case was the paradigm altered; constraints were imposed for short-term instrumental political purposes.

GROUP-LEVEL DECISION MAKING

The second group of modes of decision making focuses on the social dimension: groups of individuals interacting to produce foreign policy. Cohen identifies the modes of bureaucratic politics, multiple advocacy, and democratic processes. Examples for each of these modes are given to permit categorization of the micro-level perspective; they help us understand both the locus of the debate over specific policy alternatives and different modes of implementation. However, these modes neither permit discussion of the liberal economic paradigm as presented at the systemic level nor tolerate profound controversy over general objectives. The debate in the policy arena remains limited.

Bureaucratic politics is the most developed mode analytically.[1] It is based on several interrelated themes (Fuell, 1980). First, foreign policy cannot be separated from domestic politics; thus policy makers inevitably examine domestic, organizational, and personal interests, as well as external foreign policy objectives. Second, foreign policy is developed by multiple individuals; it is not made by a unitary government actor. Thus, decision making must of necessity be a process of dynamic consensus building. Third, the bureaucratic decision-making process influences the content of a decision. As Art (1973:469) explains, "The content of any particular policy reflects as much the necessities of the conditions in which it is forged—what is required to obtain agreement—as it does the substantive merits of that policy." Fourth, conflict is the central element of decision making. Under conflictual conditions, resolution is reached through bargaining, persuasion, and compromise. Hanf (1978:1) captures the dynamics of the process:

Territorial and functional differentiation has produced decision systems in which the problem solving capacity of governments is disaggregated into a collection of subsystems with limited tasks, competences and resources, whereby relatively independent participants possess different bits of information, represent different interests, and pursue separate, potentially conflicting courses of action.

The negotiations aimed at formulating a U.S. position toward the Integrated Program for Commodities (IPC) provide an excellent example of bureaucratic politics. Rothstein's (1979) analysis of the Ford and Carter administrations is especially instructive. The prevalent interpretation is that the Ford administration, dominated by officials in the Department of Treasury and the Council of Economic Advisers, reacted negatively to the IPC. The belief in the market approach remained strong as the United States anticipated the imminent disintegration of OPEC and the termination of commodity producer power. Bureaucratic dominance by the two groups was moderated in February 1975, however, when the government decided to conduct a major review of international commodity policy, to insure that "U.S. policy would be consistent, principled, and feasible" (Vastine, 1977:436–37). The NSC task force recommended that the United States engage in negotiations on a commodity-by-commodity basis. Specific approaches to the negotiations became the topic of bureaucratic maneuvering. Treasury officials fought any comprehensive approach to commodities. Some State Department officials won the "possible" concession that U.S. participation in commodity agreements was not foreclosed. The vague yet ideologically consistent wording of the stated policy symbolizes the level of ambiguity necessary to obtain interorganizational and interagency agreement.

Several close observers contend that the Carter administration desire was to "do more" for the LDCs in the area of commodities, given that certain ideological and psychological obstacles had diminished (Rothstein, 1979:127; Schechter, 1979). However, this sentiment was never translated into policy. Many of the same individuals were responsible for commodity policy; differences among organizations and bureaucracies persisted, and little deviation from the dominant paradigm was effected.

The conclusion drawn from the case is consistent with the general thesis: the irrelevancy of bureaucratic politics in terms of actual policy. Rothstein (1979:240–41) concludes:

> There were times during the commodity negotiations when the presence of different individuals in key positions or different governments in key countries would have had an appreciable effect on atmospherics (style, tone, climate), but whether the effect would have been extended to substantive outcomes is far less than clear. The difficulty that the Carter administration has had in converting improved atmospherics into acceptable agreements is probably symptomatic: something more than "good will" is necessary. Changes in personality or regime can be important,

but they are not likely to be important enough to eliminate structural and institutional obstacles that are deeply engrained and that seem to protect important interests and values.

The multiple-advocacy mode is based on assumptions similar to bureaucratic politics. Different interests and organizations bargain over the contents of policy. While bureaucratic outcomes reflect compromise in bargaining, however, the multiple-advocacy mode suggests that a "neutral" observer makes the final decision, preferably an individual not participating in initial interactions and not advocating a specific position. The decision to impose formal quotas of U.S. imports of Canadian oil in 1970 offers evidence of this mode in the commodity area.[2]

In 1969, President Nixon ordered a comprehensive reassessment of the oil import policy. The task force recommended relaxation of import controls and the imposition of tariffs; however, the secretaries of Interior and Commerce and the chairperson of the Federal Power Commission dissented, advocating instead a modification of the quota system. According to the final report, the Office of Emergency Preparedness would chair an interdepartmental policy advisory panel with State, Treasury, Defense, Interior, Commerce, Attorney General, and chairperson of Council of Economic Advisers (CEA). The State Department would be responsible for dealing with the Canadian portion of the policy. When the Canadians became reluctant to guarantee security of supplies, the State Department recommended that formal import controls be put on Canadian oil. Both the Department of the Treasury and Interior concurred. The Council of Economic Advisers opposed restricting oil imports from Canada, favoring instead trade liberalization.

Because of the conflicting recommendations, the policy debate moved to the Oil Policy Committee (OPC). OPC members admit they contributed little to the policy options, listening instead to the multiple-advocacy arguments made by the respective organizations. The OPC recommended allocation criteria for instituting an import quota system. These recommendations were forwarded to Nixon's special assistant, and President Nixon announced formal restrictions on Canadian crude oil imports.

What makes this case less than stereotypic of the multiple-advocacy mode is the fact that the OPC was, essentially, confronted with only two options. Other suggestions proposed early in the bureaucratic process had been eliminated. The effective choice was between doing nothing or imposing controls. Under a multiple-advocacy model, other alternatives would have been fully debated and then the "neutral" observer (OPC) would make the final determination. In this sense, OPC may have served more a legitimizing role. The final decision was taken at the presidential level, as stipulated in the Trade Expansion Act of 1962. In this decision, neither the Congress nor the public had any impact on the final decision.

In contrast to decisions that emerge from direct or indirect bureaucratic maneuvering, the domestic politics mode permits participation from additional actors, Congress, domestic interest groups, and the public. Few commodity decisions follow the mode. Those that do tend to be on issues where national security concerns are nominal and commodities in question are produced in the United States. With U.S. production, there is greater likelihood of domestic interest groups, mobilized publics, and congressional involvement. The case of the 1974 attempt to renew the U.S. Sugar Program provides an excellent example.[3]

At the executive level, an Interdepartmental Sugar Study group under the Council on International Economic Policy was the locus of bureaucratic bargaining. Representatives from State, Treasury, Commerce, Agriculture, Labor, OMB, CEA, Domestic Council, and NSC were included. The study group listed three policy options: (1) retain the current sugar act with modifications (more market flexibility in pricing); (2) support a two-tiered system, with price supports for domestic producers if the price fell below a USDA established target price and the elimination of foreign quotas; (3) a compromise between options 1 and 2.

These policy options represented the culmination of bargaining in which the various departments and subunits voiced divergent perspectives. Two agencies supported option 1; five, option 2; and four, option 3. The administration decision emerging from the bureaucracy was support of a three-year act having greater price flexibility with retention of the country-quota system. While this policy illustrates bureaucratic compromise, other groups became instrumental in the outcome.

The Sugar Bill H.R. 14747 (the administration proposal) emerged from committee with overwhelming support. Once on the floor, however, several labor amendments were appended, causing traditional supporters of the Sugar Program to balk. The bill was defeated. Essentially the administration had exerted no influence to ensure passage of the act; Latin America had been accorded low priority. Differences within the sugar industry over both the price goal and the specific provisions of the act made their lobbying virtually ineffective. This case illustrates the important check exerted by Congress on executive decision making and the potential influence of domestic industry. The presence of both these actors differentiate the domestic politics from the bureaucratic politics mode.

The last four modes of policy making focus on groups of decision makers. Two major criticisms of this emphasis are pertinent. First, all the decision makers probably share a common structure of beliefs and assumptions or common understandings. When conflict is accentuated, however, minor differences are underscored while important commonalities are never articulated. With respect to commodity policy, there are few conflicts of understanding, few conflicts over fundamental tenets of policy, few conflicts over the paradigm. Rather, there are conflicts of interest, reflections of institutional differences, of differences on resource distribution and responsibilities, and differences relating to technical features of a decision. Fundamental conflicts of understanding represent circumstances where there is an absence of general consensus on the definition of the situation; this type of conflict will be most evident during periods of paradigm institutionalization; once the paradigm is established, decision makers rarely return to this level again. Conflict is circumscribed.[4] This argument does not underrate the importance of these conflicts of interests; it only seeks to situate them in proper systemic perspective.

Second, the assumptions behind the group process models are squarely congruent to pluralist interpretations. Destler (1980:16–17) clearly enunciates the pluralist argument:

> Assuming pluralism in U.S. foreign economic concerns, this study sets out first to determine the *form* pluralism takes in particular issue areas. What are the predominant concerns; which officials, departments, and agencies represent them; how do the trade-offs among these concerns present themselves to officials; and how are these trade-offs, in practice made? Second, what is the effect of the coordinating institution on the *resolution* of pluralism: are they relatively neutral and objective vis-a-vis competing concerns or do they raise certain ones to prominence and neglect others?

Furthermore, the pluralist model from a political perspective is compatible with the liberal economic model. There are many suppliers and consumers of a particular commodity as there are many groups competing over different interests. The method through which an agreement is reached between buyers and sellers is price, while for pluralists, the bargaining and compromise process produces the outcome. The congruence in assumptions mutually reinforces the political and economic components of the paradigm. Our micro-level modes of decision making are useful for analytical purposes, and they reinforce the strength of the liberal economic paradigm.

SYSTEMIC AND MICRO-LEVEL IMPACT ON POLICY SUBSTANCE

Do the systemic shared understandings and the contending decision-making modes at the micro level make any difference for the substance of policy? Cohen (1977:114) suggests that certain types of policy seem to predominate: "All too much of U.S. international economy policy has been in the nature of *protective* reaction. Policy makers have been mainly on the defensive, putting out a series of brush fires." To answer this inquiry more specifically, we introduce a typology of commodity policy.[5] Although the typology is applicable to other policy issues, the scheme is equally suitable for discussion of commodity policy. After delineating the typology, we analyze the impact of process on substance.

Four types of policy are feasible; they reflect different temporal sequencing between an event or set of conditions and a policy. *Reactive* policies attempt to reduce damage or detrimental side effects of conditions after these effects are being experienced. Typical commodity conditions may be a temporary shortfall or glut, caused by weather, transportation bottlenecks, or labor unrest. Reactive policies might include *ad hoc* suspension of purchase and sales. *Regulatory* policies seek to avoid potentially damaging outcomes before the evidence is clear. The same conditions causing reactive policies can lead to regulatory ones. However, the political responses are apt to include permanent measures. For example, a commodity price range might be determined, above which purchasers should not buy and below which purchasers can add to the stockpile. *Confounding* policies result from logically inconsistent or uncoordinated policies, usually emanating from either the reactive or regulatory mode. Such policies develop because of confusion and conflicting goals in the domestic political process. When the existence or magnitude of a problem is disputed, or the appropriateness of certain responses is questioned, confounding policies often occur. *Anticipatory* policies are designed to provide a decision algorithm before problems arise. Such policies attempt to predict the direct and potential consequences of systemic changes and to provide a repertoire of appropriate responses. For example, in commodity policies, such responses may include maintaining a predetermined level of domestic and international prices to achieve desired social ends.

Illustrations of three of these types of commodity policy can be found in the American experience. Reactive policies characterize the recent history of copper and oil policy. Although both commodities are produced in the United States, foreign suppliers are critical. Thus, when labor strikes or transportation bottlenecks occuring in Zambia or Zaire play havoc with the international copper market, the U.S. government's reaction may be to release stockpiles to compensate for shortfall. No consistent pattern to this policy choice can be discerned, however. It is based on an overall evaluation of price levels, industrial pressure, and the strength of supplier lobbying. Petroleum policy may have been approached similarly, yet the failure to even enact a reactive policy is stunning. Beginning with the oil embargo in 1973–74 by the organization of Arab Petroleum Exporting Countries and the Iranian cutoffs in 1979–80, the United States has been unable to develop even the most reactive of policies. Similarly, regulatory examples abound, previously in agriculture support prices for U.S. grain producers and more recently in critical minerals not found in the United States (e.g., chromium and tin). In the former case, a national stockpile assures supply at target prices; in the latter case, an international buffer stock has operated within negotiated price markets. Confounding policies are prominent in commodities where there is an uncompetitive domestic sector and politically favored imports (e.g., sugar and cotton). On the one hand, price supports augment the income of producers in key U.S. agricultural regions; yet on the other, lower-priced supplies are allowed to enter the United States. The result is inconsistent policies, emanating from conflicting domestic policy goals. In contrast, there is a dearth of anticipatory policy. The policy followed by many Western European governments in response to their acknowledged petroleum dependency is the best example: High taxes are levied on petroleum use in order to lower consumption and stabilize oil dependency. Such policies anticipated the rise of OPEC and the escalation of oil prices.

All three types of policy have not been employed with the same strength or frequency in the United States. This chapter suggests that U.S. commodity policy is dominated by reactive and confounding decisions, with some instances of regulatory policy and virtually no examples of anticipatory policies. Why are specific types of policy more prevalent than others? First, all commodity policies are guided by the understandings of the dominant liberal economic paradigm. When market forces function according to supply and demand, the first three policies are plausible. If the market fails to operate smoothly, if either too few buyers or sellers are present, then incremental market adjustments may be employed retroactively. If market signals are either ambiguous, or are evaluated with conflicting results, then reactive policy responses may become confounding. If underlying market dynamics undergo longer-term alterations, perhaps regulatory policies can mitigate conditions more permanently after the fact. Anticipatory policy by its basic nature is antithetical to the classical free functioning of the market and in all probability never occurs given the shared assumptions of the paradigm.

Second, types of policy are determined by the different modes of decision making at the micro level. Seldom is a commodity issue the subject of top priority requiring presidential attention. Yet, consensus for an anticipatory policy is unlikely to emerge without strong, individual support. Groups, particularly those sharing a restricted paradigm, are unlikely to take bold action to anticipate trends and develop probable responses for the future. Group-level planning in the economic policy area is clearly antithetical to the liberal economic paradigm.

The more numerous the participants in the decision-making process, the more that policies are apt to be either reactive or confounding. By the time that the various affected groups are mobilized for the bureaucratic, multiple-advocacy, or democratic process mode, the groups are reacting either to events or to policies that their counterparts have already instituted: The former leads to reactive policy; the latter, to confounding policy. While regulatory policies may be rare, they are probable if there is consensus among the various groups that the set of conditions evoking the response is apt to be recurrent. Thus, the analysis of both the systemic and decision-making modes suggests what types of policies are most likely to occur. However, an analysis of commodity characteristics is a more reliable indicator.

The third factor that determines the relative potency of a type of policy depends on two variables related to specific commodity characteristics: (1) the degree of competitiveness of U.S. production; and (2) the extent to which the United States trades the commodity. The first variable concerns the ability of American producers to compete economically in an international market. The more competitive U.S. production, the more the policy is apt to be reactive. There is scant motivation to respond in advance to market conditions. When U.S. producers are not economically competitive, U.S. policy is apt to be confounding. The interests of domestic producers must be weighed against the norm of international market efficiency.

The second variable measures the relative trade position of the United States in markets for a specific commodity. Trade status indicates the *degree* to which the policy will be reactive or confounding. If the United States is an economically competitive commodity producer and is a net exporter of the commodity, the policy is apt to be *most* reactive. Protection of the export market, the accruement of vital foreign exchange, and the maintenance of a stable balance of payments need to be assured. The policy will be *less* reactive if, given the same economically competitive situation, the United States is a net importer of the commodity and no overriding social need dictates such a reactive policy. If the United States is not an economically competitive producer and is self-sufficient in the product, the policy is apt to be the most confounding. Domestic producers and their representative constituencies will advocate price supports and subsidies equal to or above the international market prices. The policy will be less confounding if, given the same uncompetitive status, the United States is a net importer. The domestic processors and manufacturers would support a system of relatively guaranteed supply designed to maintain international market prices as low as possible; that policy would be compatible with consumer interests. Thus, U.S. trade position suggests *how* reactive or *how* confounding that policy ought to be.

Finally, an analysis of the changing position and role of the United States in the international system leads us to similar conclusions regarding the prevalence and potency of certain types of commodity policy. Between World War II and the end of the 1960s, the United States enjoyed economic, military, and political hegemony. Under these conditions, all three types of policy are possible, although anticipatory policy will continue to contradict the liberal economic paradigm. By the 1970s, however, with U.S. hegemony eroding (see the essays by Krasner, Keohane, and Chase-Dunn in this volume), it is logical to expect a resurgence and reaffirmation of reactive and confounding policies. Confronted with a declining economic position, policy makers react to protect entrenched and

eroding markets. The resultant reactive and confounding policies reinforce the critical factors analyzed above.

The American commodity policy-making process, as well as the content of the resulting policy, have clearly been circumscribed by the requirements of the dominant liberal economic paradigm. Like the outer
layer of an onion, the paradigm is largely impenetrable. While it can be
peeled away layer by layer, there are retardants to the peeling between
each layer. The process and policy is managed and given coherence by
the presence of the liberal economic paradigm. Too much is at stake in
terms of both domestic and international politics for that skin to be
peeled away.

The decision-making modes can be compared to two segmented cores
cut into the onion; the larger core is the group decision-making mode.
Although the dynamic interactions within each core may differ, each is
circumscribed by the same parameters. The logic of the liberal economic
paradigm suggests that policies could be reactive, confounding, or regulatory; however, by the time that the bisected core is cut, the logical
choices are further limited. Given the predominance of the group decision-making people, policies are apt to be either reactive or confounding.

The core of the onion can be compared to two variables related specifically to the policy issue: the commodity characteristics of the degree of
competitiveness of the U.S. production and the extent to which the
United States trades the commodity. The first variable suggests *whether* the
policy will be reactive or confounding *and* the second, the *degree* to which
the policy will be reactive or confounding. Thus, as we peel away the
thick-layered skin and bisect the core of the onion, we are able both to
predict a range of likely policies and to assess their relative potencies as
formulated by the United States for internationally salient commodities.

NOTES

1. For presentation of the bureaucratic approach, see Graham Allison and
Morton Halperin (1972), "Bureaucratic Politics: A Paradigm and Some Policy
Implications," *World Politics* 245 Spring Supplement, 40–79; Morton H. Halper-
in and Arnold Kanter (1973), "Introduction," in *Readings in American Foreign
Policy: A Bureaucratic Perspective* (Boston: Little, Brown). For suggestions for
change, see Graham Allison and Peter Szanton (1976), *Remaking Foreign Policy/
The Organizational Connection* (New York: Basic Books).

For a critique of the bureaucratic position, see Robert J. Art (1973),
"Bureaucratic Politics and American Foreign Policy: A Critique," *Policy Sciences*
4, 467–90; and Stephen D. Krasner (1972), "Are Bureaucracies Important? (Or
Allison Wonderland)," *Foreign Policy*, Summer, 159–79.

2. The information on the Canadian oil case is drawn from Kathryn Young
Voight (1974), "U.S. Oil Import Policy: The Decision to Impose Formal Quotas
on U.S. Imports of Canadian Oil (1970)," in *Commission on the Organization of*

the Government for the Conduct of Foreign Policy, vol. 3, Appendix J, *Foreign Economic Policy*, 33–52.

3. The information on U.S. sugar policy is drawn from Robert A. Pastor (1974), "U.S. Sugar Politics and Latin America: Asymmetries in Input and Impact," in *Commission on the Organization of the Government for the Conduct of Foreign Policy*, vol. 3, Appendix J, *Foreign Economic Policy*, 221–23.

4. This general argument developed for a different setting is given by Thomas D. Lairson (1979), "Decision-Making in Groups: Social Paradigms and Postwar American Foreign Policy" (unpublished dissertation, Department of Political Science, University of Kentucky).

5. The ideas for the typology are drawn from Dorothy Nelkin (1976), "Trends in Science Policy: The Search for Controls," *Policy Studies Journal* 5, no. 2 (Winter), 180–85. She differentiates among participating, reactive, and anticipatory policy for issues in science.

REFERENCES

Andrews, Bruce. 1975. "Social Rules and the State as a Social Actor." *World Politics* 27 (July), 521–40.

Art, Robert J. 1973. "Bureaucratic Politics and American Foreign Policy: A Critique." *Policy Sciences* 4, 467–90.

Brown, Michael Barratt. 1974. *The Economics of Imperialism*. England: Penguin Books.

Choucri, Nazli, with Vincent Ferraro, 1976, *International Politics of Energy Interdependence. The Case of Petroleum*. Lexington, Mass.: Lexington Books.

Cohen, Stephen D. 1977. *The Making of United States International Economic Policy. Principles, Problems, and Proposals for Reform*. New York: Praeger.

Destler, I. M. 1980. *Making Foreign Economic Policy*. Washington, D.C.: Brookings Institution.

Fisher, Bart S. 1972. *The International Coffee Agreement. A Study in Coffee Diplomacy*. New York: Praeger.

Fuell, Lawrence D. 1980. "Food-Aid Decision Making: A Test of the Bureaucratic Politics Approach." Unpublished paper, University of Kentucky, Lexington, February.

Hanf, Kenneth. 1978. "Introduction." In *Interorganizational Policy Making. Limits to Coordinations and Central Control*, Kenneth Hanf and Fritz W. Scharpf, eds. Beverly Hills: Sage Publications, pp. 1–15.

Hveem, Helge. 1978. *The Political Economy of Producer Associations*. Oslo: Universitetsforlaget.

Katz, Julius. 1976. *Joint Hearings Before the Subcommittees on International Resources, Food, and Energy; International Economic Policy; International Organizations; and on International Trade and Commerce of the Committee on International Relations*. House of Representatives, 94th Congress, 2nd sess. *United States Commodity Policies*, 26 April.

Kisiel, Theodore. 1970. "Ideology Critique and Phenomenology: The Current Debate in Germany Philosophy." *Philosophy Today* (Fall), 151–60.

Krasner, Stephen. 1978. *Defending the National Interest: Raw Materials Invest-*

ments and United States Foreign Policy. Princeton: Princeton University Press.

———. 1973. "Business Government Relations: The Case of the International Coffee Agreement." *International Organization* 27, no. 4 (Summer), 495–516.

Lairson, Thomas D. 1979. "Decision-Making in Groups: Social Paradigms and Postwar American Foreign Policy." Unpublished dissertation, Department of Political Science, University of Kentucky.

Mikdashi, Zuhayr. 1976. *The International Politics of Natural Resources*. Ithaca: Cornell University Press.

Mingst, Karen A. 1974. "The Process of International Policy Making in Regulation of Tropical Agriculture Products: Coffee and Cocoa." Unpublished dissertation, Department of Political Science, University of Wisconsin.

Parsky, Gerald L. 1976. *Joint Hearings Before the Subcommittees on International Resources, Food, and Energy; International Economic Policy; International Organizations; and on International Trade and Commerce of the Committee on International Relations*. House of Representatives, 94th Congress, 2nd sess. *United States Commodity Policies*, 26 April.

Robinson, J. 1962. *Economic Philosophy*. Harmondworth, England: Penguin.

Rothstein, Robert L. 1979. *Global Bargaining. UNCTAD and the Quest for a New International Economic Order*. Princeton: Princeton University Press.

Schechter, Michael G. 1979. "The Common Fund: A Test Case for the New International Economic Order." Paper presented at the Annual Conference of the International Studies Association/South, 5 October, Athens, Georgia.

Vastine, J. Robert. 1977. "United States International Commodity Policy." *Law and Policy in International Business* 9, no. 2, 401–76.

10

U.S. Foreign Economic Policy Formation: Neo-Marxist and Neopluralist Perspectives

Stephen G. Walker and Pat McGowan

An understanding of how foreign policy is made is one route to knowing why the policies have the content they do. This is as true of foreign economic policy as of any other aspect of a nation's external relations. In the preceding four chapters the authors have described U.S. policies regarding international trade in food grains and other commodities, the policy-making process itself, and attempts to reform it. In this chapter we present two contrasting images of the policy process—what we term neo-Marxist and neopluralist perspectives—and then proceed to show how the insights and findings of Cohen, Mingst, Paarlberg, and Porter may be interpreted from the point of view of these perspectives. Because U.S. foreign economic policy impacts on the lives of all Americans and most other inhabitants of the globe on a daily basis, there is a great need for better understanding of the sources of these policies and their resulting contents. We believe that aspects of the neo-Marxist and neopluralist perspectives can be combined in a fashion that will provide just such understanding.

Before we present the two perspectives we shall work with in this chapter, the differences between Marxist and conventional approaches to political studies must be examined so that readers appreciate the genuinely contrasting character of neo-Marxism and neopluralism. Four differences are of special importance in our view. First, most Marxist researchers make a sharp distinction between explanation on the one hand and description and prediction on the other hand. This is necessary because social phenomena exist at two levels, that of "appearances" and that of "essences."[1] The level of appearances, or *immediately observable phenomena*, is the realm of events, kinship networks, demographic trends, economic variables, concrete institutional arrangements, and so on.[2] Conventional methodologies permit one to describe and even predict appearances, but not to explain them. For many Marxists, explanation is based on the analysis of underlying social reality—the realm of essences—which by its operation generates the phenomena of everyday life. Both levels are important, for as Erik Olin Wright notes, "[p]eople starve 'at the level of appearances' even if that starvation is produced through a social dynamic which is not immediately observable."[3] The paradigmatic instance of such explanation is Marx's analysis of commodities as the carriers and encapsulations of the social history of capitalism in volume 1 of *Capital*.[4]

The second key difference from conventional approaches is very well known and equally controversial. Marxist social science is a critical approach in which theories and results are ultimately to be judged on the basis of their relevance for political action.[5] Most conventional social scientists are political *liberals* believing in incremental change in the direction of greater equality or *leftists* who advocate sharp reductions in differences in power, wealth, and privileges among classes and strata. Marxists and many other radicals claim to be *revolutionaries* who advocate "fundamental and discontinuous change in political and economic institutions that takes power away from one class or group of classes and gives it to another class or classes."[6] Individuals committed to such distinct political philosophies will obviously view each other's writings in sharply different fashions and in this important sense, no synthesis between neopluralist and neo-Marxist approaches is possible.

The third difference we wish to highlight is the differing conception of the state or political system held by radical and conventional social scientists. Most American political scientists study government and politics from one of three perspectives—pluralism, structural functionalism, or elite theory.[7] The starting point of the Marxist theory of the state is entirely different and is found in Marx and Engels' famous dictum that "[t]he executive of the modern state is but a committee for managing the common affairs of the whole bourgeoisie." This conception of modern government in capitalist societies implies a distinctly different image of the state.

All Marxists would agree that the capitalist state is a class government ultimately serving the interests of one small sector of society—the capitalist class. It would also be agreed that if there are common capitalist affairs, there are also special capitalist interests that do not concern the whole bourgeoisie. Monopoly capitalism is complex and contains a variety of sectors, each with its special interests regarding tariffs, quotas, export promotion and subsidies, investment abroad and in the United States, monetary policy, inflation, control of technology, and so on.[8] Capitalists also share a common overriding interest in the reproduction of the capitalist system. A state that acted at the *behest* of every conflicting special interest could well be torn apart and therefore could not act on *behalf* of capital in general. The state *must be relatively autonomous* from the economic structure if it is to reproduce the main features of that structure (i.e., its capitalist character). It is therefore either a conscious distortion by opponents or an ill-conceived or vulgar deformation by adherents to say that for radicals economics entirely determines politics.[9]

The fourth and final difference is the much greater emphasis neo-Marxists place on the economic functions of the capitalist state in comparison to the political-legal activities emphasized by conventional political science. One detailed discussion of state activity is provided by Szymanski, who begins by assuming that the capitalist state necessarily acts to promote the survival and advance of the capitalist mode of production.[10] To do this, the state must first ensure its own maintenance as a *capitalist state* by raising tax money, by personnel recruitment and socialization into capitalist values, and by securing itself against threats from other states, particularly other competitive advanced capitalist states. Second, via ideological apparatuses and interest aggregation, the state legitimizes the capitalist system, particularly its property relations, and helps form and moderate the capitalist-class will.[11] Finally, the state implements this class will to ensure continued capital accumulation and business profitability. It is clear to us that if one believes that a basic function of the state is to foster capitalist accumulation and profits, one will ask quite different questions about foreign economic policy formation than if one assumes, as do most neopluralists, that the state is a neutral power broker as regards the interests of various sections of capital, labor, agriculture, and consumers.

A NEO-MARXIST PERSPECTIVE

Since the late 1960s there has been a remarkable revival of interest in Marxist approaches to the study of politics and policy formation. Not all Marxists think alike, and therefore as many as five different approaches can be distinguished—instrumentalist, structuralist, materialist, Hegelian-Marxist, and world-systems. In our view, the common elements of these neo-Marxist perspectives outweigh their differences. Therefore, using ideas drawn primarily from so-called instrumentalist and structuralist writers, we present a single neo-Marxist perspective in this chapter.[12]

Writers in the instrumentalist tradition argue that the state serves the interests of the capitalist class because it is controlled by that class. The basic logic of the instrumentalist position may be summarized as follows: (1) Policy making is dominated by the big corporations, other groups such as labor or small farmers having a distinctly subordinate role; (2) corporate interests have many institutions such as the Council on Foreign Relations or the Committee for Economic Development to forge common capitalist positions that are often implemented during periods of crisis; (3) strategic or broad-gauge policy formation occurs within such groups, seldom publicly; (4) policy thus formulated is implemented by the state apparatus because of personal interlocks and informal networks—decision makers are disproportionately from the capitalist class and almost without exception open to corporate influence; (5) the state normally does not have an independent or initiatory role because power derives overwhelmingly from economic strength; (6) "while divisions between large and small corporations, conservative and liberal viewpoints, and immediate and long-run interests may occur . . . over time the largest and most long-run interests tend to prevail."[13] These working hypotheses suggest a research agenda for instrumentalists involving studies of the sociology of the ruling class, studies of the personal and institutional linkages between this class and the state, and concrete and detailed analyses of how current policy is shaped by capitalist class interests and reinterpretations of past episodes of state action.[14]

In sharp distinction to the instrumentalist position, the basic thesis of the *structuralists* is that state activity is determined by the structures of society and not by people in positions of state power. The late Nicos Poulantzas has articulated this point most strongly:

> The relation between the bourgeois class and the state is an *objective relation*. This means that if the *function* of the state in a determinate social formation and the *interests* of the dominant class in this formation coincide, it is by reason of the system itself: the direct participation of members of the ruling class in the state apparatus is not the *cause* but the effect, and moreover a chance and contingent one, of this objective coincidence.[15]

In their research, then, structuralists focus on what functions the state must perform in order to reproduce capitalist society. Starting with classes and class struggle, inquiry is directed at how state policy and organization displace the contradictions generated by given economic structures and class interests.

But if it is true that state activity is determined by the structures of society, what does this mean? What are "structures" and how do they "determine" or "cause" collective and organizational behavior? As an undifferentiated concept, structural causality is highly abstract and has proven extremely difficult to use in empirical investigations. To use a term from the philosophy of science, structural causality needs to be "unpacked" so that the various modes of determination may be identified. Eric Olin Wright has done this in a fashion to permit us to outline a structural model of U.S. economic policy. Within the "global concept of structural causality" he distinguishes six "modes of determination."[16]

1. **Structural Limitation**: This constitutes a pattern of determination in which some social structure establishes limits within which some other structure or process can vary, and establishes

probabilities for the specific structures or processes that are possible within those limits. That is, structural limitation implies that certain forms of the determined structure have been excluded entirely and some possible forms are more likely than others.

2. **Selection**: Selection constitutes those social mechanisms that concretely determine ranges of outcomes, or in the extreme case specific outcomes, within a structurally limited range of possibilities.... There are two complementary forms of "selection," which can be termed "positive" and "negative" selection. Negative selection involves those mechanisms which exclude certain possibilities. Positive selection ... involves mechanisms which determine specific outcomes among those that are possible.

3. **Reproduction/Non-reproduction**: To say that one structure functions to reproduce another implies that the reproducing structure *prevents* the reproduced structure from changing in certain fundamental ways.... Reproduction thus is also a kind of limiting process: it maintains the reproduced structure within certain limits of variation. The essential difference from structural limitation is that in the latter case there is no presumption that the determined structure would necessarily change in the absence of the specific structural limitation process, whereas in the case of reproduction such changes would normally occur.

4. **Limits of Functional Compatibility**: [Limits of functional compatibility determine] ... which forms of the state [and state policy] will be reproductive and which non-reproductive. Stated in somewhat different terms, limits of functional compatibility determine what the effects of a given structure of that state [and state policy] will be on economic [and political] structures.

5. **Transformation**: Transformation refers to a mode of determination by which class struggle (practices) directly affect the processes of structural limitation, selection and reproduction/non-reproduction. Transformation is thus fundamental to the dialectical character of patterns of determination as understood in Marxist theory: Class struggle, which is itself structurally limited and selected by various social structures, simultaneously reshapes those structures.

6. **Mediation**: A mediating process must be distinguished from what is commonly called an "intervening" process or variable in sociology.... An intervening variable is simply a variable which is causally situated between two other variables. X causes Y, which in turn causes Z. A mediating variable, on the other hand, is one which shapes the very relationship between two other variables: Y causes the way in which X affects Z. In a

sense a mediating process can be viewed as a "contextual variable": Processes of mediation determine the terrain on which other modes of determination operate.

The purpose of Wright's effort is to clarify the questions a neo-Marxist would ask in studying a phenomenon such as U.S. foreign economic policy. For example, what are the *limits* generated on policy by the structure of the U.S. and international capitalist economies? Within these limits, how are given economic policies *selected* by the state structure (federal government) and class struggle (politics)? Do these policies *select* certain class-struggle processes? Do they help *reproduce* the state and capitalist economic structures or are they *nonreproductive* because of *functional incompatibilities* generated by these same structures?

A NEOPLURALIST PERSPECTIVE

In contrast to the neo-Marxist contentions that a monolithic ruling class or an overarching state structure determine the process of U.S. foreign economic policy-making, neopluralists assert that the characteristics of the policy process depend significantly upon the characteristics of the values that are the focus of the process. The most creative synthesis of the neopluralist perspective for the analysis of foreign policy is by Zimmerman, who integrates the issue typologies of Rosenau and Lowi with a variant of the power politics model articulated by Wolfers.[17] Zimmerman hypothesizes that when an issue involves the relatively intangible and indivisible goods of power, security, and prestige, then the policy process will correspond to a rational actor model in which the maker of government policy is a relatively monolithic rational decision maker. However, if an issue involves only the distribution, regulation, or redistribution of more tangible goods such as tariffs and export subsidies, then the policy process begins to resemble the domestic interactions of several actors described by the organizational process models of foreign policy analysts and the pluralist models of American government scholars such as Dahl.[18]

Our adaptation of Zimmerman's paradigm appears in figure 10.1. In the upper-left quadrant, *distributive politics* is defined as occuring when "the political goods are readily subject to being parceled out to the major units."[19] That is, the issue involves tangible goods, such as policies regarding foreign investment by U.S. corporations, which can be disaggregated in a relatively symmetrical fashion so that the outcome is non-zero-sum,"...everyone who counts politically [gets]...a piece of the action."[20] The patterns of interaction associated with distributive politics are characterized by logrolling and alliances among actors with otherwise uncommon interests. These actors tend to be limited to specialized socioeconomic elites plus their support groups.

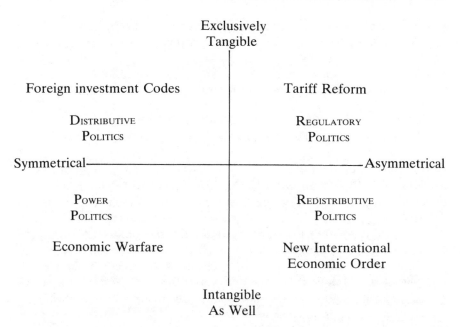

FIG. 10.1   A GRAPHIC FORMULATION OF THE NEOPLURALIST PARADIGM.

In the upper-right quadrant, the political goods are still tangible, but they are not as amenable to division as in the case of tariff reduction policies. "Where it is often difficult in the distributive arena to identify specific losers, there are always losers in the regulatory arena."[21] The interaction patterns of *regulatory politics* involve coalitions of bureaucratic agencies, interest groups, and legislators according to shared, actor-based interests. The process involves moderately intense bargaining among a much more diverse and numerous set of actors.

In the lower-right quadrant in the figure is the *politics of redistribution*, such as Third World demands for a New International Economic Order. Here the political goods begin to involve intangibles, such as power and prestige. "Relative status and power . . . is thought to be at stake— the political goods being both tangible and nontangible—disaggregation is extremely limited."[22] The limited possibilities for disaggregation make the policy impact likely to be asymmetrical, creating winners and losers. The inclusion of power and prestige add to the significance of the outcome and invoke system-based considerations as well as actor-based interests. There is the potential for an intense conflict between an elite and a counterelite over the structure of the existing system.

In the lower-left quadrant fall those foreign policy issues that almost exclusively concern power, security, and prestige, as in cases of economic warfare in the form of embargoes, boycotts, and blockades. Here the stakes are the survival of the entire national political economy. In this *power politics* process the patterns of interaction are highly elitist and based upon "team norms" (i.e., a shared symmetrical interest in the survival of the existing system for allocating both tangible and intangible political goods). Individuals act 'without their institutions" (i.e., they base their actions upon systemic rather than actor considerations).[23]

THE INTERFACE BETWEEN NEO-MARXIST AND NEOPLURALIST PERSPECTIVES

In our view any attempt to combine neo-Marxist and neopluralist perspectives of U.S. foreign economic policy making will depend upon the dependent variable(s) of interest and their rates of change. If one is interested in short-run, incremental changes in U.S. foreign economic policy, then the neopluralist perspective sensitizes the analyst to the immediate surface causes of these fluctuations. On the other hand, if one is interested in identifying the outer parameters of change in American policy, then a neo-Marxist perspective identifies the constraints that limit the range of variation and provides insights into the deeper structural changes that appear to be required in order to reshape U.S. foreign economic policy.[24] Our overall analytical goal, therefore, should be to retain the major features of the neo-Marxist model, subject to qualifications suggested by the nature of the issue according to our neopluralist model.

Our initial integration of ideas from Marxist and pluralist models is depicted in figure 10.2. The picture of the U.S. foreign economic policy-making process in this diagram is characterized by high resolution and low magnification. Resolution and magnification refer to the properties of distinguishability and enlargement in the science of optics, where these properties are inversely related. For example, if the focus of a microscope is adjusted to enlarge the image of the object under observation, the distinctions among the individual parts of the object are lost (low resolution). Conversely, if the focus is adjusted to enhance the distinguishability of the object's major components, then the reduced size of the image obscures some details of each part (low magnification). The optimum focus for our purposes is that point of maximum magnification wherein the entire policy-making process still remains in view.

The view in figure 10.2 is labeled high resolution/low magnification because its level of magnification is not great enough to show the processes associated with the models of distributive, regulatory, redistributive, and power politics in the neopluralist paradigm. Instead, it reveals the adjacent institutional layers of economic policy making and some of the processes (modes of determination) neo-Marxist theorists have distinguished to explain the interrelationships among them. The arrows in the diagram suggest that the state selects policies under the influence of the network of special interests and the class struggle (i.e., politics). The capitalist structure of the U.S. economy and the world-system limit the

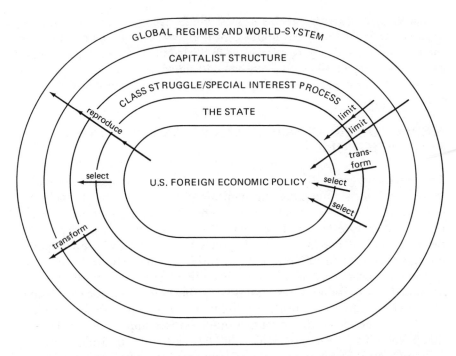

FIG. 10.2 A HIGH-RESOLUTION/LOW-MAGNIFICATION VIEW OF THE U.S. FOREIGN ECONOMIC POLICY-MAKING PROCESS.

nature of U.S. economic policy and the modal choices of the state (negative selection) so that the policy consequences tend to reproduce the capitalist features of the domestic and international systems. Only a decisive change in the class struggle can transform the state or the existing capitalist structure.

If the magnification in figure 10.2 is increased slightly to enlarge the issue areas within the class-struggle/special-interests process, then it may be possible to supplement the neo-Marxist analysis with the neopluralist perspective. However, if our focus becomes magnified so much that only the state and the issue areas are distinguishable, then we will pass the optimum point of adjustment and experience high magnification at the expense of low resolution.

In the remainder of this chapter we will appraise the other analyses of U.S. foreign economic policy making in an attempt to discover evidence of structural limitation, reproduction, positive and negative selection, transformation, and the mediating effects of variations in the tangibility and symmetry of the issues involved in these case studies. Our working hypothesis to link neo-Marxist and neopluralist perspectives in the appraisal is that a magnification of the class-struggle/special-interests process within the state and capitalist economic structures in figure 10.2 will reveal that the intensity of this process varies according to the tangibility and symmetry of the issues under consideration. As the issues shift from the distributive through regulative and redistributive to the power politics quadrants in figure 10.1, the class struggle intensifies and acquires the features of the political process associated with each quadrant of the neo-pluralist paradigm.[25]

MEDIATION PROCESSES IN AMERICAN FOREIGN ECONOMIC POLICY

The preceding essays by Porter and Cohen focused upon those organizational and decision-making mechanisms of the executive branch that shape U.S. foreign economic policy. Porter's emphasis upon organizational reform to establish a multiple-advocacy system is one response to the dilemmas of making economic policy in a context where competing interest groups want different policies to be adopted. However, once the multiple-advocacy system is established, there still remains the need to account for variations in the intensity of the multiple-advocacy process. In our view, a focus upon the tangibility and symmetry of the issues that are on the agenda of the executive branch offers important insights into this puzzle. This focus also inables us to resolve the difficulty posed by Cohen (page 150) who notes, "Since bureaucratic actors and the nature of the official actions required will vary from issue to issue, it is difficult to determine the existence of a significant number of uniform principles." It is precisely our contention that mediating properties of the issues do shape the relationships among other variables in the policy process and do form the basis for the formulation of a "significant number of uniform principles," which are listed below and have already been presented graphically in figure 10.1.

1. **Distributive Politics Proposition**. If the issue is tangible and symmetrical, then
    a. The number of actors tends to be small.
    b. The identity of the actors tends to be specialized.
    c. The decision-making process tends to be characterized by logrolling.
2. **Regulatory Politics Proposition**. If the issue is tangible and asymmetrical, then
    a. The number of actors tends to be large.
    b. The composition of the actors tends to be diverse.
    c. The decision-making process tends to be characterized by moderately intense bargaining and the establishment of a dominant coalition.
3. **Redistributive Politics Proposition**. If the issue is intangible and asymmetrical, then

  a. The number of actors is relatively few.
  b. The identity of the actors tends to be large aggregates (i.e., the chiefs of large departments, congressional leaders, or leaders of peak associations).
  c. The decision-making process tends to be characterized by the unilateral use of power and influence rather than by negotiation or consensus-building, and the potential for intense conflict is high.
4. **Power Politics Proposition**. If the issue is intangible and symmetrical, then
  a. The number of actors tends to be small.
  b. The identity of the actors tends to be individual elites acting "without their institutions."
  c. The decision-making process tends to be based upon "team norms" rather than the representation of bureaucratic or special interests.

With these four propositions it is possible to account for the association between Cohen's various models of policy-making in the executive branch and the major cases he uses to illustrate them.

Cohen's first model (page 152) is decision making by "presidential fiat," which he associates with President Nixon's personal intervention to decide U.S. balance of payments policy and American textile trade policy toward Japan.

> In this model, the White House participates and dominates from the early formulation of policy through the effort to achieve the objectives selected. Such continuity differentiates this model from instances when the President is drawn into an issue merely to ratify a bureaucratic consensus or to arbitrate at the last minute a dispute among the line departments.

Cohen (page 152) dismisses the President's role in the textile issue as an exception to fulfill a campaign pledge for political support, noting that "the stamp of presidential pressure is relatively seldom found in trade policy."

However, Mr. Nixon's 1971 decision to end dollar-gold convertibility and establish an import surcharge continued a pattern of active presidential participation in U.S. balance-of-payments crises. Cohen's description (page 153) of the Nixon balance-of-payments decision conforms to proposition's 3 and 4 regarding redistributive and power politics.

> This drastic, abrupt shift in economic policy was constructed by the President and a handful of senior advisers during a single fateful August weekend at Camp David. . . . U.S. policy was formulated quickly and enunciated at the highest level. Objectives were then pursued ruthlessly

and unequivocally by the President's men with relatively little regard for foreign political sensitivities or foreign policy considerations. Once again, the United States extracted maximum concessions from other countries while yielding relatively little.

The decisions to terminate dollar-gold convertibility and impose an import surcharge addressed an issue with properties of intangibility and, depending upon the level of analysis, had the potential for symmetrical or asymmetrical impact. The issue involved U.S. power and prestige as well as having the effect of redistributing wealth in the international system by devaluing the dollar. Consequently, within the U.S. government the President and his advisers shared symmetrical interests in the maintenance of U.S. economic power, while at the international level the policy impact was asymmetrical in favor of the United States. Viewed from within the U.S. government and the context of the power politics proposition, this national-level decision was taken by a small number of individual elites acting on "team norms" independently from bureaucratic or special interests. Viewed at the international level of analysis and the perspective of the redistributive politics proposition, the U.S. decision represented a unilateral use of American power rather than a policy reached by negotiation or consensus-building with the heads of other countries.

A second, "multiple advocacy" model is introduced by Cohen, who associates it with major trade legislation and control of the export of hazardous items. These two cases create issues dominated by the properties of tangibility and asymmetry; tariffs and export controls will result in gains for some actors and losses for others. Consequently, we should expect that the regulatory politics proposition should describe the number and type of actors involved in the decision as well as the dynamics of the decision-making process. In both cases Cohen (pages 155–57) characterizes the number and diversity of actors as high. Each case required congressional consultation and public hearings. Within the executive branch "the number of bureaucratic entitities in 1972 with an overall or specific interest in major trade legislation was enormous. More than a dozen departments and agencies...and about twenty-five persons reportedly attended a typical [interagency] meeting." Elsewhere, the author cites the difficulty of gaining a consensus among over twenty-two bureaucratic actors assembled to draft the hazardous exports Executive Order. In both instances, the President ultimately either ratified bureaucratic and congressional consensus or arbitrated a deadlock by use of presidential authority.

Cohen's third, "bureaucratic politics" model focuses upon commodity cartel policy and trade with less developed nations. The cases are part of the larger package of issues assembled under the rubric of the New International Economic Order (NIEO). In addition to wealth, these issues engage questions of power, prestige, and status. Since the impact of the decision also has definite asymmetrical possibilities, the redistributive politics proposition is relevant here. As another analyst has argued, the nations of the Third World have pursued a two-track strategy regarding NIEO. On one track they pursue goals related to economic well being, while on another track they try to deal directly with their lack of real power in the present international political economy.[26]

The dual nature of these issues is partly reflected by the contending perspectives and missions of the various agencies of the U.S. government who compete for influence over the policy to be adopted. The Treasury Department, whose principal concern is the health of the U.S. economy, reacted to NIEO proposals by opposing the use of government authority and funds "to rig the international economic system to favor the LDCs." The State Department, which is concerned with the overall political mileu and general U.S. relations with other nations, was more "sensitive to the political implications of an angry group of nations capable of disrupting the international order [and was] ... anxious to develop a serious dialogue wherever and whenever possible." (Cohen, page 158). The bureaucratic infighting associated with the subsequent series of speeches by Secretary of State Kissinger and officials in the Treasury Department regarding commodity agreements "became a symbol of the larger and oversimplified ideological question as to the need to occasionally circumvent the market mechanism with negotiated price fixing as a means of assuaging the economic demands of the poorer countries." (Cohen, page 160). This preoccupation with precedent is an indicator of the intangible and asymmetrical properties of this issue at both the national and international levels of analysis.

Cohen's fourth major model, "shared images and perceptions," applies to the many U.S. international economic policies that do not elicit important differences of opinion within the U.S. bureaucracy. This model is illustrated by U.S. policy in such areas as private international investment and international energy policy. It appears to us that this model really compounds two types of political processes, the distributive politics process and the power politics process. On the one hand, international investment is a distributive (tangible and symmetrical) issue for the United States, in which major American multinational corporations and their bureaucratic allies can logroll and support a free market investment system to go along with a liberal trading system. On the other hand, the consensus on the general principles of the U.S. international energy policy is probably the result of its intangible and symmetrical properties as a national security problem, which inclines decision makers to act "without their institutions" regarding a power politics issue. In the case of international investment the shared images and perceptions were based upon overlapping constituent interests, while international energy involved a collective interest incapable of disaggregation.

Finally, Cohen identifies another important feature of the decision-making process, one that has also been recognized by other authors. The "linkage factor" refers to the subordination of an economic policy issue to broader policy questions such as national security concerns. Cohen illustrates this model by arguing (page 167–68) that "the net economic cost-effectiveness of restricting grain exports to the USSR was judged incidental in 1980 to the national security imperative of imposing financial (if not dietary) costs on the Soviets for their actions in Afghanistan." Krasner makes the more general point that the state's chief decision makers may transform an issue by linking it to national security and thereby bestowing properties of intangibility and symmetry, which alters the number and identity of the actors and the decision-making process to conform with the power politics proposition.[27]

If we impose the results of our analysis of the Cohen essay upon a graphical presentation of the four issue propositions, we obtain the patterns in figure 10.3. The location of the various issues in the four quad-

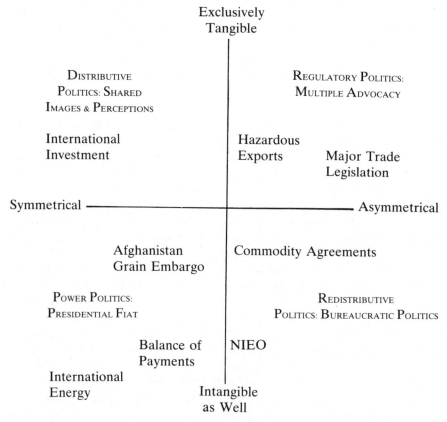

FIG. 10.3   THE MEDIATING EFFECTS OF ISSUE PROPERTIES UPON THE U.S. FOREIGN ECONOMIC POLICY-MAKING PROCESS

rants is consistent with our analysis of their decision processes described by Cohen. As the issue properties change from distributive through regulatory and redistributive to power politics, the number and type of actors change along with the actions in the decision process as summarized in the distributive, regulatory, redistributive, and power politics propositions.

OTHER MODES OF STRUCTURAL DETERMINATION IN THE FORMATION OF U.S. INTERNATIONAL ECONOMIC POLICY

While Cohen's essay has provided many examples of the mediating effects of issue properties upon the U.S. foreign economic policy process, other modes of determination are more aptly illustrated in the essays by Mingst and Paarlberg. *Structural limitation* is a mode that neo-Marxists define as a pattern of determination in which some social structure establishes limits within which some other structure or process can vary. This form of structural determination is performed by the "liberal economic paradigm," the subject of the Mingst essay, to the extent that the principles of this paradigm correspond to the way in which the actual domestic and international economic systems function. As long as a free market economy operates, certain forms of trade and investment policies are more likely than others. This range of policies in the trade sector, for example, would extend from mild versions of neomercantilism through reciprocal free trade relations.

The internalization of these norms by policy makers as a paradigm illustrates another mode of determination, *reproduction*. Reproduction differs from limitation as follows: In the case of limitation there is no presumption that the determined structure or process would necessarily change in the absence of the limitation source, but in the case of reproduction such changes would normally occur. Mingst argues, in effect, that internalization of the liberal economic paradigm disposes policymakers to resist proposals for a New International Economic Order and instead adopt policies that reproduce the existing system.

A third mode of determination, *selection*, constitutes those social mechanisms that concretely determine specific outcomes or types of outcomes within a structurally limited range of possibilities. These selection mechanisms include the various models of economic policy making in the Cohen essay. We have argued earlier that the type of issue determines which of these selection mechanisms is activated, but we did not account for the range of outcomes produced by a given model. The evidence complied by Mingst indicates that the reproductive effects of the liberal economic paradigm act to constrain selection within a range of policies which are consistent with the assumptions of that paradigm.

Whereas the *mediation* effects of issue properties accounted for *variations* in the U.S. foreign economic policy-making process, the *limitation*, *reproduction*, and *selection* modes of determination explain *continuity* in the parameters of substantive economic policies. Two other modes of determination account for *changes* in policy parameters. The first mode is the *limits of functional compatibility* principle, which addresses the problem of contradictions between a particular economic policy and the economic structure of the country. An example of a U.S. policy that was becoming functionally incompatible with the American economy at the end of the 1960s was the American balance-of-payments deficits associated with the U.S. dollar-gold convertibility policy. As we have already learned from the Cohen essay, the Nixon administration took drastic action in 1971 to eliminate this contradiction by changing the policy.

In the absence of policy change, another mode of determination operates as the limits of functional compatibility are exceeded. *Transformation* occurs, which directly affects the processes of limitation; selection, and reproduction. The result is a new economic order. The sources of transformation in Marxist theory stem from ineffective (nonreproductive) policies by decision makers in the face of pressures for change emanating from the class struggle. As Wright has put it: "Transformation is thus fundamental to the dialectical character of patterns of determination as understood in Marxist theory: class struggle, which is itself structurally limited and selected by various social structures, simultaneously reshapes these structures."[28]

In the preceding chapters there are three main examples that expose symptoms of structural transformation associated with U.S. foreign economic policy. One is the chronic U.S. balance-of-payments crises of the late 1960s and early '70s. A second is the set of challenges to U.S. economic policy posed by the calls for a New International Economic Order. A third is the crisis in the world grain market, which Paarlberg analyzes extensively in his chapter. Each of these examples illustrate symptoms of the decline of U.S. hegemony and the rise of new and potentially powerful actors in the international economic system. Although in each case the sources of these problems lay in the interplay of contending policies by governmental and nonstate actors, the structural context for their resolution is different in the 1970s and '80s than it would have been in the previous era of American hegemony. This point is made most forcefully by Paarlberg (page 142) who concludes:

> The political logic of the world grain market seems in an awkward phase of transition. The structure and condition of that market, until now, have been largely a byproduct of separate and separately determined national policy actions. . . . [A]t a moment when some importers cannot afford deeper participation in such a market . . . the dominant exporter, the United States, has fewer international means to ensure the stability and security of that market. What the logic of national politics hath wrought, the international system, which lacks a confident hegemonic leader, must now seek to manage.

The decline of American hegemony has created the conditions for the emergence of these redistributive issues in the international economic system and has increased the potential for further transformation in the existing international economic and political order. The extent and rate of transformation is difficult to forecast. Our more modest goal in this essay has been to provide our readers with insights from neo-Marxist and neo-pluralist perspectives, which will enhance their understanding of continuity and change in U.S. foreign economic policy during this turbulent era.

NOTES

1. R. L. Heilbroner, *Marxism: For and Against* (New York: W. W. Norton, 1980), pp. 16–18, 44–51.

2. E. O. Wright, *Class, Crisis, and the State* (London: New Left Books, 1978), p. 14.

3. Ibid., p. 11

4. Heilbroner, *Marxism*, pp. 95–105.

5. A. Wolfe, "New Directions in the Marxist Theory of Politics," *Politics and Society* 4 (1974): 131–59.

6. A. Szymanski, *The Capitalist State and the Politics of Class* (Cambridge, Mass: Winthrop, 1978), pp. 30–31, n. 31.

7. For expositions and critiques of these perspectives by Marxists, see R. Miliband, *The State in Capitalist Society* (London and New York: Basic Books, 1969), *passim*; and Szymanski, ibid., pp. 1–20.

8. See J. R. Kurth, "The Political Consequences of the Product Cycle: Industrial History and Political Outcomes," *International Organization* 33 (Winter 1979): 1–34.

9. R. Miliband, "Poulantzas and the Capitalist State," *New Left Review*, 82 (November–December 1973): 85.

10. Szymanski, *Capitalist State*, pp. 25–26.

11. L. Althusser, "Ideology and Ideological State Apparatuses" in *Lenin and Philosophy*, ed. L. Althusser (New York: Monthly Review Press, 1971), pp. 121–73.

12. For a brief exposition of all five neo-Marxist approaches see Pat McGowan and Stephen G. Walker, "Radical and Conventional Models of U.S. Foreign Economic Policy Making," *World Politics* 33 (April 1981): 347–82.

13. J. Mollenkopf, "Theories of the State and Power Structure Research," *Insurgent Sociologist* 5 (1975): 245–64; see also Miliband, *The State in Capitalist Society*, p. 22, and McGowan and Walker, ibid.

14. D. Gold, C. Lo, and E. O. Wright, "Recent Developments in Marxist Theories of the State," *Monthly Review* 27, nos. 5 and 6 (1975): 29–43, 36–51. See also McGowan and Walker, ibid.

15. N. Poulantzas, "The Problem of the Capitalist State," *New Left Review* 58 (November–December 1969): 245. For a review of structuralist theory, see McGowan and Walker, ibid.

16. Wright, *Class, Crisis, and State*, pp. 15–23, 66–67; Claus Offe, "Advanced Capitalism and the Welfare State," *Politics and Society* 2 (1972): 479–88; McGowan and Walker, ibid.

17. W. Zimmerman, "Issue Area and Foreign-Policy Process," *American Political Science Review* 67 (December 1973): 1204–12; J. Rosenau, "Pre-Theories and Theories of Foreign Policy," in *Approaches to Comparative and International Politics*, ed. R. B. Farrell (Evanston, Ill.: Northwestern University Press, 1966), pp. 27–92; T. Lowi, "American Business, Public Policy, Case-Studies, and Political Theory," *World Politics* 16 (December 1964): 677–715; T. Lowi, "Making Democracy Safe for the World," in *Domestic Sources of Foreign Policy*, ed. J. Rosenau (New York: Free Press, 1967), pp. 295–332; A. Wolfers, *Discord and Collaboration* (Baltimore: Johns Hopkins Press, 1962). See also McGowan and Walker, "Radical and Conventional Models."

18. McGowan and Walker, ibid.; see also R. Dahl, *Who Governs?* (New Haven, Conn.: Yale University Press, 1961).

19. Zimmerman, "Issue Area and Foreign-Policy Process," p. 1206.

20. Ibid.

21. Ibid.

22. Ibid.

23. Ibid.

24. McGowan and Walker, "Radical and Conventional Models."'

25. For the rationale which developed this hypothesis, see McGowan and Walker, ibid.

26. S. Krasner, "North-South Economic Relations: The Quests for Economic Well-Being and Political Autonomy," in *Eagle Entangled: U.S. Foreign Policy in a Complex World*, ed. K. Oye, A. Rothchild, and R. Lieber (New York: Longman, 1979), pp. 123–45.

27. S. Krasner, *Defending the National Interest* (Princeton, N.J.: Princeton University Press, 1978), p. 87.

28. Wright, *Class, Crisis, and State*, p. 21.

Conclusion

11

America in the World Political Economy: Prognoses, Prescriptions, and Questions for Future Research

David P. Rapkin and William P. Avery

The contributors to this volume provide a variety of insights and findings regarding American international economic policy from the perspectives of the systemic and national levels of analysis. We stated earlier that both levels are necessary for a thorough understanding of American policy. That policy cannot be adequately comprehended without prior knowledge pertaining to the position of the United States within the larger world political economy. As the chapters in Part 1 demonstrate, both the world political economy and the structural position of the United States within it are undergoing substantial change, much of which is predictable from the standpoint of systemic-level theory. That body of theory is not capable, however, of predicting the American response to these changes. Part 2 provides considerable understanding of the organization, process, and to a lesser extent content of American international economic policy; but it too falls short of enabling us to predict the substantive direction of American policy that will, in large part, determine the country's future global role. To be sure, the volume does not approach an integration of the two levels of analysis. Rather, the products of the research conducted at each level need to be additively considered as complementary types of information.

Given the partial nature of both world system theory and theories of policy making, prescription for and prediction of the future course of American international economic policy are necessarily problematic tasks. Adding to the difficulty is the fact that the major systemic changes discussed in the introductory chapter are still unfolding. Are these changes unique to the contemporary period or are they interpretable as elements of the longer-term cyclical processes identified by Modelski and Chase-Dunn? To the extent that the latter is the case, the systemic context of future American policy, if not its content and direction, should be easier to anticipate.

In this concluding chapter we compare the prognoses and prescriptions derived by the authors from their respective theoretical points of departure. What form will the future world political economy take? What role will the United States occupy within it? Will the United States be able to make the internal adjustments necessary to arrest the erosion of its structural position in the world political economy? Is further decline imminent, or is there scope for a renascence of American leadership?

It would have been impossible of course for the essays in this volume, taken collectively, to have exhaustively covered the broad topical concerns they address. As is the case in most joint endeavors, the volume raises, implicitly and explicitly, at least as many questions as it resolves. Thus, another purpose of this chapter is to suggest some research questions relating to the volume's principal concerns.

PROGNOSES AND PRESCRIPTIONS

The four systemically oriented chapters, though differing in terminology and explanatory emphasis, provide interpretations of the post-World War II period that are, in broad contour, consistent with one another. Collectively the four provide a composite sketch of the period that involves the establishment, rise, and some degree of decline of American hegemonic leadership. All view the United States as emerging from the war with an extraordinary margin of superiority across virtually all categories of power resources and capabilities. While the authors might disagree about the character of American hegemonic leadership, they all agree that the United States applied its varied resources to a range of system-ordering activities in the late 1940s and early 1950s. Under U.S. hegemony in the 1950s, the world economy underwent a phase of relative stability combined with intensive and extensive growth. The implementation of liberal ordering principles resulted in sizable increases in the aggregate global product, stimulated a marked expansion of international trade, and facilitated the rapid reconstruction of the industrial economies of Western Europe and Japan.

But the enormous power disparities that originally enabled U.S. hegemony were short-lived, in part inevitably because they derived from the temporary, war-induced weakness of Europe and Japan and in part, as Keohane argues, because U.S. policy failed to sustain the necessary bases of American power. The consequent leveling of capabilities has reduced American incentives to invest resources in system-ordering tasks while also reducing the incentives for other states to accept and follow American leadership. This *relative* decline in the structural position of the

United States has been accompanied by contraction in the world economy, increased interstate competition stemming from surplus global capacity in key industrial sectors, and the deterioration or collapse of many institutional arrangements that had previously ordered international economic interactions. In short, all four authors acknowledge a correlation between hegemonic leadership and order (though they differ as to the normative valuations they attach to American hegemony and its attendant world order).

The predictive power of the systemic approach remains in question. What can this approach tell us about the future of the world economy and the U.S. role within it? How far has the United States traveled down the path of hegemonic decline? Is the decline reversible? If so, what would be the necessary and sufficient conditions for such a reversal? If not, what lies in store for the United States and for the world economy? If indeed the world system is characterized by cyclical processes, are disorder, collapse, and/or global war lurking in the foreseeable future? If so, what steps might be taken to avoid these outcomes?

For Modelski, the question of future U.S. leadership is not amenable to systematic prediction. Since his historical analysis "suggests that the sheer size of the economy is not a reliable guide to the performance of world leadership" (page 113), he does not regard the relative decline of American capabilities as a crucial consideration. Rather, the prospects for American leadership hinge on the ability of the United States to remain a "lead economy," a qualitative status defined by high rates of investment, technological innovation, and the creation of leading sectors. The verdict is open, in Modelski's view, on whether the United States will be able to retain its position as lead economy.

Modelski's long-cycle model indicates that the global system is entering the mid-cycle "delegitimation" phase that, in previous cycles, has been characterized by political and economic instability. The model also suggests that global war should not be an immediate concern; by extrapolation of the long-cycle framework, global war for purposes of resolving the "succession" problem lies several phases of the cycle into the future. Modelski asserts that the present situation constitutes a "crisis of legitimacy, arising out of the waning of the leadership of the United States" (page 114). It is similar to previous "crises of expectations and crises of confidence, hence tests of a political system unable to meet them and of a culture unable to restrain them"; these tests "need to be met principally as political and moral phenomena" (page 114). Modelski's concluding prescription for resolution of the crisis exhorts that "this is the period in which stategic emphasis needs to be placed on political innovation" (page 114).

While the other contributors would certainly acknowledge the need for bold political innovations, their analyses lead neither to the expectation that they will be forthcoming nor that they would suffice for purposes of resurrecting American leadership. Their pessimism in this regard stems from several conceptual and analytical differences between their formulations and that advanced by Modelski.

One question on which Modelski's analysis diverges from those of the other contributors concerns specification of the requisite capabilities for leadership. Modelski deemphasizes purely quantitative considerations, such as the size of the American share of the world product (or other capability indicators), and instead stresses the qualitative properties associated with lead economy status. While Krasner and Keohane fully recognize the significance of qualitative considerations, such as the nature and rate of investment, technological innovation, and the development of leading sectors, they regard their presence as a necessary but not sufficient condition for hegemonic leadership. An additional necessary condition is a wide (though as yet empirically unspecified) margin of quantitative superiority over lesser states. This specification of requisite capabilities derives from the public goods interpretation of hegemony and order. Just as the incentives for the exercise of leadership are a function of the relative size of the stake that the would-be hegemon has in the functioning of the world political economy, so also is the ability to exercise leadership a function of the disparity in capabilities between leader and followers. The relative decline of American capabilities, as reflected in Krasner's cross-time data, strongly suggests that a wide margin no longer obtains. This is not to imply that Modelski's approach is necessarily incorrect, since we still lack precise knowledge of how large a margin of quantitative superiority, or what mix of quantitative and qualitative superiorities, will suffice.

Another difference concerns the degree of specificity that the contributors apply to factors internal to the United States. Modelski operates exclusively at the systemic level of analysis and thus implicitly treats the United States as a unitary, homogeneous entity. Krasner, Keohane, and Chase-Dunn, by way of contrast, depart from a strictly systemic approach and give more detailed attention to the shifting and often conflicting domestic pressures encountered by U.S. leaders in their attempts to implement leadership strategies. This difference also relates to the logic of the public goods conception of the problem. If indeed the structure of the global system has altered such that the United States no longer occupies a superordinate position atop it, then the set of constraints and incentives that the system poses for the United States has also altered in the sense that this set now more closely resembles the mix encountered by more normal, "ordinary" states. The chapters by Krasner, Keohane, and Chase-Dunn all look—albeit through different lenses—*within* the United States (as a hegemonic state and society) and find that different domestic interests (groups, classes, segments of capital) have reacted in different ways to these shifting systemic constraints and incentives. In the context of America's extraordinary position at the outset of the postwar period, the incentives for investments in order and bold leadership strategies were sufficiently strong to enable those state managers and societal interests favoring a leadership role for the United States to check the counterpressures of nationalist and isolationist interests.[1] Over time, however, as the country's structural position (and its associated constraints and incentives) has changed, so too has American behavior; the United States has retreated from its leadership role to the extent that policy is increasingly oriented toward the satisfaction of short-term, particularistic American interests, rather than toward the more diffuse goals of global order and stability. Perhaps this is the point at which political innovations could be decisive in rejuvenating American leadership, but the implication of the public goods interpretation is that the structure of incentives has shifted so as to render this outcome unlikely.

A final difference involves the authors' views of the current world situation. For Modelski, the essence of the problem—a crisis of world order—is subjective, a moral phenomenon, a matter of expectations and confidence and will. For the other contributors to the systemic section, the problem derives from sources that are more objective and material: Without the necessary capabilities, and without the mix of incentives that results from a highly skewed global distribution of capabilities, the exercise of hegemonic leadership becomes more difficult and thereby less likely. Krasner's argument to this effect succinctly expresses the differences we have been discussing:

> the American adoption of policies directed more toward clearly identifiable national economic interests means that there is no effective leader in the present system. Appeals for greater political will and wisdom will not change this basic fact, for American behavior is not a function of short-sightedness or chauvinism but of a fundamental change in the world political position of the United States (page 47).

Krasner reasons that the recession of American leadership leaves only the binding force of interdependent national interests to maintain an international economic order with some modicum of stability. The current situation, in consequence of the American decline, is both "messier" and "more fragile." It is messier in the sense that, for all states, "*ad hoc* calculations of interest increasingly determine national behavior. The result is a more confused and complicated international economic system" (pages 43–44). It is more fragile insofar as there is no leader willing to absorb political shocks (e.g., another oil embargo, a Persian Gulf war, widespread crop failures) for purposes of sustaining economic order.

Krasner, though exuding no great confidence, acknowledges that the binding force of national interests may well suffice to preserve the rudiments of the extant international order: "The absence of leadership does not mean any necessary change in the basic shape of the vessel—the body

of rules, norms, and behavior that constitute the global economic order —
but it does imply that the vessel has become more fragile, more likely
to be suddenly shattered" (page 47). If "messier" and "more fragile"
seem roundabout ways of saying "disorder" and "unstable," Krasner's
concluding statement is more straightforward: "We are returning to normalcy, but normalcy in international politics is much less stable than the
world we have known for the last thirty years" (page 47).

Keohane's conclusions are a bit more sanguine than Krasner's in that
he allows the possibility of regeneration of American leadership. Just as
Keohane's account of hegemonic leadership in petroleum stresses the internal sources of contemporary American weakness, his prescriptions
underscore the need for internal correctives. It would be difficult to argue
with Keohane's maxim that "any strategy that is viable in the long term
has to re-create the conditions for its own existence.... Any hegemonic
leadership strategy... must seek to maintain the national base of resources upon which governmental influence, and leadership, rest" (page
67). His analysis of American oil policy leads to the judgment that
the United States failed this test: A critical component of America's resource base was needlessly dissipated, and thereby the conditions necessary for maintenance of hegemonic leadership were not reproduced.[2]
Since it was internal weakness—the inability to force adjustment on
domestic oil interests—that proved to be the Achilles heel of American
hegemony, it follows for Keohane:

> Internal measures—to adjust to change, to build up industrial strength
> through investment and technological development to bring energy con-
> sumption and production more closely into balance—are necessary con-
> ditions for successful reassertion of U.S. leadership.... If capabilities
> are lacking, slogans about leadership will be to no avail (page 71).

Chase-Dunn's analysis of the cycle of core competition leads him to
the conclusion that "we can expect the United States to maintain its economic and political centrality in a world economy experiencing slower
and less even rates of growth; but it can never recover the heights of hegemony reached during the score of years following World War II" (page
91). He suggests that a logical course for the United States would be to
try to engineer a corewide solution to managing international economic
order, but cautions that this outcome is unlikely given the contradictory
economic forces that are operative both within and between the United
States and other core states.[3] With no apparent hegemonic successor on
the immediate horizon, another and perhaps more likely variation on the
same theme would be a coalition between two or more core states to fill
the hegemonic role.[4] But Chase-Dunn, who has no normative predilec-
tion for "saving the empire," correctly reminds us that "U.S. hegemony
has not been a picnic for everyone" and argues that "the hegemony of a

particular state is less important than the dynamics of a socioeconomic system that produces both rapid and uneven development and extremely destructive wars. . . . It is this system which should be changed rather than the preservation of a particular hegemony within it" (page 93).

By way of prescription, Chase-Dunn advocates movement toward forms of economic democracy designed to produce collectively rational structural changes within the American economy. While such measures would provide no immediate solution to the problems of the world economy, Chase-Dunn views them as necessary first-steps toward an admittedly utopian "democratic world government that could control the anarchy of military conflict and promote a collectively rational approach to world economic development" (pages 93–94).

A common theme that emerges from both the systemic and national perspectives represented in this volume is the likelihood of rising nationalistic policy concerns, as U.S. policy makers face the problems posed by America's declining world economic position. Krasner, Keohane, and Chase-Dunn each note the insertion into the policy process of particularistic national interests at the expense of larger world economic concerns. The occurrence of sustained periods of slow growth has perhaps caused many national interests to anticipate zero-sum outcomes arising from declining U.S. hegemony, leading them to seek protective measures against such outcomes. In consequence, policy makers display increasing sensitivity toward domestic pressures for policy adjustments that benefit short-term national economic interests. Adjustments are indeed necessary, as Keohane stresses, but they must be directed toward increasing America's industrial strength and capabilities rather than merely toward insulating U.S. industry against the challenges emanating from changes in the world economy.

The contributions to the second part of this volume all share broadly a common perspective on this problem: namely, that as redistributive issues deriving from systemic economic alterations become more salient, the U.S. policy-making process tends increasingly to embrace more actors in order to accommodate the growing number of national interests affected by these issues. The result is a continuing trend toward bureaucratic, multiple modes of decision making. There is little expectation that a unified theory will emerge to guide U.S. policy making; rather, each author points to greater complexity in the decision-making process. Cohen argues that multiple modes of decision making are inevitable, that international economic policy making must reconcile the internal and external aspects of economic and political objectives. Policies incorporating long-range systemic goals will usually seek to minimize the disruptive impact of such goals on U.S. business and labor. The precise manner in which these policies are reached is not always clear because "the need for short-term compromises frequently necessitates detours in the form of compromise" (page 150). Different bureaucratic perspectives, "the irregular casts of decision makers and the heterogeneity of the issues involved in the entire gamut of U.S. international economic relations preclude construction of a universally applicable mode of policy making" (page 150). Cohen would no doubt agree that it is altogether likely, therefore, that compromises to incorporate short-term domestic interests will result in defensive or protective policies.

In their discussion of neo-Marxist and neopluralist conceptions of state policy making, Walker and McGowan (drawing on prior work by Zimmerman) hypothesize that the policy-making process will more closely approximate pluralist models of decision making when the issues involve relatively tangible and divisible goods—as, for example, issues concerning tariffs and export subsidies. Put alternatively, "when an issue involves the relatively intangible and indivisible goods of power, security, and prestige, then the policy process will correspond to a rational actor model in which the maker of government policy is a relatively monolithic rational decision maker" (page 212). Issues involving tangible goods that are asymmetrically divisible (i.e., rendering zero-sum outcomes) are likely to include large numbers of diverse actors and to be characterized by a pluralistic, bargaining mode of decision making. The contributors to this volume are in basic agreement that many of the issues currently confronting U.S. policy makers are of this variety.

In a directly prescriptive vein, Porter argues for the need to deliberately factor pluralism into the decision-making apparatus. He proposes the creation of a broadly integrative economic advisory council that would ensure that the President is not left to integrate all the issues and that policy makers would operate in a decisional context transcendent of their own departmental concerns. Further, he states that such coordination should be organized around those institutions and officials concerned primarily with domestic economic policy. This recommendation stems from his belief that international economic issues are more closely tied to domestic economic policy than to foreign policy.

Departing from the position of Porter, Mingst seems to cast group-level decision making (i.e., multiple advocacy, bureaucratic) in a somewhat negative light. This mode of decision making, which she notes has characterized much of American international economic policy making, has resulted from the dominant liberal economic paradigm upon which U.S. policy is based and has led to the formulation of less than optimal reactive and confounding policies. It will be recalled that she defines reactive policies as those which seek to dampen detrimental side effects of conditions ensuing from U.S. participation in the world economic system after these effects have become evident. Confounding policies arise from "confusion and conflicting goals in the domestic political process" (page 201) and from inconsistent or uncoordinated policies. More desirable policies are of the anticipatory variety, those which seek "to predict the direct and potential consequences of systemic changes and to provide a repertoire of appropriate responses" (page 201). As the structural position of the United States erodes in the world economy, she suggests that America can no longer afford the ideological luxury of avoiding anticipatory policies.

Paarlberg, while not directly addressing the question of what the United States ought to do, feels nonetheless that this country will very likely be drawn into an internationalization of its grain trade policies. This is so, he maintains, because of the likelihood that continuing instability in the world market will prompt poor, food-deficit countries "to search for ways to hedge against the costs and risks of still deeper participation in such a market" (page 142). Thus, as the dominant exporter, the United States may find it desirable "to influence world grain conditions toward stability and growth . . . for the first time quite consciously, in hopes that the United States will be the largest beneficiary of stable growth" (page 142). In short, American policy makers will probably be unable to continue policies based on national concerns alone. He adds, however, that "it must only be hoped that U.S. power, in the grain market and beyond, has not eroded so far as to discourage or to defeat these leadership efforts" (page 142).

QUESTIONS FOR FUTURE RESEARCH

An important aspect of hegemonic systems, and the role of leadership within them, not directly addressed in this volume is the systemic rate of economic growth. That growth and expansion is essential to the smooth and sustained functioning of hegemonic systems seems apparent in the sense that "a rising tide floats all ships." With a satisfactory rate of global economic expansion, the hegemonic state is able and willing to bear the costs of leadership, more inclined to invest in order and less inclined to extract resources from the balance of the system. Of equal import, other states are likely to be complaisant with respect to the hegemon's leadership (and the liberal form of order that the hegemonic state is attempting to build or maintain) if the rate of growth is adequate to reward their support and compliance. Simply stated, we are referring to the familiar positive-sum, "larger pie to divide" rationale of liberal theory extended to the global realm. As Charles Maier argues:

> Hegemony remains successful . . . only when it achieves advances for the whole international structure within which it is exercised. Hegemony imposed in a zero-sum cockpit, that is at the expense of the secondary members of the system, must finally prove less durable. The quarter-century of relatively frictionless American domination depended partially upon the fact that the technologies of the era . . . permitted the growth that was its underlying premise.[5]

Maier adds that "once the system ceased to pay off, it began to founder."[6] In the absence of the positive-sum rationale, the legitimacy of the hegemon and its order loses force. The incentives for lesser states to adhere to open trading arrangements wane, and the temptations for individual states to employ mercantilistic policies in pursuit of national gain become strong enough to result in a more generalized systemic retrogression toward closure.[7] Protectionism, in turn, exacerbates the problem of economic contraction.

There are two ways of approaching the relationship between hegemony and growth. One view is that the liberal hegemonic order itself is the source of global economic expansion. The fact that the peak periods of the British and American hegemonies coincided with dramatic expansions of world trade and rapid economic growth provides strong evidence of association but does not exhaust the range of possible causation (i.e., these relationships are not sufficient to establish hegemony as the primary cause of growth).

Maier's reference to the "technologies of the era" suggests an alternative explanation in which Schumpeterian long waves of economic growth are triggered by clusters of technological innovations which revolutionize capitalist production and produce new leading sectors. From this perspective, we might hypothesize that hegemonic systems, in the fashion of a surfer catching a wave, (fortuitously?) ride long waves of economic growth. Unfortunately, the genesis of technological innovation is not well understood, and the question remains whether long waves can be induced by political action or whether they are exogenously determined by forces intrinsic to global capitalism (with the implication that the fate of hegemonic systems is ultimately exogenously determined). Mandel, who argues that the rate and character of technological innovation is a function principally of cyclical movements in the rate of profit, asserts that we are at present entering the second, *stagnating* stage of a long wave triggered in the 1940s "by the generalized control of machines by electronic apparatuses."[8] Mensch locates the causes of technological change in market processes, but allows that basic innovation can be facilitated by microeconomic (but not macro-) policies. He offers a more optimistic scenario, projecting that a new long wave will be generated by a surge of innovations in the 1980s.[9] Rostow, operating within the analytical context of the price variant of Kondratieff long waves, advocates large-scale public investment in scientific and technological research and development in order to stimulate a period of growth.[10]

Despite the theoretical ambiguity surrounding the phenomenon of long waves, the two alternative hypotheses linking hegemony and growth are not logically incompatible. It is plausible to combine the two and hypothesize that a hegemonic system functions so as to accelerate the growth effects stemming from an exogenously determined long wave (as if our surfer could accelerate the speed of the wave he is riding). In any event, it seems clear that the connection between hegemony and growth is not fully understood and thus warrants further exploration.

The role of the global division of labor in hegemonic systems is another question that is in need of further scrutiny. It is widely agreed that hegemonic systems eventually produce a systemic leveling of capabilities as the hegemonic state's initial productive superiority (as embodied in techniques, expertise, and the capacity for innovation) is diffused via the mechanisms of exchange and capital movements (and to a lesser degree by emulation). More generally, hegemonic systems accelerate the rate of change in the global division of labor. The implications are several. First, since hegemonic leadership is predicated on capabilities, the leveling of those capabilities implies that the hegemon's ability to exercise leadership will be constrained accordingly; insofar as leveling changes the hegemon's incentives, it also reduces its willingness to undertake the costs of leadership. Second, the diffusion of core production results in global surplus capacity in former leading sectors (e.g., steel, automobiles, chemicals). This in turn alters the incentives for other core states and leads to competition, protectionism, and often enmity between the hegemon and its competitors, as well as among the latter. Third, in consequence of these developments, the institutional and ideological bases of the hegemonic order itself are undermined.

This discussion suggests that one key to understanding the dynamics of hegemonic systems is the rate of change in the global division of labor. It seems evident that the erosion of the American hegemony (and perhaps also that of Great Britain) could have been predicted prior to its actual occurrence by observation of change in the division of labor. While we beg here the problem of precise operational definition (changing shares of core production would be a likely place to start), the relationship between the rate of change in the division of labor and the rate of hegemonic erosion—along with the question of temporal leads and lags—poses an interesting direction for further research.

A related factor that contributes toward understanding hegemonic systems concerns the ability and willingness of the hegemonic state to adjust to these inexorable shifts in the division of labor. Keohane's chapter in this book stresses the refusal to adjust to change in oil and monetary relations as a crucial element of American decline. The ability to adjust domestic production, to shift factors from one sector to another, in response to a changing global industrial geography, is a somewhat different and perhaps more difficult matter insofar as it raises highly politicized domestic issues that involve large, geographically concentrated segments of both capital and labor. This is not to say that such adjustments are impossible—surely no one would want to argue that the antiquated condition of much of the American industrial base is an outcome that could not have been avoided. More generally, the question of hegemonic adjustment underscores the need to examine processes internal to the hegemonic society; the systemic level of analysis alone offers little explanatory or predictive potential with respect to this question.

A final research problem, which combines the concerns of the book's two parts, involves developing a theory of the hegemonic state and the processes by which its global policy is formed. While considerable advances have been made in theories of *the* capitalist state (see Walker and McGowan's essay in this volume), there are at least several distinct categories of capitalist states; the need for a differentiated theory of dependent capitalist states has been already recognized and addressed.[11] There is no shortage of reasons to doubt that a single theoretical orientation is equally tenable in application to both "ordinary" and hegemonic capitalist states. First, the point that hegemonic and secondary states encounter different mixes of systemic constraints and incentives implies that a single theory of how responses to those constraints and incentives are formulated will not suffice. Second, the global policies of the hegemonic state are unique in terms of content when compared to the policies of other states. Third, the hegemonic state faces the unique task of mobilizing domestic support for long-term global policies aimed at vaguely defined objectives (order, stability) and not always in harmony with immediate, tangible national interests.

The basis for such a theory lies in the structural Marxist's emphasis on the functions of the state in reproducing the essential elements of capitalist society. We simply suggest that the hegemonic state spatially extends, or at least attempts to extend, these reproductive functions to the entire capitalist system. In other words, the hegemonic state assumes the role of reproducing the essential features of global capitalism. The manner in which the United States was able to accomplish these reproductive functions within the *tabula rasa* of postwar Western Europe and Japan is well illustrated in Maier's essay concerning the outward projection of American values and beliefs in the postwar period.[12]

Several problems that have emerged in the above discussion—hegemonic adjustment to a changing division of labor, inducement of technological innovation, the creation of new leading sectors—bear on the prospects for a regeneration of U.S. hegemony. We are in fundamental agreement with the longer-term, theoretical arguments of Krasner, Keohane, and Chase-Dunn, which suggest that this is an unlikely outcome. We find this conclusion to be reinforced in the short-term by recent developments in U.S. domestic and international economic policy. In our view, it requires heroic faith in the singular efficacy of "autonomous" market forces (as opposed to political action) to suppose that such a regeneration will ensue from the policies of the Reagan administration. The disdain of American capitalists and incumbent state managers for sectoral (or industrial) policies is a major case in point that does not lead us to optimism. We acknowledge the argument of free market advocates that there is no guarantee that state-imposed sectoral policies will be able to "pick winners" (i.e., new leading sectors). But nor is there any guarantee that further removal of state constraints on the behavior of American capital will produce any winners. Certainly the case of Japan, which indicates that supply-side economies is not incompatible with extensive state involvement, has established that winners can indeed be picked. More generally, the major capitalist competitors of the United States are tending toward increased coordination between state and capital in attempts to rationally determine industrial sectors that will be viable in the long term. In such an environment, reliance on the (very) short-term profit calculi of American capitalists to restore international competitiveness does not seem a good bet.

It may be incorrect to assert that the United States lacks sectoral policies; rather, it seems patently clear that the Reagan administration's remilitarization efforts constitute a *de facto* sectoral policy. The administration's further concentration of scarce capital and research and development resources in the strategic-military sector does not augur well for the restoration of growth-based American hegemonic leadership in the economic realm. Moreover, for a variety of reasons, the reassertion of American military power will surely be an insufficient condition for a renewal of leadership. This conclusion is bolstered if one believes that in the contemporary world, strategic superiority vis-à-vis the Soviet Union is unattainable, as well as undesirable and unusable if it were attainable.

In conclusion, we note once again the extraordinary role played by the United States in the reconstruction of world capitalism following World War II. Once its particular form of world order had been established and set in motion, however, the extraordinary role of the hegemonic state became less necessary (though not entirely unnecessary) and less accepted (though not entirely unaccepted). The inability of the United States to eventually reduce its hegemonic role in a more graceful and orderly fashion provides an invaluable key to understanding the contemporary world political economy.

NOTES

1. We would be remiss if we did not point out that the perceived threat of Soviet expansionism and international communism was also instrumental in American state managers' efforts to muster domestic support for their plans for the postwar international economic order. For the argument that American leaders were unable to sell their idea of American leadership of a liberal, open international order on its own merits until the perception of Soviet threat in 1947, see Stephen D. Krasner, "United States Commercial and Monetary Policy: Unravelling the Paradox of External Strength and Internal Weakness," in Peter J. Katzenstein, ed., *Between Power and Plenty* (Madison: University of Wisconsin Press, 1978), pp. 72–75. More generally, the ramifications of the conjunction between bipolarity in the global security realm and (unipolar) hegemony in world capitalism have yet to be fully and systematically examined.

2. Keohane argues that American monetary problems, as in the case of oil, stem from the failure to make necessary domestic adjustments; American trade difficulties derived largely from shifts in the global division of labor and thus have been harder to avoid (via internal adjustment) than problems in the oil and money issue areas (page 68). For a more detailed account of differences across the three issue areas, see R.O. Keohane, "The Theory of Hegemonic Stability and Changes in International Economic Regimes, 1967–1977," in *Change in the International System*, ed. Ole R. Holsti, Randolph M. Siverson, and Alexander L. George (Boulder, Colo.: Westview Press, 1980).

3. For an interesting prognosis that envisages increased "international corporatism" among core states, see Walter G. Seabold and N. G. Onuf, "Late Capitalism, Uneven Development, and Foreign Policy Postures," in *The Political Economy of Foreign Policy Behavior*, ed. Charles W. Kegley and Pat McGowan, Sage International Yearbook of Foreign Policy Studies, vol. 6 (Beverly Hills: Sage, 1981).

4. Cf. the suggestion of an American–West German "bigemony" in C. Fred Bergsten, *Toward a New International Economic Order* (Lexington, Mass: Lexington Books, 1975), chap. 23.

5. Charles S. Maier, "The Politics of Productivity: Foundations of American International Economic Policy After World War II," in Katzenstein, ed., *Between Power and Plenty*, pp. 47–48.

6. Ibid., p. 48.

7. For a discussion of the relationship between hegemony and the openness of trade regimes, see Stephen D. Krasner, "State Power and the Structure of International Trade," *World Politics* 28 (April 1976).

8. Ernest Mandel, *Late Capitalism* (London: New Left Books, 1975), p. 121; for his treatment of long waves, see chaps. 4 and 6.

9. Gerhard Mensch, *Stalemate in Technology: Innovations Overcome the Depression* (Cambridge, Mass.: Ballinger, 1979).

10. W. W. Rostow, *The World Economy: History and Prospect* (Austin: University of Texas Press, 1978), Chapter 54.

11. For a theoretical discussion of the dependent capitalist state, see Raymond D. Duvall and John R. Freeman, "The State and Dependent Capitalism," *International Studies Quarterly* 25 (March 1981).

12. Maier, "The Politics of Productivity."

Index